Happy Birthday, Carrie
July, 1991
Uncle George

GLORIOUS HARVEST

GLORIOUS HARVEST

Francesco Bianchini   Francesco Corbetta

CRESCENT BOOKS
New York

Copyright © 1973, 1975, 1990 Arnoldo Mondadori Editore S.p.A., Milan
English translation copyright © 1975, 1977, 1990 Arnoldo Mondadori Editore,
S.p.A., Milan

Text by Francesco Bianchini and Francesco Corbetta
Artwork by Marilena Pistoia
Design by Simona Aguzzoni
Photographs Mondadori Archives, Milan

This 1990 edition published by Crescent Books,
distributed by Outlet Book Company, Inc.,
a Random House Company,
225 Park Avenue South, New York, New York 10003

ISBN 0-517-03313-5

8 7 6 5 4 3 2 1

Photoset in Great Britain by
Rowland Phototypesetting Limited, Bury St Edmunds, Suffolk
Printed and bound in Italy by
Arnoldo Mondadori Editore, Verona

Contents

Introduction

The current renewal of interest in the natural world is reflected in the ever increasing use of words such as "green," "herbal," and "ecology." As man realizes the need to establish a more responsible relationship with the world surrounding him, he is turning more and more to simple wholesome foods, as well as to herbal remedies. These are now regaining the important position which they once held before the advent of the industrial era.

This book contains numerous color illustrations with more than 300 plants. These are grouped according to their use: as a food, or for medicinal purposes (vegetables, fruit, cereals, medicinal plants, etc.).

Because of the limitations a book necessarily imposes, we have illustrated the varieties of plant that are most commonly found today and which are readily available in the shops. However, we have also included some illustrations of less well-known plants which are worth rediscovering.

Our collection of plants thus contains wild herbs, flowers, and fruit. Despite their lack of renown they are rich in flavors and unusual aromas and are almost impossible to purchase. In order to enjoy them they just have to be picked at the right time of year, perhaps on a walk in the country.

The illustrations are accompanied by information on the origins and distribution of the various plants, their nutritional value, and their different uses in cooking or as herbal remedies. Simple recipes are also included for a healthy natural cuisine. Both text and illustrations aim to show the reader all that nature has to offer and how best to appreciate her gifts.

VEGETABLES

Tomato

The tomato originated in South America, but its botanical name *Lycopersicum esculentum* was once applied to an Egyptian plant, and only later transferred to the American fruit. The first names given to the tomato, in the sixteenth century, "Peruvian apple" or "Apple of Peru," would seem to indicate a Peruvian origin. Most botanists agree with the theory that Peru was an important area of early cultivation. The term "tomato," by which the plant is known in many European languages (French, Spanish, German, English), derives from an ancient Mexican word, *tomatl*. The more romantic French name of *pomme d'amour* that was given to the tomato when it first came to Europe has remained as a little used synonym in English, "love apple." It was introduced into Europe by the Spanish and Portuguese, who used it as a vegetable. Its cultivation quickly spread throughout the Mediterranean and, more slowly, in the northern part of central Europe. In the second half of the eighteenth century, it was listed in the catalogs of a famous Parisian horticultural firm as an ornamental plant. Now it is grown all over the world, and, because of the highly refined techniques of hothouse cultivation, is available throughout the year at a relatively moderate price, compared with other out-of-season vegetables. The wild parental form is thought to be *Lycopersicum cerasiforme*, which grows wild in Peru, the Antilles, and Texas. The many cultivars known today are derived from this wild species through a long succession of hybridizations and selections. Commercially the large, round, smooth or ribbed tomatoes are

Some of the most popular varieties of tomato: Prince Borghese, small and full of flavour; opposite, the Salad, Beef-heart, and Yellow tomatoes, all firm and flavorsome eaten raw, and the plum-shaped Marzano tomato, ideal for sauces.

FRESH TOMATO SAUCE

Clean, skin, and chop 2 lb (1 kg) ripe tomatoes. Finely chop 1 carrot, 1 stick celery, 1 large onion, and 3 cloves garlic and fry gently in 2 tbsp olive oil. Add the tomatoes and season with salt, freshly ground pepper, and dried oregano. Cover and cook gently for 20 minutes. Stir in 1 tbsp chopped fresh basil before serving.
This sauce is ideal for traditional pasta dishes or it can be sieved to obtain a smoother pouring sauce.
When tomatoes are in season, prepare large quantities and freeze or bottle.

Tomato

suitable both for immediate use and for the canning industries, and the pear-shaped tomatoes, among them the classical San Marzano, are also good for the table or for canning, especially when peeled. However, the cherry tomatoes, strictly related to the *L. cerasiforme*, which represent the original form, have been little cultivated in the past, but are now becoming popular in the United States. These tomatoes have red or yellow skin when completely ripe. Golden Jubilee is one of the most widely used in the United States.

The tomato can be eaten raw when still slightly unripe, as a salad flavored with a little garlic or a pinch of oregano, or cooked in many different ways. Commercially it is used to make tomato paste, catsup and tomato juice, which is widely drunk, both on its own, and mixed with alcohol. The raw tomato has a modest nutritive value, water representing the largest part of its weight, more than 90%; protein less than 1%; carbohydrates 4–5%, and ash 1%. The calories in 3½ oz (100 g) are 23–24. From a vitamin standpoint 3½ oz (100 g) of tomatoes provide 1 mg of vitamin A, traces of thiamin and riboflavin, and a moderate amount of vitamin C (30 mg).

The easiest way to skin tomatoes is to lower them into a bowl of water, which has just been boiled, and leave them for about a minute. Lift them out and drain. Remove the calyx by cutting it away with a small part of the core around it. Make a cut across the other end of the tomato and start to peel back the skin. Alternatively, you can remove the calyx, make the cut, and hold the tomato over an open flame for about 15 seconds; the skin will come away easily.

Chicory · Endive · Escarole

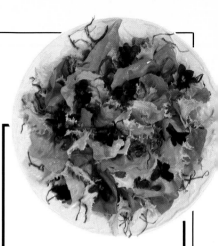

These tender green-leaved vegetables are generally used to make up delicious salads, often combined with other leaves and flavored with a fine dressing. They are among the more bitter-tasting of the salad greens and make a pleasing combination with the sweeter varieties of lettuce. Pick crisp, fresh-looking specimens. Rather than discarding the outer, tougher leaves, chop them up and add them to the ingredients of a vegetable soup. Alternatively, these traditional salad vegetables can be braised and used as a hot vegetable or to make soups.

The cutting-type chicories are popular in domestic cooking. They are planted close together and cut near the base at regular intervals. Similar to the true chicories in their use and characteristics are escarole and endive, both belonging to the species *Chichorium endivia* which is believed to be native to India. There is no proof that the endive was known to the ancient Greeks and Romans, but some botanists believe that its use dates back to those times. We know that in France *C. endivia* appeared at first as a medicinal plant and only in the fourteenth century was it considered a food. Within the species *C. endivia* some authorities identify a *crispa* variety with curly, deeply

dentate leaves (endive) and a *latifolia* variety with only slightly denticulate leaves, slightly curled at the edges (escarole).

There are many forms of the variety *crispa* with curly, deeply cut leaves: Full Heart Batavian, Broad-leaved Batavian, Salad King, Pancalier, Ruffec, and Green-curled. These are used only in salads. They are sometimes blanched in the field. The various forms of escarole, Florida Deep Heart, Florida Giant, and Florentine Big, can be either blanched for use in salads or cooked like Catalonia chicory. The nutritional value of these plants is the same as those of other chicories.

COUNTRY SALAD

This quick and easy recipe uses a mixture of salad greens in an interesting combination of flavors. Simply tear up the leaves of one small green lettuce and one small curly endive; add a dozen sorrel leaves, chopped up, and a bunch of freshly picked sweet violets; toss with a dressing of oil, cider vinegar, salt, and pepper.

The broad-leaved chicory varieties escarole, right, and grumolo, left. Like many salad plants, they are not difficult to grow in the garden, although care should be taken to keep snails from eating them.

Lettuce

The cultivated lettuces, perhaps the plants most widely used in salads (to such a degree that in some countries salad and lettuce have become synonymous), belong to the *Compositae* (daisy or thistle family) and to the genus *Lactuca*. The majority of botanists agree that the garden lettuce is a variety (*sativa*) of the species *Lactuca scariola* which is found in the wild state in Asia, Europe, and northern Africa, and has become naturalized in North America and Argentina. Lettuce has been cultivated since very early times and was known not only to the Greeks and Romans, but, even earlier, to the Chinese. The Romans were familiar with several different forms that were mentioned by Pliny and Columella, while the authorities of the Dark Ages and of the Renaissance seem to have known fewer forms. At least three principal forms are recognized: head or cabbage

lettuce (var: *capitata*), cos or romaine (var: *longifolia*), and the curled or leaf lettuce with leaves somewhat deeply incised, belonging, according to some botanists, to the varieties *crispa* and *palmata*. Head lettuce comes in many forms. The typical round head is a large bud, the development of which is helped considerably by transplanting. Lettuce is primarily a salad plant. It is highly refreshing and contains several vitamins, such as vitamin A, riboflavin, thiamin, and above all, vitamin C. Its calorific value is extremely

low, its composition being mostly water, 1% protein, only traces of fats, and 2–3% carbohydrates. One of the lesser known but highly recommended uses of lettuce is in the preparation of a delicately flavored soup.

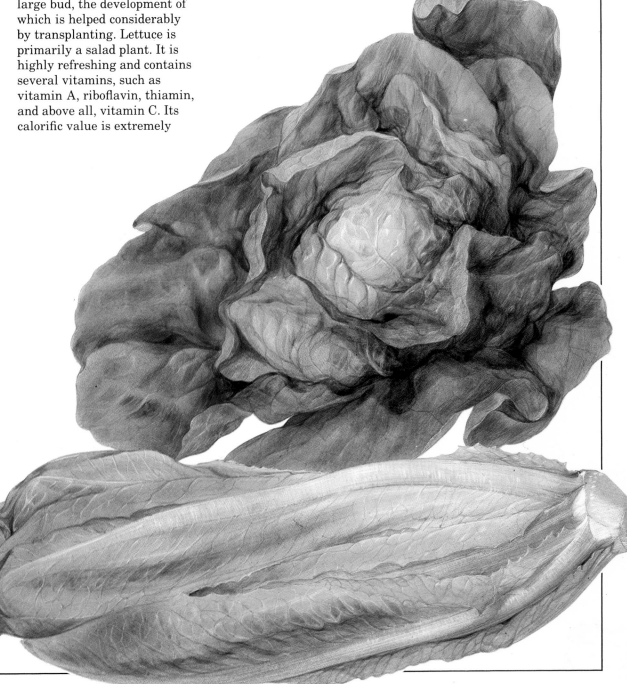

Butter-head lettuce, above right, is traditionally eaten as part of salad but it can also be used to make a delicious soup with a delicately sweet flavor. The cos lettuce, right, is a tall variety with crisp leaves with a thick central rib. This is a very popular salad lettuce.

Eggplant or Aubergine

Eggplant (*Solanum melongena*) belongs to the *Solanaceae* (potato family) and is said to have originated in India. Unknown to the Greeks and Romans, it appeared in Europe in the fourteenth century, probably via Africa, where its cultivation was supposedly introduced and spread in the Middle Ages. In the thirteenth century it was mentioned by an Arab physician. Furthermore, modern travelers now find the eggplant growing in the region of the Nile and in Guinea. From Europe its cultivation spread to America. Old documents show that it was cultivated in Brazil in 1658. The classic areas of growth are around the Mediterranean, as a warm climate is needed, and it is therefore not well known in the north. It is still grown in the warm regions of India and also in Japan, and in North and South America. Its cultivation requires warmth and constant and abundant irrigation. In addition, the eggplant is very hardy and is not usually afflicted either by parasitic insects or disease. It is a perennial plant, but is cultivated as an annual, growing to about 24 inches; the stem is lignified at the base; the leaves coarse, ash-gray, whole or simply lobed, sometimes spinescent on the main rib. The flowers are star-shaped and very beautiful, of a typical blue-violet color, with five sepals and five petals and the stamens joined at the center of the corolla. The edible fruits are large berries, varying in shape from round to oblong, and in color from white to purple. They contain numerous seeds for which reason the fruit should not be allowed to become overripe; the fruit is attached to the plant by the fruit-stalk and the persistent calyx, both of which are often covered with sharp spines which can hurt one's fingers.

Eggplants can be cooked in numerous ways, but cannot be eaten raw. Two classic recipes for eggplants are ratatouille *from Provence and* imam bayildi *from Turkey. Ratatouille is a vegetable stew of coarsely chopped eggplants, onions, zucchini, red and green peppers, garlic, and a few crushed coriander seeds, cooked in olive oil. For* imam bayildi *the eggplants are stuffed and simmered slowly for 3 hours in olive oil which should almost cover them. They are then left to cool for 24 hours, and eaten cold as an appetizer.*

In recipes using eggplants in small slices, the preparation involves a salting process to remove the bitter juices inside the fruit. First clean and dry them and remove the calyx with a knife. Cut into slices and place in layers in a colander, lightly sprinkling with salt as you go. Weigh the layers down with a dish or bowl and leave for 1 hour to draw out the juices. Lastly, rinse and dry the pieces on a clean cloth.

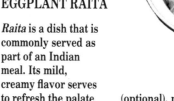

EGGPLANT RAITA

Raita is a dish that is commonly served as part of an Indian meal. Its mild, creamy flavor serves to refresh the palate between the other spicier dishes. An eggplant *raita* is made with 10 oz/300 g eggplant, 2 cups/ 12 fl oz/300 ml natural yoghurt, 1 finely chopped mint leaf, pinch chili powder (optional), pinch black pepper, salt, and a few mint leaves. Peel the eggplants, cut into small slices and steam. Beat the yoghurt with the chopped mint, chili powder, and black pepper and place in refrigerator. When the eggplant slices are ready, cut them into small cubes and lay on a plate to cool. Mix together the yoghurt and eggplant and garnish with the mint leaves.

Cardoon · Artichoke

Artichokes may be eaten hot or cold, but either way they must first be boiled vigorously for 30–40 minutes. The saucepan should be left uncovered during boiling, otherwise they will take on a bitter flavor. The smaller heads, picked at the end of the season, can be preserved in oil. This is a simple process: clean the heads, removing the tougher scales, cut off the tops, then cut the heads twice lengthwise, thus obtaining four pieces for each head. Boil them in a mixture of water, white wine, salt, and vinegar. Drain, put in jars, and cover with olive oil flavored with capers, oregano or chili peppers.

There is some confusion regarding the origin of cardoons and globe artichokes. Some European botanists believe that both vegetables were derived from a wild perennial herb (*Cynara cardunculus* var. *silvestris*) that grows in southern Europe and northern Africa. Current American taxonomists think that they are two distinct species, cardoon (*C. cardunculus*) and globe artichoke (*C. scolymos*). Others consider the globe artichoke to be a cultivated form of cardoon. The wild species of cardoon is of medium size, growing up to about 3 ft (0.9 m). It has many thorns and its flowers are much smaller than those of the globe artichoke. The cultivated cardoon (*C. cardunculus* var. *altilis*) is very different from the original form. It is much taller (6–7 ft [1.8–2.1 m]) with fleshier leaves and fewer thorns. The flowers are deep blue with large inflorescences. Cardoons look even more different when they arrive on the market because they are

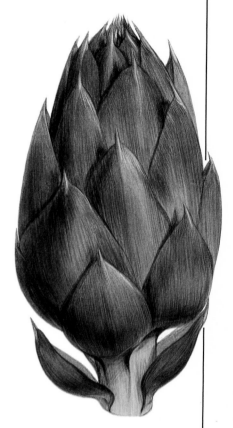

artificially blanched. Although the cardoon is a perennial plant, it is cultivated as an annual. It is sown in spring in cold frames and the seedlings are transplanted later to the field. At the beginning of the fall, at the height of its vegetative development, it is subjected to blanching through various processes. One of the older methods was to tie the leaves at the top into a bunch and draw the soil up around the base of the plant. Today it is more convenient to cover the plant with canvas or opaque plastic or cardboard packing. The leaves that are gradually forming inside the rosette are white and very tender, suitable for eating raw. But generally cardoons are eaten hot, and are first boiled so that the leaf stalks will be tender. Often they are seasoned with cheese or white sauce, and are also good when breaded and fried. Cultivated artichokes (*C. cardunculus* var. *scolymus*) are taller than cardoons, although with smaller heads. The leaves are wider and fleshier.

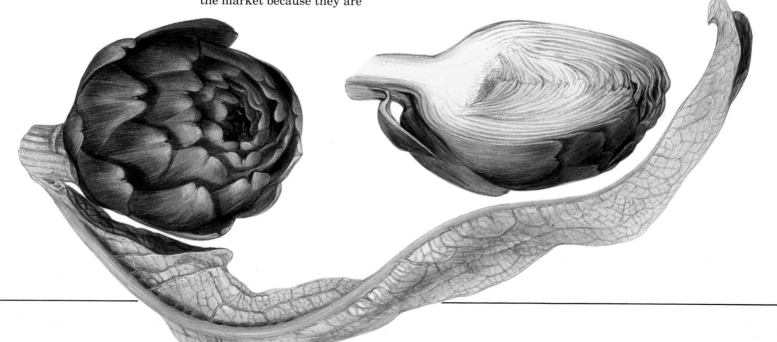

Zucchini or Courgette

Two globular zucchini. Young, tender fruits can be cooked with their flowers. Place straight in a saucepan with a piece of butter and a touch of garlic. Cover and stew for 5–10 minutes.

Zucchini (*Cucurbita pepo*) belong to the *Cucurbitaceae*. In Britain they are called courgettes. Their fruits are eaten when unripe, and since the younger ones are preferred they are often sold still bearing the flower. Zucchini are annual herbaceous plants with sturdy running stalks which can easily grow up to 3–4 ft (0.9–1.2 m) or more in length. The leaves, large, hispid, wrinkled, and lobed, are supported by long, thick, completely hollow petioles. Like the majority of *Cucurbitaceae*, zucchini bear staminate and pistillate flowers separately on the same plant. They are therefore monoecious plants with unisexual flowers. The pistillate (female) flowers have small ovaries just behind the flower that develops into the fruits. The staminate (male) flowers have large and showy corollas with petals fused together, and are a beautiful golden-yellow color. They can

be distinguished from the pistillate flowers because they have longer and thinner peduncles and, of course, no ovaries. These flowers are sometimes sold in continental markets in little bunches. They are good dipped in a batter of milk and flour and then fried.

The fruits of the cultivars used when still unripe, called by the Italian name, zucchini, are for the most part smooth and cylindrical, sometimes also globular. They are, in general, uniformly dark or light green; but some cultivars are variegated. Some botanists, including Naudin, have subdivided the polymorphic category of the exponents of *C. pepo* into seven groups. Today, within the zucchini, there are numerous, very popular cultivars. Some of the best known are the Apulia striated, the green round, the Bolognese or the Faenza gardener with long ovoid fruits; various new American varieties with

Zucchini should first be washed and then the ends sliced off so that they do not absorb the water. They can be sliced either thinly or thickly for stewing or boiling; alternatively, cut into sticks for frying. The flowers can be dipped in batter and fried. They can also be chopped and used in omelets.

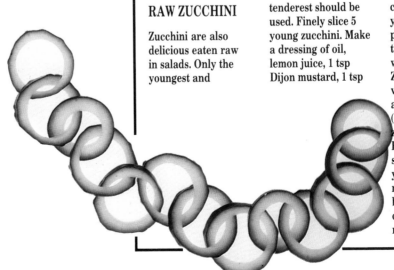

RAW ZUCCHINI

Zucchini are also delicious eaten raw in salads. Only the youngest and tenderest should be used. Finely slice 5 young zucchini. Make a dressing of oil, lemon juice, 1 tsp Dijon mustard, 1 tsp cream, 1 tsp natural yoghurt, salt, and pepper. Pour over the zucchini and mix well.

Zucchini are also a versatile and attractive garnish (see below). Cut the zucchini into rounds. Remove the pulp and slice finely so that you are left with thin rings. Link together by making a small cut in each alternate ring.

Zucchini or Courgette

PICKLED ZUCCHINI

Cut the fresh, young zucchini into medium-sized slices. Put 2¼ cups/1 pint/ 500 ml water into a saucepan together with the same amount of white wine vinegar. When the liquid has started boiling add the zucchini and parboil for 3 minutes. Remove the slices with a slotted spoon and leave on kitchen paper to dry. Arrange the slices neatly in a preserving jar, sprinkling a little finely chopped parsley, oregano, fennel seeds, and garlic between the layers. Once the jar is filled cover the zucchini with olive oil and cover the jar with a cloth. Add a little oil each day until the level remains the same. Seal the jar and store for 1 month before using.

cylindrical, dark green fruits, such as the Ambassador, the various Black Jack, Store's Green, Super Diamond, and others.
Boiled and seasoned with oil and lemon juice they are easily digestible and therefore good for convalescents or people on strict diets. Zucchini are thought to have a considerable diuretic action and to be effective against constipation because of the mucilage they contain. If the thought of boiled zucchini served only with oil and lemon juice appears unappetizing, there are numerous other ways in which they can be prepared. They are very good dipped in batter or in egg and breadcrumbs and then fried; stuffed; stewed separately or with other vegetables such as eggplants, tomatoes, potatoes, peppers, etc. A typical dish of southern Italy is *tenerume*: the very young shoots, together with flowers and leaves, are picked, cleaned, boiled and then sautéed with garlic and chili pepper.

Zucchini flowers have to be very fresh. They are delicious fried in a light batter made with a little flour, warm water, and a pinch of salt.

Squashes · Pumpkins · Gourds

The fruits of this family vary greatly in size, shape, and color: Yokohama, chayote (with spines) and cushaw (cut in half). Chayotes can be stewed, stuffed, fried, boiled or cooked in many other ways. It is also possible to cook the young shoots in the same way as asparagus. Even the tuberous roots, rich in starch, are edible.

The gourd family (*Cucurbitaceae*) includes the pumpkin, squash, cucumber, zucchini, and melon. The curious variety of forms and bright hues of the fruits of this family make an interesting and colorful display. The species of the genus *Cucurbita* are herbaceous plants of great size with long vinelike shoots bearing tendrils. They are monoecious, that is, with male and female organs in different flowers on the same plant. The fruits of curbitaceous plants generally have a fleshy, many-seeded interior with a hard or firm rind. The colors vary enormously from rich, dark green to bright yellow and burnt orange. Some fruits are used for decoration only, but most are edible.

The two main types of squash are summer squash and winter squash. Summer squash are generally small, fast-growing with soft seeds and thin skin. Zucchini (courgettes) are characteristic of this type. Summer squash can usually be cooked without peeling or removing the seeds. The pumpkin is characteristic of winter squash. Both seeds and thick skin must be removed before cooking. Winter squash is best when fried, baked or used in stews. Winter squash can be stored for months providing only the best are used, and they are kept in a relatively warm, humid place. There are many shapes, colors, and sizes of the different types of fruit. The chayote (*Sechium edule*), illustrated left, is a slightly elongated pear-shape with green spiny skin. It is a rampant climbing plant with shoots sometimes several yards

From left: sea or Chioggia squash, Ohio squash, and two turban squashes. The turban squash has a lovely, deep orange flesh which is often used for its decorative effect.

long. The fruit hangs down evenly spaced. Uncharacteristically each fruit contains only one seed which has the unusual property of germinating while inside the fruit. They are best eaten when young and tender. They can be cooked like zucchini, without peeling, and served with a simple dressing of olive oil and lemon juice. Older and larger chayotes can be stewed, stuffed, fried, boiled or cooked in other ways. Some of the most classic and best known examples of the larger fruits of the gourd family (*Cucurbita maxima*) are illustrated above:

the Sea or Chioggia squash with a coarsely wrinkled rind, generally metallic gray or greenish, and Turban squashes (var. *turbaniformis* or *pileiformis*). In the last few years a form of turban squash with rather small and brightly colored fruits, the expanded part bright red, and the tapering part lemon yellow, has become very popular as ornamentals. The sea squashes have very mealy flesh: they can be boiled, baked or puréed, and also used in soups. Sometimes the unripe fruits are used for relishes and preserves.

If you purchase a whole squash, quarter it and scrape out the seeds and loosest fibers with a sharp knife. Cut the flesh into chunks and remove the skin. The chunks of flesh should be cooked in as little water as possible as the squash itself contains its own liquid. Alternatively, the flesh can be baked and either mashed with butter or used as stuffing. Squashes also make excellent soup.

Squashes · Pumpkins · Gourds

Naples stuffed squash (*Cucurbita moschata*) is commonly grown in southern Mediterranean regions. The fruit is cylindrical with bronze, greenish or brightly variegated skin. The flesh is a beautiful orange-yellow. The largest fruits can reach up to 3 ft (0.9 m) and weigh 44 lb (20 kg).

Scallop gourd (*Cucurbita pepo* var. *melopepo*) has a variety of forms and colors. It is particularly interesting for its ornamental uses. Some cultivars are known as pattypan or custard squash, and are also excellent baked or boiled, and mashed with butter.

Bottle gourd (*Lagenaria siceraria*) is a very popular variety because of the many shapes and colors: some are metallic green, others have dark green variegations. In the past the dried shells of the fruit were used to make bottles and gunpowder flasks; today they are used exclusively as ornaments. The dry fruits can also be decorated by painting or fire branding.

Crookneck squash and *Brazilian pumpkin* are two forms of *Cucurbita maxima*. They should be eaten when fully ripe. They can therefore be stored, though not for too long, for the fall and winter seasons. Both can be stewed or, more generally, cooked in the same way as the chayote.

Cocozelle is a variety of summer squash with a green skin that is usually striped with a lighter green or yellow. This is a form of zucchini and is cooked in the same way.

American pumpkin, a cultivar of *Cucurbita pepo*, has similar

Squashes · Pumpkins · Gourds

qualities to the Naples stuffed squash. Despite its name it is most commonly grown in southern Europe. Pumpkins are much in demand for making the famous American pumpkin pie and are also used at Hallowe'en for the making of jack-o'-lanterns. Illustrated on page 20 are some specimens of winter squash (*C. maxima*) with roughly tapered or spherical shapes. Squashes are easily hybridized, so that the range of colors and forms that can be

obtained is very wide and it is difficult to tell one variety from another. Some of these tapering or oval squashes are ascribed to the variety *ohioensis* and are commonly called Hubbard or Ohio squashes. Very large specimens are also known as Mammoth squashes or Whale pumpkins. These can weigh up to 110–132 lb (50–60 kg). Because they have less flavor and a high water content, they are used almost exclusively to feed livestock.

Illustrated on page 20

A simple, delicious way of cooking squash is by chopping it into small cubes and frying them in oil for 10 minutes. Remove from the oil and place on kitchen towels to absorb excess oil. Season before serving.

Opposite: a selection of squasnes and gourds: Naples stuffed squash (large, orange-colored), winter crookneck squash (bright yellow), cocozelle (very elongated, pale green), and a small scallop gourd.
Right: more examples of squashes and pumpkins: Ohio squash (dark green with crinkly skin), crookneck squash (yellow with very curved neck), American pumpkin (spherical with orange skin), and a small yellow Brazilian pumpkin.

Asparagus

HOW TO COOK ASPARAGUS

Asparagus should be tied in a bunch, and steamed in a high-sided saucepan with the tips uppermost, out of the water. Cook for 10–15 minutes, or until tender.

The edible part of the asparagus (*Asparagus officinalis*), a genus of the *Liliaceae*, is provided by the very fleshy and tender "spears" or young sprouts. Cultivated asparagus is derived from a wild form still commonly found in sandy places, woods, and along river banks in south-central Europe, western and central Asia, and in northern Africa. The plants can be started from seeds, or, better, from the so-called "crowns," the subterranean stems (rootstocks) which are provided with a cluster of white, fleshy roots. The spears, usually sold at very high prices, arise from the crowns in the following spring, or, because of forced growth, also in the fall and winter. Asparagus has a long historical record. Proof of its use in ancient Egypt has been found on old bas-reliefs. It was also used by the Greeks and Romans. Its use seems to have disappeared in the Middle Ages, except in Arab countries. It started again in Europe during the reign of the Sun King, Louis XIV of France, spreading especially in regions characterized by fertile and sandy soils where it grows best. Later, through repeated selections, asparagus has evolved from the forms still close to the wild species, with thin, green spears, to those with fleshier and larger spears, variously pigmented. The commercial names of asparagus are derived primarily from the places where it is intensively cultivated and from the color of the spears. So there are the Argenteuil asparagus, which is white and considered to be the best, the purple Holland asparagus, the white German asparagus, the purple Genoa asparagus, and the Mary Washington of America. Its uses in cookery are varied.

Right: wild asparagus, which is just as delicious as the cultivated varieties. The culinary applications of asparagus are varied: it can be used in soups, or steamed and served with butter and Parmesan cheese, or oil and lemon juice.

Carrot

The uses of the carrot for food date from the sixteenth century when some better varieties were obtained from the wild form. The carrot is an important garden vegetable as shown by the continuously growing number of cultivars recently introduced. In cultivation it is considered an annual plant, but its natural cycle is really biennial. This means that the root is developed during the first year, while flowers and seeds are produced during the second year. The edible part of the carrot is supplied by the conical, thick, and fleshy root. The very numerous cultivated varieties are divided into two large groups, according to either the color of the root (red, yellow or white) or its size (short, medium or long). The best quality carrots are the orange-yellow ones of medium or short size.

Carrots have considerable medicinal and nutritive properties, having a large amount of sugar and being rich in vitamins, particularly in alfa-beta-gamma carotene, which is responsible for the typical coloration. The beta carotene, also called provitamin A, is transformed into Vitamin A, thus becoming part of the growth vitamins. The beta-carotene content of 1 lb of carrots is about $4\frac{1}{2}$ times the minimum daily requirement of the human body. There is a considerable amount of vitamins B_1 and C, which helps to increase the body's resistance to certain illnesses. Carrots also contain an essential oil, rich in vitamin E and carbohydrates. Conversely, they are low in protein and lipids.

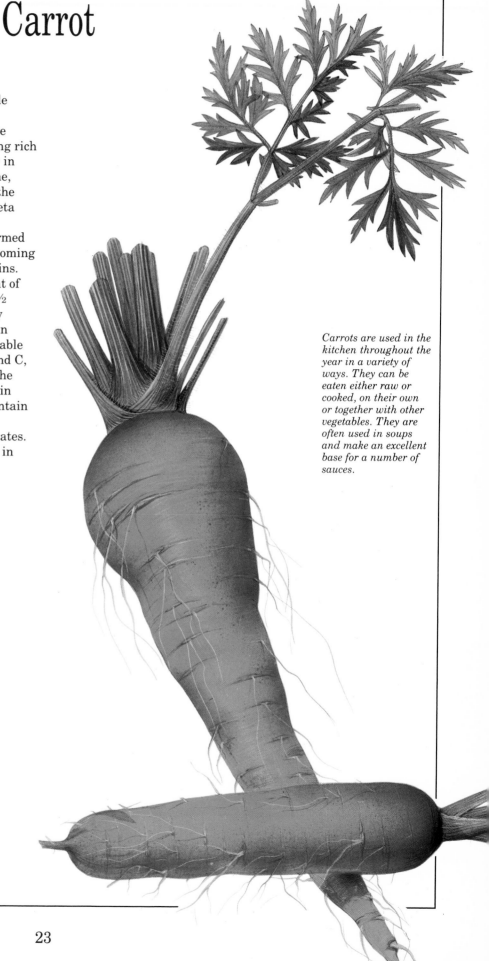

Carrots are used in the kitchen throughout the year in a variety of ways. They can be eaten either raw or cooked, on their own or together with other vegetables. They are often used in soups and make an excellent base for a number of sauces.

INDIAN CARROT JELLY

$1\frac{1}{4}$ lb/600 g carrots; 1–$1\frac{1}{4}$ pints/ 600–700 ml milk; 1 envelope saffron; 2 oz/50 g clear, runny honey; $\frac{1}{2}$ tsp cinnamon; $\frac{1}{2}$ oz/15 g gelatin.

Grate the carrots and boil in the milk for up to 1 hour, until creamed. Add the saffron, butter, honey, and cinnamon and mix into the carrot cream. Pour into individual molds and chill until set.

Garlic

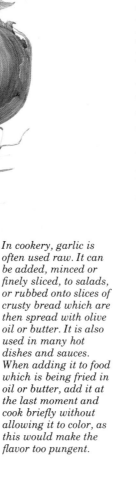

In cookery, garlic is often used raw. It can be added, minced or finely sliced, to salads, or rubbed onto slices of crusty bread which are then spread with olive oil or butter. It is also used in many hot dishes and sauces. When adding it to food which is being fried in oil or butter, add it at the last moment and cook briefly without allowing it to color, as this would make the flavor too pungent.

At the mention of garlic (*Allium sativum*) sensitive people might turn their heads away in disgust. This is more likely to happen in Anglo-Saxon than in Latin countries, where it is the king of herbs and is used extensively with meat, fish, and other vegetables. The Latin genus name, *Allium*, is probably derived from the Celtic word "all," meaning hot, burning, which is exactly the sensation that garlic produces on the palate. Among the several different hypotheses about the place of origin of garlic, the most likely is central Asia. Garlic has been known and cultivated in China since time immemorial and, according to Herodotus, was widely used by the ancient Egyptians. From Egypt it was introduced to the Greeks and Romans.

This herb is used almost exclusively to season foods. Its aromatic properties are due to a crystalline amino acid called alliin contained in its oil that converts to allicin by enzymatic action, thus releasing the characteristic odor. Besides being very important in the preparation of food, garlic is thought by many to be a truly medicinal plant; it is said to promote hypotensive and cardiovascular activity and to be beneficial to the respiratory system. Pliny had great admiration for it, and believed it to be a cure for consumption. Mohammed recommended it as an antidote to the bites of snakes and scorpions. It was said to reduce lethargy, and Aristophanes told of athletes eating garlic before exercising in the stadium. Culpeper, the great seventeenth-century English herbalist, used it to cure almost everything, including the plague. He advised that "it be taken inwardly with great moderation; outwardly you may make more bold with it," believing that it accentuated characteristics already present in a person's personality; "in choleric men it adds fuel to the fire; in men oppressed by melancholy, it will attenuate humour. . . ." Wreaths of garlic hung outside the door were supposed to ward off witches in medieval times. Garlic is now used a great deal pharmacologically.

GARLIC BUTTER

3½ oz/100 g butter; 6 cloves garlic; 1 tbsp lemon juice; salt and pepper.

Peel the garlic cloves and mince. Beat the softened butter with a wooden spoon, add the minced garlic and lemon juice, and season to taste with salt and pepper.

Spread on French bread and bake in foil, or add to steamed fish or vegetables.

Minced garlic, fried in butter with a little fresh rosemary, can be added to boiled rice as a subtle flavoring.

Onion

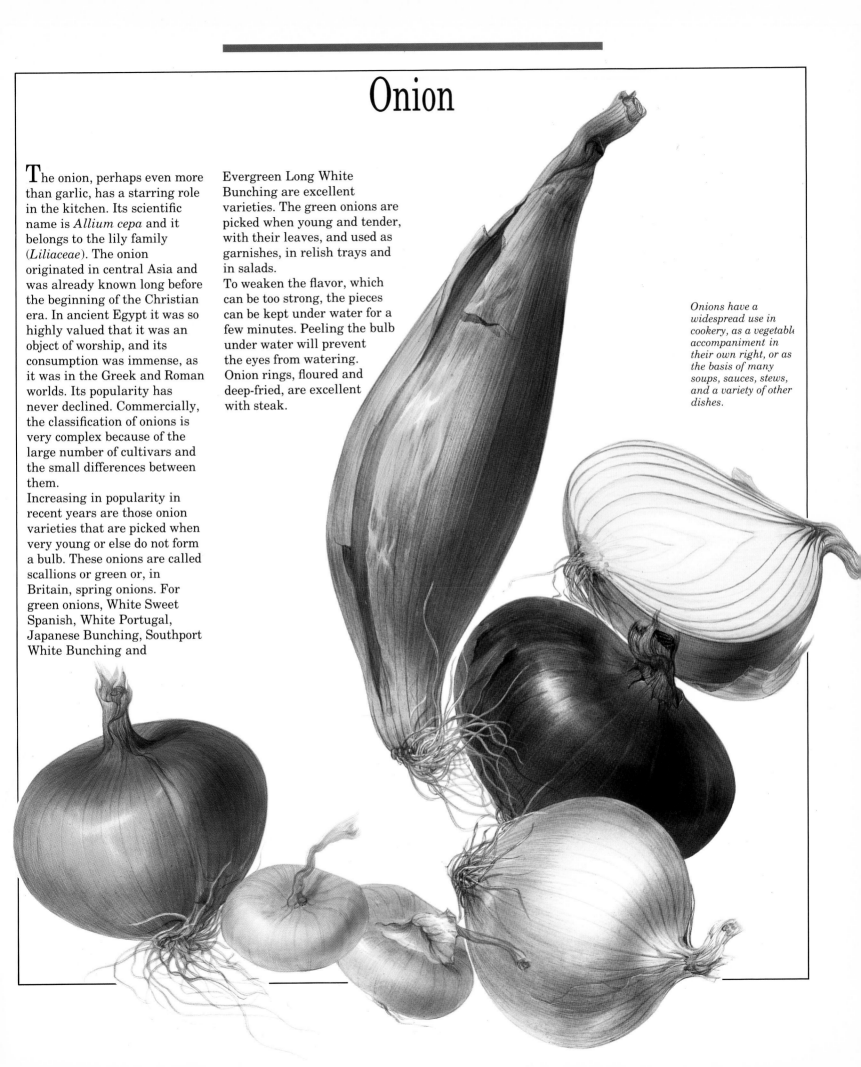

The onion, perhaps even more than garlic, has a starring role in the kitchen. Its scientific name is *Allium cepa* and it belongs to the lily family (*Liliaceae*). The onion originated in central Asia and was already known long before the beginning of the Christian era. In ancient Egypt it was so highly valued that it was an object of worship, and its consumption was immense, as it was in the Greek and Roman worlds. Its popularity has never declined. Commercially, the classification of onions is very complex because of the large number of cultivars and the small differences between them.

Increasing in popularity in recent years are those onion varieties that are picked when very young or else do not form a bulb. These onions are called scallions or green or, in Britain, spring onions. For green onions, White Sweet Spanish, White Portugal, Japanese Bunching, Southport White Bunching and

Evergreen Long White Bunching are excellent varieties. The green onions are picked when young and tender, with their leaves, and used as garnishes, in relish trays and in salads.

To weaken the flavor, which can be too strong, the pieces can be kept under water for a few minutes. Peeling the bulb under water will prevent the eyes from watering. Onion rings, floured and deep-fried, are excellent with steak.

Onions have a widespread use in cookery, as a vegetable accompaniment in their own right, or as the basis of many soups, sauces, stews, and a variety of other dishes.

Leek

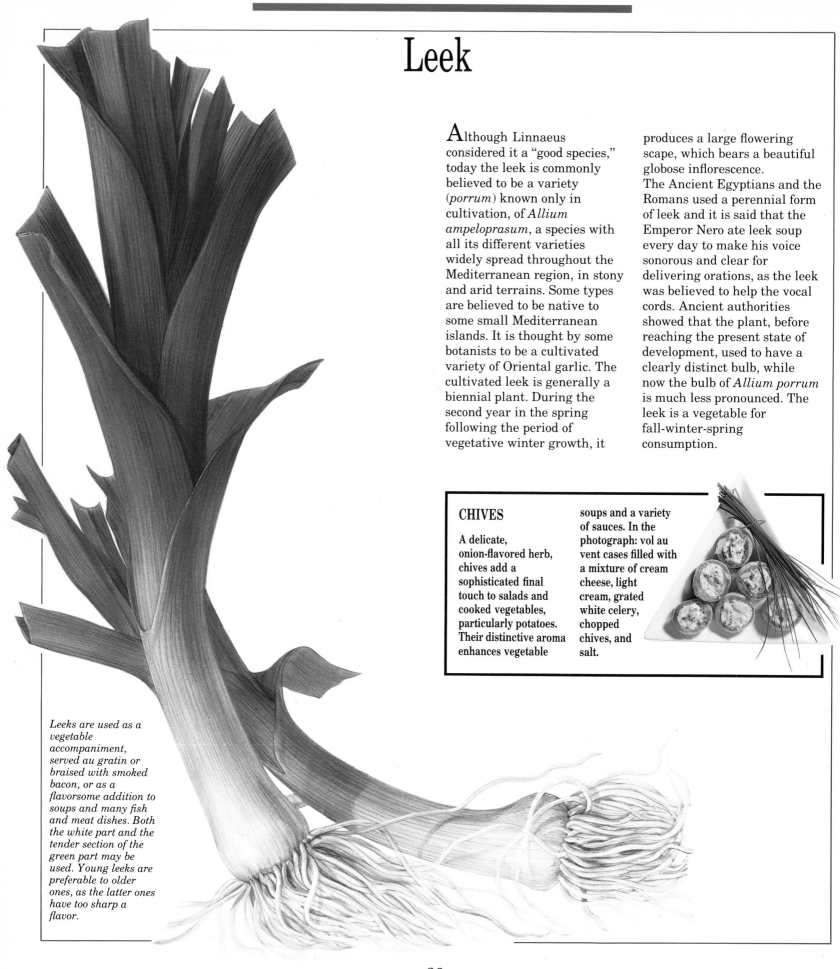

Although Linnaeus considered it a "good species," today the leek is commonly believed to be a variety (*porrum*) known only in cultivation, of *Allium ampeloprasum*, a species with all its different varieties widely spread throughout the Mediterranean region, in stony and arid terrains. Some types are believed to be native to some small Mediterranean islands. It is thought by some botanists to be a cultivated variety of Oriental garlic. The cultivated leek is generally a biennial plant. During the second year in the spring following the period of vegetative winter growth, it produces a large flowering scape, which bears a beautiful globose inflorescence.

The Ancient Egyptians and the Romans used a perennial form of leek and it is said that the Emperor Nero ate leek soup every day to make his voice sonorous and clear for delivering orations, as the leek was believed to help the vocal cords. Ancient authorities showed that the plant, before reaching the present state of development, used to have a clearly distinct bulb, while now the bulb of *Allium porrum* is much less pronounced. The leek is a vegetable for fall-winter-spring consumption.

CHIVES

A delicate, onion-flavored herb, chives add a sophisticated final touch to salads and cooked vegetables, particularly potatoes. Their distinctive aroma enhances vegetable soups and a variety of sauces. In the photograph: vol au vent cases filled with a mixture of cream cheese, light cream, grated white celery, chopped chives, and salt.

Leeks are used as a vegetable accompaniment, served au gratin or braised with smoked bacon, or as a flavorsome addition to soups and many fish and meat dishes. Both the white part and the tender section of the green part may be used. Young leeks are preferable to older ones, as the latter ones have too sharp a flavor.

Grape hyacinth · Shallot

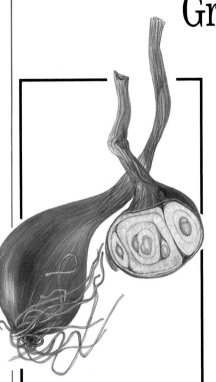

SHALLOT SAUCE

Shallot bulbs should be peeled and chopped. Use raw or cooked as an aromatic addition to a variety of dishes, sauces, and salads. For a simple but delicious sauce, melt a piece of butter and fry 1 chopped shallot until soft. Add the chopped yolk of 2 hard-boiled eggs and the juice of 1 lemon. Blend well and cook over low heat for a few minutes. When creamy, add black pepper and a sprinkling of chopped parsley. Serve with meat or fish.

The use of the grape hyacinth (*Muscari atlanticum* or *Leopoldia comosa*) is characteristic of the cooking of the regions surrounding the Mediterranean, especially Greece. Today, however, it can easily be found in northern markets and is exported in quantity to North America, probably because of the large Italian population established there. The bulbs of the grape hyacinth, which constitute the edible part, have a slightly bitter flavor. It is necessary, therefore, to boil them in a large pot of water with a few drops of vinegar. Afterwards, they can be preserved, either pickled or in oil, and served as antipasto or as a relish. They are thought by many to have diuretic qualities and to be helpful in stimulating the appetite.

The shallot (*Allium ascalonicum*) has never been found in the wild state; its place of origin is therefore unknown. It is very similar to the onion in the shape of the bulb and in the tubular leaves. Little is known about the origin of the shallot. It was not known in ancient times. The only sure fact is that it was known around the twelfth or thirteenth century. There are two types of shallot: the common shallot with pear-shaped bulb about the size of a walnut, and the Jersey shallot with more compressed bulbs, sometimes larger in width than in length. Its flavor is more delicate than the onion's and it is more digestible.

The only edible part of the grape hyacinth is the bulb. The leaves and purple-blue flowers are inedible.

Water chestnut

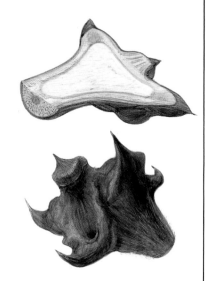

In the search for food plants which are now obsolete or little known, a prominent place should be given to the water chestnut. This is the fruit of an annual herbaceous plant, *Trapa natans*, belonging to the *Onagraceae* or evening primrose family. It is a water plant, growing anchored to the bottom of lakes or ponds, and sending up to the surface a thin stem which will produce a rosette of floating leaves. The fruit has oddly shaped sharp thorns and is filled with starchy tissues. The typical species is widely dispersed throughout the world, in Europe, western Asia, India, northern and tropical Africa, and northern Italy, and it has become naturalized in North America. Within the species, various forms, supposedly endemic, have been distinguished.

The strange fruits look very unusual. Under the tough skin, water chestnuts have a sweet and tender pulp, rich in starch, which was greatly in demand in the past. They have an agreeable and delicate flavor, very similar to that of boiled chestnuts. The water chestnut is still celebrated as the main ingredient of a famous Italian risotto, invented by a citizen of Bologna. Brown some shallots in oil and butter, add the rice and sauté, stirring, for a few minutes. Add some warm meat stock and cook, uncovered; when the rice is half done, add thin slices of water chestnut. Let the rice cook, adding more stock if necessary.

A *T. bicornis* called *ling kio* is known in China, and a *T. bispinosa* is used in tropical regions, Asia, Ceylon, Africa, and in India where it is called *singhara*. The fruits of *T. bispinosa* are eaten boiled or made into flour used for making confections with sugar and honey. They are served as a vegetable in Chinese restaurants. The water chestnut is another plant connected with the Jesuits, and is sometimes called Jesuits' nut.

The edible part of the water chestnut is the inner bulb. The tough skin that encloses the tuber should be removed. Widespread in Chinese cookery, the water chestnut may be bought canned.

Sweet potato · Jerusalem artichoke

The origin of the sweet potato (*Ipomea batatas*) causes some confusion. It is not related in any way to the true potato. This name was given to it when Columbus brought it back from America to Europe. However, it cannot be stated definitely that the sweet potato is native to America because some authorities maintain that Asia, where it was extensively cultivated before arriving in Europe, is its true place of origin. Whether American or Asiatic, the sweet potato is a plant of nutritional interest, as it can sometimes substitute for the common potato, with which it shares some properties, such as the high percentage of starch. Although in Europe its use is limited, in some regions of Asia, in particular Indochina, the sweet potato is one of the most important crops from the economic point of view. In the United States it has wide use as a vegetable, cooked, in the same way as yams. It is often featured a lot in Creole cookery, where it is made into cakes and sweet soufflés.

The Jerusalem artichoke (*Helianthus tuberosus*) is native to America. It is a close relative of the sunflower, but unlike that plant it is not cultivated for the extraction of oil, but only for its edible tubers. It originated in North America and was introduced to France during the seventeenth century. The flavor of the cooked tuber is similar to that of the artichoke; the appearance is that of a knobby potato which, at the moment of harvest, being covered with dirt, vaguely resembles the truffle. The tubers are harvested at the beginning of October and throughout the winter months. This plant spreads rapidly, and the few specimens of one year can multiply enormously in the following one. The use of these tubers in cookery is very varied and they can satisfy many palates. Cleaned, washed, and sliced they are very good in a sauce of anchovies and garlic. They can also be sautéed with parsley, or slowly boiled and then dipped into cold water, drained and fried.

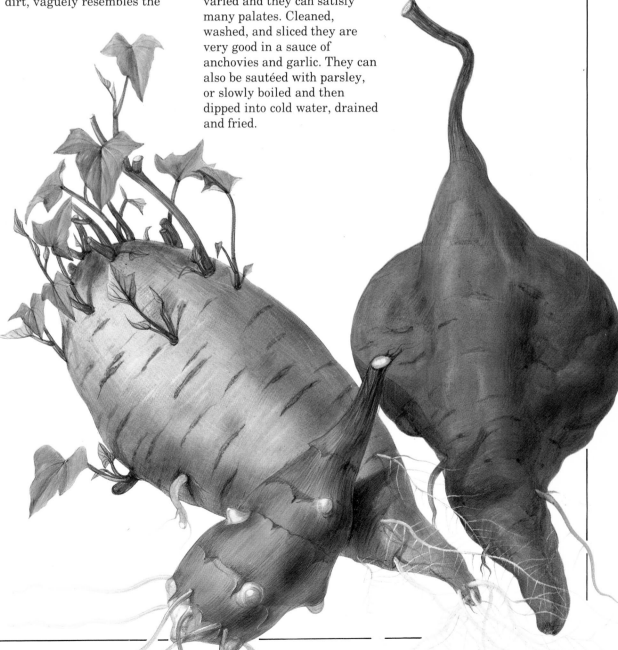

A white sweet potato (left), a red sweet potato (right), and, below, a Jerusalem artichoke.

Potato

There are many commercial varieties of potato to choose from. White (floury) potatoes lend themselves well to mashing, whereas yellow (waxy) potatoes are best fried or roasted. Potatoes may be kept for a considerable time once dug up, and are therefore always available in the shops. Small, new potatoes should be eaten at once.

Among the food plants of great economic interest that the American continent has offered to the Old World (including corn, tomatoes, peppers, and eggplants), the potato (*Solanum tuberosum*) is probably the most important. Its centers of origin can be found in some areas of Peru, Bolivia, and Mexico, where it is believed to have been cultivated during the Aztec and Inca civilizations. It was introduced into France and Spain during the second half of the sixteenth century, and in the early years was sometimes grown as an ornamental for its flowers. Sir John Hawkins is thought to have first brought the potato to England in 1563, but it was not until twenty years later, after Sir Francis Drake had reintroduced it to Britain, that its highly nutritious value was recognized and its cultivation taken seriously. Sir Walter Raleigh grew potatoes in Ireland. It was realized that the potato could be very important in human nutrition. Consequently an intensive campaign was begun to spread and increase its cultivation. Sometimes, in periods of scarcity or war, the potato was used as a substitute for wheat and other cereals, which was another reason for further extension. Today it is cultivated in every continent, and the yearly world production is now around 300 million tons, half of which comes from Europe. Russia, Poland, and Germany are in the lead for the quantity and quality of the production. In some countries, like the United States and Britain, the potato is a complementary food, suitable for the preparation of a large variety of excellent dishes (fried, baked, boiled, mashed, dumplings, etc.). But in countries such as those of central and eastern Europe,

POTATO SKINS

Traditionally, cooks were taught to boil potatoes in their skins so none of the vitamins and minerals would be lost. More recently, however, the skins have been found to contain substances that could prove toxic and provoke headaches, nausea or, in some cases, even intestinal problems. The safest method of cooking is to steam peeled potatoes.

Potato

the potato substitutes, partly or totally, for the starchy food generally included in the daily diet. The dry tuber contains an average of 66% starch, the principal component of its calories; 4% sugars; 9% protein; and about 0.5% potassium, phosphorus and lipids. The potato can provide the human body with such useful elements as copper and iron that are, for example, in minimal percentage in milk, which is considered a complete food. For those who are overweight, the potato could take the place of bread, because as far as calories are concerned, the equivalent of 3–4 oz of bread corresponds to approximately 1 lb of potatoes. It would be impossible during a meal to eat a quantity of

potatoes corresponding in calories to the amount of bread that the people of some nations normally eat. Because of its low percentage of salts, the potato is often eaten by those suffering from high blood pressure. It also has some vitamins, especially vitamin C and thiamin (B_1), riboflavin (B_2), and pantothenic acid. Besides human nutrition, the tubers of *S. tuberosum* have many other uses: some varieties, rich in water, are grown for forage, others are used for the extraction of starches and the production of alcohol. In Poland a vodka, almost 100% proof, is produced from potatoes. For these secondary uses, the flavor of the tubers is obviously not important.

HOW TO SERVE POTATOES

Roast potatoes
Peel the potatoes, and cut into even-sized pieces. Parboil for 5 minutes, drain, and place in a roasting tin with oil or melted shortening. Roast at 425°F for about 40 minutes or until done.

Sauté potatoes
Slice peeled potatoes into thin rings. Boil for 15 minutes, drain, then cook in a skillet in butter or oil until crisp all over.

French fries
For thin, crisp French fries use a special cutter known

as a mandoline. Deep-fry until golden brown.

Noisette potatoes
Use a melon baller to cut out small potato balls. Boil for 5 minutes, then sauté gently in butter for 3 minutes.

Broccoli · Cauliflower · Brussels sprouts

Vegetables belonging to the cabbage family have been cultivated since very early times. They are derived from a wild form native to central and western Europe, and western Asia. Some botanists ascribe these wild plants to the variety *silvicola* which grows on rocks. They are all included in the diffuse and polymorphic species *Brassica oleracea* of the *Cruciferae* (mustard family). Today, because of selections started many centuries ago, the cultivated forms differ greatly, not only from the original type, but also from one another. They can be classified simply and concisely as follows:

var.: *acephala*, including the headless cabbages, with long stems, broad green leaves, at times bearing leafy appendices on the primary or secondary ribs. These cabbages are mostly used as livestock feed, and very occasionally for human consumption, as in the case of the black cabbage or Tuscany Black;

var.: *gemmifera*, which produces the Brussels sprouts; the sprouts are large adventitious buds, with tightly compact leaves, which develop along the stem at the axil of the leaves;

var.: *sabauda* or *bullata*, known as Savoy cabbage, with short stem and leaves crimped, blistered and closely appressed, forming a compact

The odor of cabbage and cauliflower during cooking is very pronounced. Many believe that a little vinegar, a piece of stale bread or a peeled potato added to the cooking water will keep the odor at bay. Be that as it may, it is good for us to eat these vegetables occasionally, rich as they are in potassium, phosphorus, and calcium.

and globose head, usually until flowering time;

var.: *capitata*, or common cabbage, with smooth, pale green leaves (but also red or purple) which are tightly appressed to form an even more compact head than that of the Savoy;

var.: *gongyloides* or *caulorapa*, called kohlrabi, with a fleshy, swollen stem, globe-shaped;

var.: *botrytis*, the cauliflower, in which the edible part is provided by the large, hypertrophied inflorescence, still unripe, with fleshy branches which form a generally globular structure, the head being sometimes pointed at the top;

var.: *cauliflora*, commonly called broccoli, with leaves less broad and thick than those of the cauliflower, and less tight floral peduncles, forming a more open head which expands like an umbrella.

In Europe, the ancient Germans made great use of the cabbage. The varieties of greatest economic and commercial importance today are the Savoy, the common cabbage, and the cauliflower. The Savoy and common cabbage show a consistently parallel behavior. In the course of time, selection has brought about great changes in the appearance of these vegetables compared with the wild varieties. The leaves have become very broad and tightly appressed, forming the so-called head, which can be spherical, oblong, or slightly depressed. The more firm and compact the head, the more valuable is the cabbage commercially, as the internal leaves will be smoother,

whiter, and more tender. The external leaves are tougher (those of the Savoy being more crimped and blistered), more deeply colored, and often having a soft bloom that gives them a characteristic waxy appearance. A longitudinal section shows that the head is a very large terminal bud. In the spring (cabbages are late summer and autumnal crops, lasting until the next spring) when the many dormant axillary buds start blooming, the head loses its compact shape and breaks down completely. From a dietary viewpoint both the Savoy and the common cabbage, like many plants of the mustard family, have been highly recommended, especially during winter, either raw or cooked. Raw cabbage has a high vitamin content, especially of vitamin C. Cooked cabbage is low in fat, medium-low in protein, a good diuretic agent and, because of

Opposite: broccoli and Brussels sprouts. Right: cauliflower. Brussels sprouts and cauliflower take 10–15 minutes to cook, broccoli a shorter time.

33

Cabbages · Greens

Common cabbage (top); Savoy cabbage (center); red cabbage (bottom); sea kale (bottom left).

its high content of cellulose fibers, effective as roughage in stimulating the intestines. Gastronomically, the Savoy variety is the base for many different soups and stews. It is also a good accompaniment to goose or duck. By using only the inner part of the head, it is possible to prepare very good winter salads and coleslaw. Both sauerkraut and braised red cabbage are better if simmered for 4–5 hours the day before they are to be eaten, and then reheated very slowly. For cooking purposes other varieties of cabbage, with the exception of broccoli and cauliflower, have similar characteristics to those of the Savoy and common cabbages. Brussels sprouts are usually boiled or steamed. Broccoli, after the basal part and tougher leaves are removed, should be boiled and served with butter or a hollandaise sauce. Broccoli has the following composition: 15–16% solid residue, with 5–6% protein, 5% carbohydrates, no lipids, 1% ash, and 43–44 calories per 3½ oz (100 g). It has almost twice as much nutritive value as Savoy cabbage.

There are also numerous varieties of cauliflower available. Cauliflowers have 8% solid residue, 2–3% protein, 1–2% carbohydrates, less than 1% ash, and no lipids. The calorific content is 17–18 calories per 3½ oz (100 g). Even after cooking the cauliflower still retains some vitamin C and small amounts of thiamene and carotene. It is eaten primarily cooked, or raw pickled in vinegar. While boiling, it is better to use very little water, leaving the head uncovered so that it will cook by steam. After cooking, the cauliflower can be eaten as an accompanying vegetable with a little butter, or served on its own with a cheese sauce. Black cabbage, which is common to Tuscany and central Italy, can be used in soups and stews. It is not much known in England or the United States.

Turnip tops (*Brassica campestris*), commonly called "greens," are the flowered tops of the turnip. For culinary purposes they are best when sautéed in oil with garlic, after boiling in the same manner as broccoli. They are one of the cheaper winter vegetables.

Sea-kale (*Crambe maritima*) is a large perennial herb of the mustard family, growing wild on the eastern and northern coasts of Europe. It is used as a vegetable in France and England, where several horticultural varieties have been developed. It should not be overcooked.

Turnip tops and black cabbage. The latter is a typical ingredient in Tuscan cuisine.

Capsicum

SPAGHETTI WITH GARLIC, OIL, AND CHILI PEPPER

14 oz/400 g spaghetti; 4–6 tbsp oil; 2 cloves garlic, finely sliced; 1 piece chili pepper, roughly chopped; salt; chopped parsley.

Boil the spaghetti in salted water. Meanwhile, prepare the sauce. Heat the oil in a skillet and gently fry the garlic and chili. Do not allow the garlic to color. Drain the pasta when done, pour over the hot, flavored oil, mix well, and sprinkle with chopped parsley. Serve at once.

Pepper varieties. Generally, the smaller, more elongated peppers are the hottest in flavor. Larger, bell peppers are suitable for eating raw in salads, roasted, or pickled.

The genus *Capsicum*, to which the pepper belongs, originated in South America, probably Brazil. Peppers have also been cultivated for several centuries in other parts of the American continent. They were introduced into Europe after the discovery of America.

They are annual or perennial herbaceous plants, but woody at the base, of modest size, and leaves with long petioles. The flowers are formed by five white petals: the fruits are hollow berries of varying shape. It is in relation to the shape of the fruit that some

botanists have proposed a classification, interesting commercially as well, which would subdivide the peppers into three groups of varieties: (1) peppers with smooth fruits and curved peduncles so that the fruits appear pendulous; (2) with more or less deeply lobed fruits and curved peduncles; (3) a group which includes forms and varieties with smooth fruits and erect peduncles. To the first group belong most of the peppers used as condiments, such as the various ordinary long red, or the similar cardinal, the Mexican long black (with long, very thin, red fruits), and the Cayenne pepper. The varieties with curved peduncles and lobed fruits include almost all the sweet table peppers which can be divided into four groups: typically square fruits; fruits tapering, like a child's

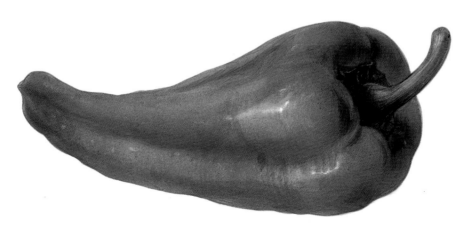

Capsicum

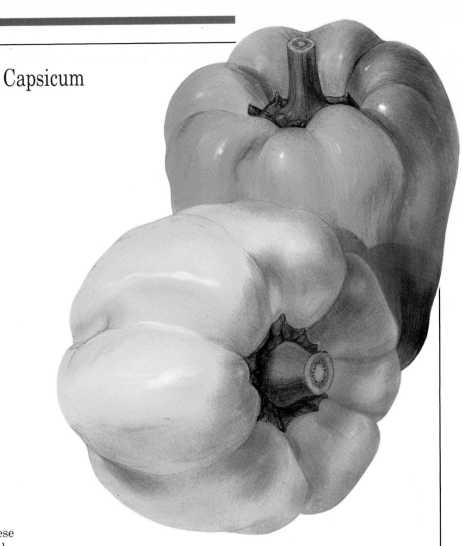

spinning top, at the apex; long, conical fruits, sometimes smooth, and sometimes contorted; and finally, not illustrated since they are no longer cultivated much, the flattened peppers known as tomato peppers. Among the best known and currently favored cultivars are the various Nocera and Asti "square" types, with yellow or bright red fruits, and the new California Wonder, Yolo Wonder, and Midway, the latter very early and edible both unripe, when it is a bright dark green, and ripe, when bright red. Also excellent for their fragrant sweet aroma and their crispness are the long peppers of "bull horn" or "of Spain" type, and the top-shaped peppers, with particularly fleshy fruits. The third category includes forms with erect peduncles; this

group includes the Chinese with conical yellow or red fruits, prized not only as a condiment but also as an ornamental fruit; the small "bunched" peppers with red, oblong, horn-shaped fruits; some other cherry peppers with spherical fruits but erect peduncles; the chili peppers, and many others. The very popular, ornamental forms also belong to this third category. In the United States, Bellringer, Bell Boy, California Wonder, Merrimack Wonder, and Worldbeater are leading varieties of sweet or green peppers for salads, which may also be cooked with various stuffings.

Sweet peppers are eaten either raw, dipped in oil; in *pinzimonio*, an oil, salt and pepper sauce; in salads, or mixed with other vegetables. They can also be cooked in

PEPERONATA

2¾ lb/1.2 kg green, red and yellow bell peppers; 1½ lb/700 g tomatoes, skinned and deseeded; 2 onions; 2–3 cloves garlic; 1–2 tbsp hot paprika; tabasco sauce; olive oil; salt and pepper.

Rinse the peppers and cut into strips. Chop the tomatoes, onions, and garlic. Place all these ingredients in a large saucepan, season with paprika, tabasco, and a little olive oil, and cover.

Cook over moderate heat for about 1 hour, stirring occasionally, and taking care the peppers do not stick to the saucepan.

Capsicum

many different ways: in combination with other vegetables, such as tomatoes, eggplants, and onions, or in the classic Sicilian *caponata* with eggplants, olives, and capers; they can also be stuffed or fried. A recipe that brings out all the flavor characteristic of peppers is to charcoal broil them, then remove the membranous skin, and season them with a few drops of olive oil, and, if desired, a little garlic. Peppers are also suitable for preserving in vinegar or, after boiling in water and vinegar, in oil. The best ones for this are the long green peppers, but all the cultivars with particularly fleshy tissues are suitable for preserving. Nutritionally, sweet peppers are low in calories and contain vitamins A, B, C, and E. The small hot peppers are used exclusively as a condiment and for seasoning meats, vegetables, and pasta. The pungent taste is due to the presence of an alkaloid called capsaicin.

Peppers should be cleaned and deseeded before use. Remove the stalk, slice the pepper in half and scoop out the seeds with a small knife. Remove the bitter white parts. Peppers may also be skinned: broil briefly or hold over a flame until the skin blackens and may easily be removed.

CHILI FLAVORING

An unusual way to use the chili pepper as a flavoring is to soak it in 2¼ cups/ 18 fl oz/500 ml sherry or vodka. Add small drops of the resulting mixture to soups. Olive oil may also be flavored with chili pepper.

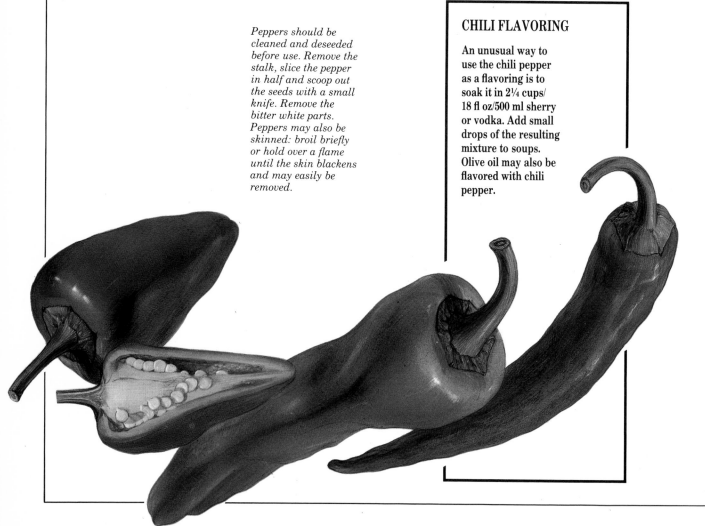

Corn salad or Lamb's lettuce ·
Bitter cress

FISH SALAD WITH LAMB'S LETTUCE

1 lamb's lettuce;
1 tomato, skinned
and deseeded; 1 can
tuna in oil; 1 can
mackerel in oil;
4 hard-boiled eggs;
1 tsp tomato paste;
1 tsp anchovy paste;

⅔ cup/5 fl oz/150 ml
mayonnaise; 1 tbsp
pickled capers;
1 clove garlic,
minced; olive oil;
juice of 1 lemon;
freshly ground black
pepper.

Lay the lettuce leaves
on a serving plate.
Finely chop the
tomato. Thinly slice
the fennel, drain and
flake the tuna and
mackerel, peel and
slice the eggs.
Arrange all these
over the lettuce. Mix
the tomato paste and
anchovy paste into
the mayonnaise, add
the capers and garlic,
and mix well. Drizzle
olive oil and lemon
juice over the salad,
season with black
pepper, and serve
with the flavored
mayonnaise.

*V*alerianella olitoria, the common corn salad (also lamb's lettuce, *Fetticus*), is one of the most prized salads for use between fall and spring. It is usually expensive, but, because of its small leaves, gives a very good yield and quite a small plant makes enough salad for two or three servings. In old treatises on food plants, many varieties of *V. olitoria* were mentioned, among which were the Etampes green with large round leaves, and a variety with spoon-shaped leaves. *V. eriocarpa* is similar to the *olitoria* and used in the same manner. So also are many other species of this genus which are common around the Mediterranean, but not well known in Anglo-Saxon countries. These salads have practically no calorific value, but their consumption, especially in winter, is thought by many to be useful for their vitamin and mineral salt content, and for the beneficial effects on the body functions (increased diuresis and stimulation of the intestines). Bitter cress (*Cardamine amara*), of the *Cruciferae* or mustard family, is found in humid places, near springs and brooks. It can be eaten alone as a salad, or, as with other plants of the mustard family such as rocket and watercress, used to enhance the flavor of other salads with its aromatic, piquant taste.

Lamb's lettuce is available from summer through the winter months until the following spring. Of little nutritional value, it is nevertheless rich in vitamins. Bitter cress has been cultivated since ancient times. It adds an interesting flavor to salads and soups, and should be added just before serving.

Borage · Wall rocket

Borage (*Borago officinalis*) is a typical plant of the Mediterranean region from whence it was introduced into America and central Europe, particularly Germany, where it has flourished. It is used in salads and as a flavoring for vegetables. It can be drunk as herbal tea or in claret cup to give a decorative and aromatic effect. It appears toward the end of winter or in the fall and lasts until the beginning of summer. The parts used are the young leaves and sometimes the flowering tops.

The less tender leaves can be cooked as a substitute for spinach, or in the preparation of omelets. Borage is considered more a medicinal plant than a food, although it can be found on sale in some large cities. It contains mucilages and saltpeter and is thought to have diuretic and emollient properties.
Wall rocket (*Diplotaxis muralis*) is never used alone in a salad because of its sharp, piquant taste. It is mostly used as a flavoring, as is another rocket, *Eruca sativa*.

Wall rocket (above) and borage (left). Easily cultivated, the edible parts of the borage are the young leaves and the flowering tops.

Swiss chard · Spinach · Field poppy

Swiss chard (*Beta vulgaris* var. *cicla*) was already known to the ancient Greeks as a food plant. Chard is excellent not only as a vegetable, but also in soups and rice dishes, prepared like spinach, with a piece of butter added at the last moment of cooking. The white ribs of the chard are the best part. They are boiled in a little salted water, drained, and then simmered in the desired seasonings.

Spinach (*Spinacia oleracea*) is thought to be of Persian origin. Its intensive and widespread cultivation in Europe started only after the eighteenth century, especially in the Netherlands, France, and England, and later in the rest of Europe and the Americas. Spinach is very rich in vitamins: it contains a high percentage of vitamin A and of the B complex, whose components are important in the development and growth of the body, and in the prevention of beriberi and anemia. The amount of vitamin C is also high, as are vitamins E and K. It also contains potassium of oxalate and some iron. Unfortunately the vitamins are soluble in water and fats, and are lost in cooking. For this reason it is advisable to cook greens in the shortest time possible. Although it was once thought that spinach could not be eaten raw it is now much in demand as a gourmet salad. With regard to protein content, spinach resembles cabbage, providing a fair amount of nitrogen compounds and only a negligible percentage of carbohydrates. The iron content of spinach, almost the same percentage as that found in fish and eggs, used to be considered its most valuable asset, especially as iron enters into the composition of the hemoglobin of the blood. However, studies have shown that it is impossible for the body to use the iron contained in spinach because it is present in a form not easily assimilated.

The field poppy (*Papaver rhoeas*), despite its leaves being slightly narcotic, can be cooked and seasoned like spinach, while the plant is still young, or be used as a herb for flavoring soups and salads.

Spinach, with Swiss chard (far right) and field poppy (below).

Turnip · Wild radish · Garden radish

The turnip (*Brassica campestris* var. *rapa*, or *B. rapa*) is botanically a close relative of cabbage (*B. oleracea*), rape (*B. napus*), and rapeseed (*B. rapa* var. *oleifera*). Another variety, sometimes called turnip, is the rutabaga, Swedish turnip, Russian turnip or Swede (*B. campestris*, var. *napo-brassica*). The turnip is a biennial plant with a characteristic edible, tuberous root of various shapes in the different cultivars (flattened and disklike or cylindrical). It is believed to have originated in Europe, where it has been grown and used as food since prehistoric times. Together with the cabbage, the turnip has been for a long time the staple food of the peoples of northern and central Europe, and its use declined only after the introduction of the potato. Trying to summarize and simplify the complex and long list of commercial varieties is very difficult. The four main types of turnip and some representative varieties of garden turnip are based on the

RADISH AND MOZZARELLA SALAD

½ lb/250 g small black olives; 2 rocket salads; 2–3 bunches small, tender radishes; 3 mozzarella cheeses, cut into cubes; 1 tbsp French mustard; 2 tbsp vinegar; 6 tbsp olive oil.

Drain the olives in a colander to dry. Wash the salad carefully and dry; chop it finely. Place in a salad bowl together with the cubed mozzarella, radishes, and olives. Beat together with a fork the vinegar, oil, and mustard. Add salt and pepper. Pour over the salad and toss.

shape of the root: (1) long types with a root three or more times as long as broad; (2) spindle-shape (tankard) with a root twice as long as broad; (3) round or globe shape; and (4) flat with roots broader than long. One other type, the foliage turnip, forms no swollen root but a cluster of leaves that are cooked as potherbs (greens). It is used

especially for the preparation of soups, in Irish stew, and as a winter vegetable. Young, white turnips are delicious boiled with butter and herbs. Wild and garden radishes are considered by some botanists as two varieties of the species *Raphanus raphanistrum*: others believe that the garden radish is a true species (*R. sativus* or *R. radicula*) and the

A turnip and two wild radishes. Turnips can be eaten either raw or cooked. Both turnips and radishes can be kept for several weeks in a cool, dark place.

Turnip · Wild radish · Garden radish

wild radish a variety (var. *niger*) of the latter, while some books list the wild radish as *R. raphanistrum*. The origin of the radish, like that of most cultivated plants, is uncertain, but it was certainly known in China and Egypt in ancient times and also to the Greeks and Romans. Today the coarser wild radish is practically no longer used, but the garden radish is popular in salads or eaten raw as a relish. In France radishes are served as an hors-d'oeuvres with fresh, crusty bread and butter. Three groups of cultivars exist: (1) the familiar red globe-shaped varieties of radish: Champion, Cherry Belle, Red Boy, Scarlet Globe,

and Comet, and the Round Black Spanish, a round-type radish with deep black skin that is excellent for storage in moist sand during the winter; (2) the long-root radish: White Chinese (Celestial), All Seasons White, Burpee White, White Icicle, and Summer Cross; (3) numerous globular ones, deeply and totally pigmented, or half and half red and white, Saxa, Perfection, and Champion.

Cultivated radishes: either round with bright red skin or white-skinned and elongated. They are often grated or finely sliced in salads.

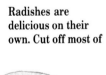

Radishes are delicious on their own. Cut off most of the leaves leaving only the freshest parts for a more colorful dish. Clean them thoroughly. Dip the radishes into olive oil, salt, and pepper. For an original appetizer, slice the radishes and serve with bread, butter, and salt.

Sugar-cane · Sugar-beet

Sugar, both from cane and beets, is a valuable source of fast energy in human nutrition. However, dieticians warn against excessive consumption.

Almost two thirds of the world production of sugar is supplied by sugar-cane (*Saccharum officinarum*), a native of the Orient, introduced into the Mediterranean basin by the Arabs. It was brought to the American continent in the sixteenth century, and spread rapidly in regions with suitable climates. The stems of the sugar-cane are cut at the base between the tenth and twelfth month of life. This is the time required by the plant to accumulate substantial sugar reserves in its tissues. After the harvest, the stems or canes are taken to the sugar refineries, having been stripped of the upper part and of the leaves. In the refinery the stems are squeezed to extract the juice (vesou). The fibrous, woody residues (bagasse) of the stems are either used as fuel, or, because of their high percentage of cellulose, to make paper, or composted to form an organic fertilizer. The syrupy, viscous cane juice is then subjected to several boilings to concentrate the sucrose, and to chemical treatment with lime water to eliminate impurities. In the concentrated, clarified solution, sugar crystalizes and is removed from the remaining syrup by centrifugation. The remaining syrup is commonly known as molasses, which is used in food or distilled to produce rum, alcohol, and vinegar. The raw crystallized sugar (about 96% sucrose) is further refined by repeated washings and recrystallization, and then delivered to the market.

The area of dissemination of the sugar-beet (*Beta vulgaris*) is very different from that of the sugar-cane. The latter is characteristic of tropical climates, while the former belongs in the maritime or continental temperate zone. The use of this plant for the extraction of sucrose dates back to the eighteenth century.

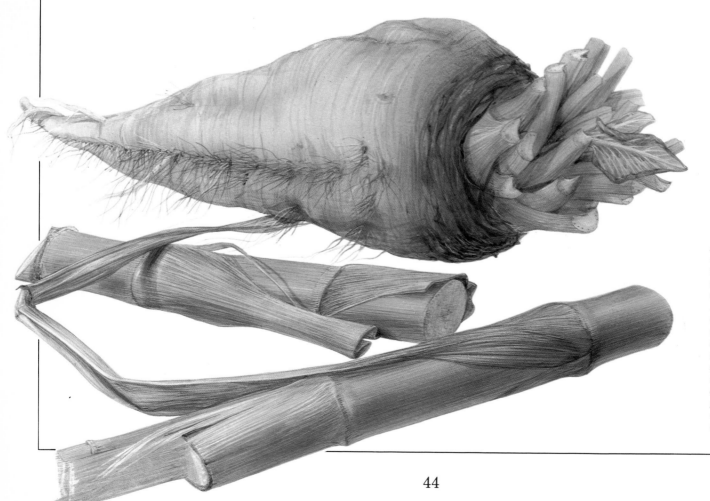

At the refinery, the beets are washed, cut into strips and put inside diffusion cells with water at about 175°F. The sugar diffuses from the strips into the water. The solution is then evaporated to a dense syrup, from which the sugar is crystalized, and then separated from the brown syrup, or molasses, by centrifugation.

Beetroot or Red beet

*B*eta vulgaris (var. *rapa*, form *rubra*), known as beets in the United States, and called beetroot in the British Isles, has been cultivated for many centuries and used not only as food for humans and animals, but also, as in the case of some varieties, for distillery purposes. The beets described by Horace and Cicero must have been vastly different from the ones used today. Those grown in Roman times were probably more appreciated for their leaves than for the rest of the plant. Our red beet, with the roundish root, cannot therefore boast a long history. Red beets in the wild state grow along the coasts of western Europe and North Africa. The plant is rather slender, and the cultivated varieties differ in the size and color of the root. The cultivated red beet originated in Germany and was then introduced into Italy around the fifteenth century. The yellow beet was favored first and only later was there an increase in the cultivation of the red beets that are the most used now. From a dietetic standpoint, the cooked beet contains up to 10% carbohydrates, mostly in the

form of sucrose. This is a considerable amount, not found in other vegetables, and makes it unsuitable for diabetics. The quantity of protein, between 1.5% and 2%, is good, the percentage varying in relation to the chemical composition of the soil and the different varieties analyzed. The high protein content makes the red beet one of the most valued vegetables. Beets also contain mineral salts, such as iron and calcium compounds. The calories supplied by 3½ oz (100 g) of beets are 46, more than double the average of other vegetables. The amount of vitamins is, however, very low, and in the case of vitamin C it is reduced to less than half by cooking.

Red beets generally arrive on the market already cooked. When prepared at home, they should be neither cut nor peeled because water penetrating the root during cooking causes a loss of nutritive substances and color.

Cucumber

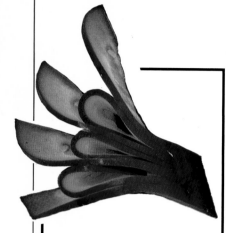

GHERKINS

Place small, immature cucumbers in a dish and sprinkle salt all over. Leave for a few hours to draw out the bitter juices. Drain and rinse in cold water, then leave to dry, preferably in the open air. When dry, cover completely with boiling vinegar. The following day, they will have turned yellow. Drain and plunge in boiling fresh vinegar with 1 onion and a pinch of salt. Allow to return to a boil, and remove from the heat. The gherkins will have turned green again. Lift out with a slotted ladle made of stainless steel, reserving the vinegar, and place in sterilized glass jars with a few peppercorns and 1 peeled clove garlic. Pour the reserved vinegar into the jars and seal when cold. Leave for 2 months before eating.

The cucumber (*Cucumis sativus*) is another member of the *Cucurbitaceae*. Some botanists believe it to be a close relative of the watermelon. The cucumber is an annual herbaceous plant, with branching and angular stems, and palmate three- to five-lobed leaves. The flowers, unisexual, are borne at the axil of the leaves and are greenish yellow in color. The edible portion of the plant is given by the unripe large berries, which have a typical elongate shape, rounded at the extremities. According to several authorities, including Naudin, who devoted his career to the study of the *Cucurbitaceae*, the cucumber, although never found in the wild state, is native to India, and, more extensively, to tropical Asia. It is one of the food plants used by Oriental populations for more than three thousand years; one proof of this long use is, for example, its Sanskrit name, *soukasa*. From the Far East the cucumber came to eastern Europe many centuries ago. It is mentioned in the Bible, and it is believed that the Hebrews imported it from Egypt to the Promised Land, where it became one of their most popular foods. It was known to the Greeks and was used extensively by the Romans. Cucumbers are almost always eaten raw, and rather unripe. The very young fruits, used whole, are suitable for pickling, but mature fruits may also be used in this way.

They are usually eaten in salads, but in some Eastern European countries they are cooked in various ways with meat. From the standpoint of food content the cucumber is very rich in water and is therefore a most refreshing vegetable, but almost completely lacking in nutritive value. It is found by some people to be very indigestible.

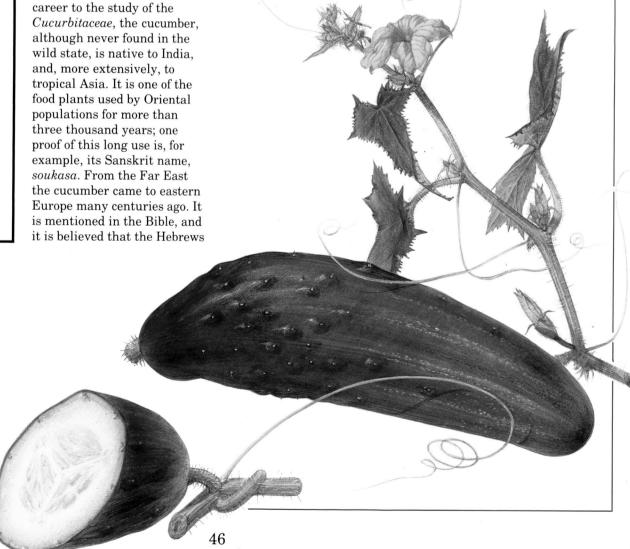

Cucumbers are usually eaten raw, and slightly unripe, although they can also be cooked in a variety of ways. Very immature specimens are suitable for pickling into gherkins (see box above).

Radicchio

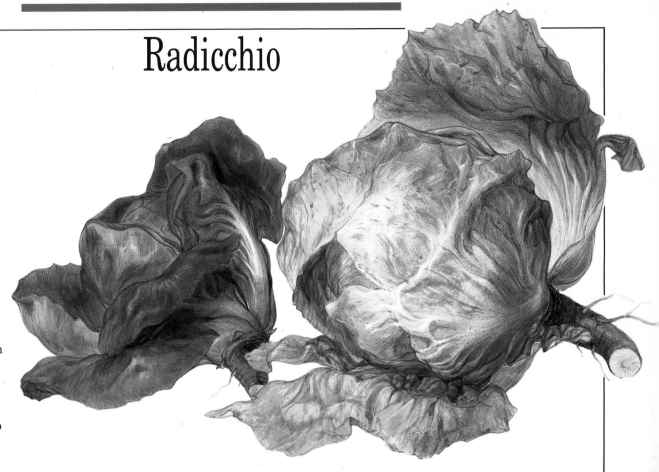

The prized wild chicory from the Venetian province, known by the name of "radicchio," also belongs to the group of root chicories, although only its leaves are used. There are three types of "radicchio": the red Verona chicory, with short leaves and rather roundish heart; the red Treviso chicory, with long and lanceolate leaves and, therefore, with tapered heart; the variegated chicory of Castelfranco, with almost globose heart and green leaves speckled with wine-red spots and streaks. It is not necessary to tie these plants for blanching although it is sometimes done for the Treviso chicory. The internal part of the rosette after the tougher, outside leaves are removed consists of a tender, crisp heart, slightly bitter to the taste but pleasantly aromatic. These "radicchi" are sold with a somewhat long piece of root that should not be discarded unless it is too stringy and tough, as it sometimes is at the end of the season. This root, cleaned of the skin, is perhaps the best part of the chicory, being very crisp because of the white and compact pith. From a nutritional standpoint, the chicories represent good eating. Raw, they supply a considerable amount of vitamins (especially vitamin C), and the bitter elements which they contain are thought to have a tonic and diuretic action. The wild chicory, common parent of the other species, has always been considered a medicinal plant. Chicories have a modest solid residue, 6–7%, with about 1% of protein and 1–2% carbohydrates, no lipids, and

only about 13 calories per 3½ oz (100 g). With the exception of the Catalonia, which is always cooked, seasoned with oil and lemon juice, or sautéed with garlic and chili, all the other chicories are eaten raw as salads and the heart chicories also in a dressing of oil, salt, and pepper. Witloof hearts are also served in this way. The

range of flavors is very varied; a strong garlic dressing with oil and vinegar is good for a coarse chicory, although it would ruin the delicate flavor of the Verona radicchio. A very unusual way to prepare the Treviso chicory is to cook it on a grill (broiled).

Three varieties of radicchio (root chicory). Above: red Verona chicory (left) and the variegated Castelfranco chicory (right). Below: red Treviso chicory, which is delicious broiled.

Celery · Celeriac

In ancient Greece the humble celery was considered worthy of crowning the heads of athletes and was also used in funeral wreaths. Celery only became a table vegetable during the Middle Ages. Today celery is widely grown because of its many culinary uses. It does not provide many calories, although it is rich in mineral salts, vitamins, and, like parsley, iron. The rootstock of the celeriac (*A. graveolens rapaceum*), called also German celery or turnip-rooted celery, increases in size near the collar, becoming turnip-shaped, with the leaves almost lying on the ground. The best roots are those of medium size, without secondary roots, and with a modest clump of leaves.

COOKED CELERY

Celery may be cooked in many different ways, and served as a vegetable accompaniment. Boil and dress with olive oil, lemon juice, and black pepper, or parboil then fry in a little oil with some chopped onion, carrot, and bacon. Celery is also delicious served au gratin, with butter, cheese, and diced ham.

Celery is an indispensable ingredient in the making of meat or chicken broth. It is also used, with onions and carrots, in a variety of braised dishes.

Salsify · Scorzonera

The swollen root of these plants is rich in reserve products and is the part which is eaten. The taste is pleasant and full of flavor. To prepare, they should be boiled and either seasoned with oil and lemon juice, or sautéed. These are sadly underrated but delicious winter vegetables which make an unusual main course accompaniment. Either can also be used as the basis of a delicious creamed soup. Both salsify and scorzonera contain medicinal properties. Inulin is their carbohydrate reserve and, as is the case with the Jerusalem artichoke, these vegetables are thought by many to be good for diabetics.

STEAMED, BRAISED OR BAKED

These excellent winter vegetables may be boiled in salted water, then dressed in oil and vinegar. Alternatively, they may be steamed or braised in butter with a little broth. Boiled salsify and scorzonera may be served hot with *béarnaise* sauce. Au gratin, they are a delicious accompaniment to all meat dishes: boil for 30 minutes, drain and place in a buttered ovenproof dish. Sprinkle with grated Parmesan or Gruyère cheese, breadcrumbs, and a few pieces of butter. Bake in a moderate oven until golden.

Both salsify and scorzonera are prepared in the same way. Top and tail the roots, scrape, and slice into pieces 2–3 in (5–8 cm) long, cutting these in turn lengthwise into four and eliminating the woody core. To prevent discoloration the prepared pieces should be kept in water acidulated with lemon juice until you are ready to use them.

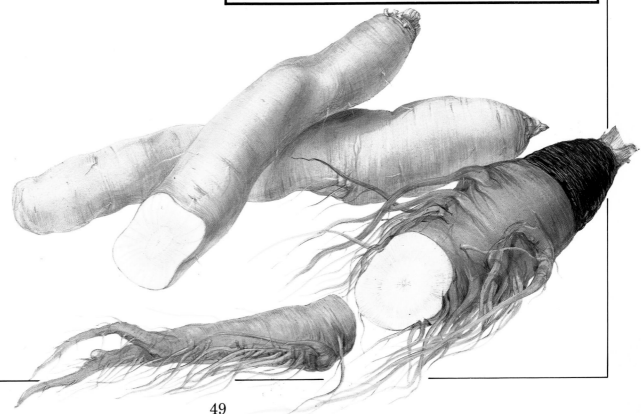

Fennel

Fennel was widely known in ancient Greece, and the name of a region, Marathon, where it grew profusely, was derived from the Greek name for fennel, *marathon*. There is even earlier information about this plant of the parsley family, in a papyrus dating back to 1500 B.C. A description of fennel can also be found in the works of Pliny, who described it as a medicinal, rather than a food plant, which, together with other essences, was used in an infusion for the eyes. However, not until the sixteenth century could some small and sparse cultivations of this sweet-smelling herb be found in Europe, particularly in central and southern Italy. Today a wild fennel (*Foeniculum officinale*) is recognized as native to the Canary Isles and has been naturalized for several centuries around the Mediterranean. A sweet fennel (*F. vulgare*), whose taste has made it a very popular garden vegetable, is also grown. The wild fennel, known as Florence fennel, is mostly used in liqueurs and pharmaceutically. The roots and seeds of the wild variety have diuretic and digestive properties, and the seeds are also used for the extraction of an essential oil. Sweet fennel, besides being used for its seeds, and eaten in large quantities as a condiment or a source of the essential oil, may also be eaten raw or cooked as a vegetable. The edible portion is provided by the leaves and the white and fleshy bulbous stem. Sweet fennel has little nutritive value, having almost the lowest number of calories of any vegetable. Fennel is essentially composed of water, cellulose, and a volatile oil, anethole, diffused in the entire plant and particularly in the seeds. It is because of its fragrance and flavor, therefore, that this plant is considered to be so appetizing. Fennel is thought to act as a stimulant, a tonic, a digestive, and an appetizer.

All types of fennel can be eaten raw or cooked, and in the latter case the bulbs should be briefly parboiled to make them more tender and digestible. Fennel can be stewed with butter, or served au gratin.

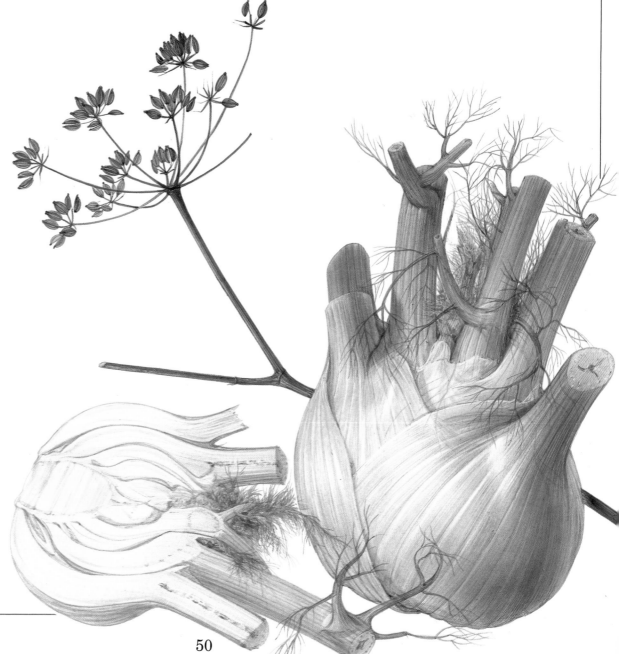

Mushrooms

The parasol mushroom (*Lepiota procera*) is common in many different habitats, woods, pastures, meadows, etc., particularly if the soil is sandy. It is practically cosmopolitan. It appears in summer and during the fall, especially in October. This is a most elegant looking mushroom, and the largest known. Only the cap should be used as the stem is tough and fibrous. From the nutritional viewpoint its value, like that of other mushrooms, is limited. Water represents about 85% of its weight; the content of nitrogen compounds is about 4–5%, and that of lipids is small. Its calorific value is very limited.

The chanterelle (*Cantharellus tubaeformis*) can also be dried and reduced to powder for seasoning purposes, or preserved in oil.

Craterellus cornucopioides, commonly called horn of plenty, grows best in the coolest and most humid parts of both broadleaf and coniferous woods. It appears from August to November, and is widely distributed in Europe, Asia, North America, and Australia. It has almost identical characteristics with the chanterelle, and can also be dried and reduced to powder, or preserved in oil. It has the great advantage of not being easily confused with poisonous species because of its distinctive black color. Together with the truffle and Caesar's mushroom, the boletus (ceps) is undoubtedly a most highly prized mushroom. The genus name *Boletus* derives from the term "bolites" that the Greeks and Romans used for the edible Amanitas

and later for all the best edible mushrooms. Afterward, the term came to be applied only to the boletus. These mushrooms are very common in both coniferous and broadleaf woods such as chestnut, oak, and beech. They are symbiotic, living in mutual association with tree roots.

Boletes can be used in many delicious dishes. The caps can be broiled, and the whole mushroom, either fresh or dried, can be used in many different ways. The dried mushrooms, previously softened in water, are particularly good for flavoring risotto, pasta, veal cutlets, and stuffing *vol-au-vent*, etc.

It is essential to avoid all species of boletus with red tube mouths (underside of the cap) as they are usually poisonous. The oyster mushroom (*Pleurotus ostreatus*) does not enjoy the same reputation and prestige as the other mushrooms already described, and yet there is no doubt about its value. Its flesh is a little tough even in the youngest

Left: a parasol mushroom, and, below, a horn of plenty. The latter is a much prized mushroom. Its texture is thin and elastic and its fragrance reminiscent of ripe fruit. It is also available dried and powdered. The parasol mushroom is dangerous, in that poisonous varieties can easily be mistaken for it.

Mushrooms

fruiting bodies, but it is precisely this "gumminess," together with the typical scent, that gives oyster mushrooms their particular sensory qualities. They are almost always stewed. The youngest fruiting bodies can be preserved in oil. The oyster mushroom is so called because of the suggestive color and shape of the cap.

Cantharellus cibarius is another well-known and widespread chanterelle, commonly called "little cockerel" or girolle. It is common in woods where it forms spots or rings, and is found in Europe, Japan, North Africa, America, and Australia.

Morels and truffles, while not true mushrooms, will be considered together for the purposes of this discussion since they have many of the same characteristics and uses. Technically, true mushrooms are *Basidiomycetes* (club fungi) and the mushroom itself is the "fruit," a basidiocarp. The

morels are therefore not mushrooms. The edible, above-ground portion is an ascocarp and so they belong to the sac fungi, the *Ascomycetes*. This is also true of *Tuber* species (truffles) and *Helvella*, called the "false morels." Morels are provided by "fruiting bodies" or macroscopic portions of the mushroom which are collected and used, and which are often identified with the entire mushroom while they actually represent only a fleeting, although important stage in the plants' life cycle.

Although they are usually thought of as something exotic and esoteric, truffles are nothing but mushrooms that produce their fruiting bodies underground. They have a symbiotic relationship with such trees as the hazelnut, beech, poplar, and willow. Morels and truffles cannot be cultivated in the same way as mushrooms. At best, their diffusion may be helped by planting acorns which have

An oyster mushroom and, right, a girolle. The latter is greatly valued, and grows exclusively in woodland, both in mountain regions and in the plain. It has a firm texture and should be cooked for at least 30 minutes. The oyster mushroom is easy to cultivate. The most flavorsome specimens are the darker ones with bluish tints.

HOW TO DRY MUSHROOMS

The simplest method of preserving mushrooms is to dry them. The mushrooms should be fresh, firm, and as dry as possible. Scrub thoroughly with a small brush, but do not wash. Slice thinly and place in full sunlight to dry out, arranging the slices well apart so they do not overlap. Turn them every 5–6 hours, and bring indoors at night so they are not exposed to damp. When dried, the mushrooms should be stored in a dry and airy place in waxed paper bags or hermetically sealed glass jars.

Mushrooms

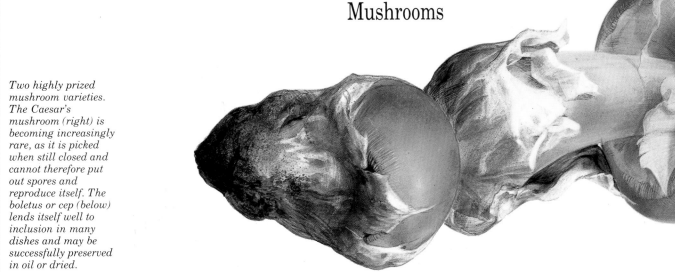

Two highly prized mushroom varieties. The Caesar's mushroom (right) is becoming increasingly rare, as it is picked when still closed and cannot therefore put out spores and reproduce itself. The boletus or cep (below) lends itself well to inclusion in many dishes and may be successfully preserved in oil or dried.

been collected under oak trees around which truffles are found.

These acorns stand a good chance of being "contaminated" with truffle spores, so there is a strong probability that truffles will form around the little oak plants that will develop from these acorns. Truffles are found with the help of specially trained dogs and, in some areas, hogs. The best known truffles are: (1) the white or Alba truffle (*Tuber magnatum*), so called because it is considered worthy of the *magnati*, that is, the very rich. It is found only in Italy, in Piedmont (Langhe and Monferrato) and in Emilia (in the Apennines in the Parma, Modena, and Bologna area), and universally considered the best among the truffles; (2) the black truffle, or Spoleto or Norcia truffle (*T. Melanosporum*), found in France, especially in the Garonne and known therefore as *Truffe de Périgord*; in Spain, in Germany (Baden) and in Italy in Piedmont, Lombardy, Trentino, and in the Apennine areas of Umbria and the Marches. Other, but less valued truffles are *T. Mesentericum, T. aestivum*

(red-grained black truffle), and *T. borchii*. No American species is considered edible. The white truffle has a penetrating, slightly garlic-smelling odor. It is very good raw. The black truffle, however, is best cooked: it is also used to flavor many pâtés. Truffles should never be washed or peeled. If it is necessary to wash them, it should be done in dry white wine.

Caesar's mushroom (*Amanita Caesarea*), so called because it is considered worthy of an emperor, is undoubtedly, with truffles and the boletus, among the best mushrooms available. Its price is always high. This mushroom is easily recognizable, at least when completely developed. It could possibly be confused with the poisonous *Amanita muscaria* although they differ in color (which is brighter in *A. muscaria*, except under heavy rains), and *A. muscaria* also has numerous warts on the cap. Caesar's mushroom is widely distributed in Europe, Asia, and Africa. It can be found in the roots of broadleaved trees, and appears in the late summer and in the fall. It was certainly known and used by the ancient

Mushrooms

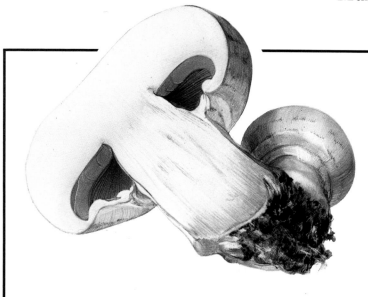

BUTTERED MUSHROOMS

1 lb/500 g button mushrooms; 2 oz/50 g butter; 1 clove garlic, peeled; salt and white pepper.

Fresh button mushrooms are best for this quick and

easy to prepare dish, although many other varieties will work just as well, providing they are tender and delicate in flavor. Clean the mushrooms and slice. Sauté over high heat

with the butter and the whole garlic clove for just a few minutes, and season to taste. As soon as their natural moisture evaporates, they are done.

Greeks and Romans. Like the truffle, the boletus, and others, it is a symbiotic mushroom, whose mycelium forms an association, known as mycorrhiza, with the roots of the tree; it cannot therefore be artificially cultivated. Caesar's mushroom can be eaten in many ways, either raw as a salad after being marinated in lemon juice for four hours, or it can be stewed or broiled. For the latter recipe the caps are stuffed with a mixture of finely minced mushroom stems, onion, parsley, breadcrumbs, salt, and pepper. Add oil and some curls of butter and cook at a low heat for about 15 minutes.

The field mushroom (*Psalliota hortensis*, *P. campestris*, *P. arvensis*), although easily recognizable, can sometimes be confused with the poisonous *Amanita verna*, but if it is remembered that *A. verna*

always bears a volva which is lacking in the *Psalliota*, lethal mistakes will be avoided. Furthermore, in *Psalliota* the color of the gills is shaded from rose to brown and the spores are dark purple, while in *Amanita* the gills and spores are both white. Unlike the symbiotic truffle, field mushrooms are saprophytes, that is, organisms living at the expense of dead substances such as straw, vegetable wastes, and manure. Because of this they can be artificially cultivated in airy caves, cellars or sheds, and on substrata such as horse manure. This is why field mushrooms are so abundant and available on the market all the year round. They can also be eaten raw but only if the very young fruiting bodies are used. They may be stewed, sautéed or preserved in oil.

Some truffle varieties and, below, two funnel-shaped chanterelles. Truffles must be neither washed nor peeled. If they are very dirty, however, clean them in dry white wine. To preserve them for a few months place in sterilized glass jars, fill with white wine, seal hermetically, and cook in a bain marie (in a roasting pan half-filled with water) for 1–2 hours.

FRUIT

Apple

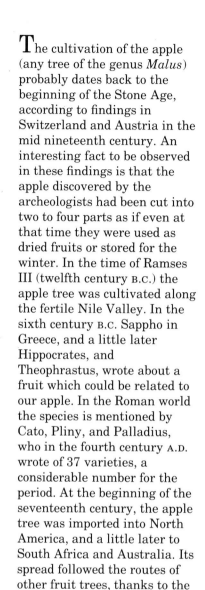

The cultivation of the apple (any tree of the genus *Malus*) probably dates back to the beginning of the Stone Age, according to findings in Switzerland and Austria in the mid nineteenth century. An interesting fact to be observed in these findings is that the apple discovered by the archeologists had been cut into two to four parts as if even at that time they were used as dried fruits or stored for the winter. In the time of Ramses III (twelfth century B.C.) the apple tree was cultivated along the fertile Nile Valley. In the sixth century B.C. Sappho in Greece, and a little later Hippocrates, and Theophrastus, wrote about a fruit which could be related to our apple. In the Roman world the species is mentioned by Cato, Pliny, and Palladius, who in the fourth century A.D. wrote of 37 varieties, a considerable number for the period. At the beginning of the seventeenth century, the apple tree was imported into North America, and a little later to South Africa and Australia. Its spread followed the routes of other fruit trees, thanks to the widespread colonization of those times.

There are thousands of varieties of apples today, generally classified on the basis of their time of maturation (summer, autumn, winter) and their color, size, flavor, etc. The many varieties can be divided into two groups: those to be eaten fresh, and those to be used for cooking. The apple is one of the most prized table fruits, but it can be used in many other ways. It is made into jelly, preserves, apple butter, and compotes. The juice is made into cider and can be distilled to produce Calvados or applejack. Pure apple juice is very popular today. In medicine its disinfectant and therapeutic qualities are highly valued. The apple must be considered a true and proper food, containing carbohydrates, vitamins, salts, and water. The carbohydrates, about 10%, are present in the form of glucose and fructose, that is, in the simplest forms, which are easily assimilated by our bodies. The vitamins contained in the apple are vitamin C and several of the B vitamins. The

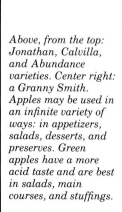

Above, from the top: Jonathan, Calvilla, and Abundance varieties. Center right: a Granny Smith. Apples may be used in an infinite variety of ways: in appetizers, salads, desserts, and preserves. Green apples have a more acid taste and are best in salads, main courses, and stuffings.

FRUIT AND SHRIMP APPETIZER

1 lettuce;
1 grapefruit; 2 green apples; 14 oz/400 g cooked large shrimp, peeled; ⅔ cup/5 fl oz/ 150 ml mayonnaise; white wine vinegar; 2 tbsp light cream; lemon juice; salt and pepper.

Wash the lettuce. Reserve the best leaves and shred the rest. Core the apples and chop. Peel the grapefruit, and skin the segments. Line a salad bowl with the reserved salad leaves and lay the fruit on top. Sprinkle with lemon juice and add the shrimp. Mix together the mayonnaise, vinegar, cream, salt, and pepper, and dress the salad with this sauce.

Apple

The apple is a highly nutritious fruit. Both the skin and the pulp have a variety of cosmetic uses, and the blossom yields an aromatic essence.

mineral salts found in apples are calcium, iron, phosphorus, and potassium. A ripe apple contains a considerable amount of water, about 85%, which makes this fruit a favorite thirst-quencher. Apples are highly digestible because they contain pectin, which helps the normal digestive processes after a meal. For people suffering from acidity, however, it is advisable to cook them, preferably by baking to retain all the flavor. The syrup obtained from apples is used to relieve chest colds and whooping cough; it is said to reduce fevers, soothe irritation, and benefit the kidneys, bladder, and liver. Gastronomically, the apple is a most versatile fruit: excellent raw, it is also delicious baked, stewed, in fritters, in pies and strudels, and especially flambéed with Kirsch or other spirits after being cooked. The numerous varieties can be divided into four categories: cooking apples, eating apples, cider apples, and drying apples. The principal categories are the first two, but it is difficult to make a sharp distinction between them because some table apples are also very good for cooking. The table varieties are in turn divided according to the time of maturation.

Apple

Further examples of the many varieties of apple. From the top: Stayman, Rennet, and Rose of Caldaro. The latter has an acid, fragrant pulp and is mainly eaten raw as a dessert apple.

early varieties.

Fall apples. The English Cellini is of medium size with a thin, yellow skin with greenish spots and streaks; its pulp is sweet-tart and mealy and it cooks well. The Autumnal Gray Rennet is also of English origin; the fruits are rather large, elongate, and angular, with wrinkled dark skin spotted with gray, and with a very juicy pulp. Like the previous variety, it is very good when cooked.

For winter storage, these cultivars are highly regarded: Stayman (Stamared), Rome Beauty (Cox Red Rome, Gallia Beauty), Baldwin and Wealthy.

Winter apples. Yellow beauty, of American origin, has yellow skin speckled with gray and with red shades on the side that has been exposed to the sun; the pulp is juicy, tender, sweet, and aromatic.

There are many other excellent apple cultivars for eating raw, and for cooking: Delicious (also Red Delicious, Starking and Richard, Starkcrimson), Cortland, York Imperial, Jonathan, McIntosh, Granny Smith, Golden Delicious, Grimes Golden, and Yellow Newtown.

BAKED APPLE

Serves 1: 1 apple; 1 piece butter; 1 tsp jam of choice; 1 sweet biscuit, crumbled; 4–5 almonds, halved; 1 tsp sugar; 1 small glass sherry or port.

Wash, dry, and core the apple. Cut out a crown shape at the top with a sharp knife, and place in a buttered ovenproof dish. Blend the jam with the crumbled biscuit and fill the hole at the top of the apple with the mixture. Put a piece of butter and the almonds over the apple and sprinkle with the sugar. Pour over the sherry or port and bake in the hottest part of the oven for 30 minutes at 350°F.

Summer apples. Some of the varieties for sale in the summer are as follows: Red Astrachan is probably the earliest variety, appearing during the first half of July. It is not very large and has yellowish green skin with red spots or streaks; the pulp is sweet, slightly acid, aromatic, and firm. Summer Rambour, which ripens between August and September, is large with smooth, light green skin spotted with red, and has good juicy pulp. Yellow Transparent and Duchess are also good

A Butter Hardy. This is a popular variety of pear, which ripens in the fall and may be preserved for several weeks. It has a rough skin and a rosy pulp.

Pear

The cultivation of the common pear tree (*Pyrus communis*), from which, over the centuries, most of the forms cultivated today have developed, dates from very ancient times. According to paleontological findings, its cultivation could date back to 35 to 40 centuries ago. It seems to have originated in western Asia and around the Caspian Sea. It has been known for many centuries in Europe. Both the Greeks and Romans prized it highly. Homer names the pear tree in listing the plants growing in Alcinous's garden. Some centuries later Theophrastus, Cato, and Pliny also mention it. Theophrastus has handed down some extraordinary information. He considers separately the wild and cultivated species, and, for the latter, describes the methods of propagation by seeds and by grafting, and the methods of cultivation. He also wrote a long and knowledgeable dissertation about the usefulness of cross-pollination, so we know that even in those times the pear's cultivation was widespread. Later, Cato identified six varieties, and Pliny nearly 40, although Virgil had written of only three. The varieties of the pear have been continuously increasing, especially since the mid eighteenth century. Today more than 5,000 varieties can be listed, some of them spread throughout the world, others found in only one country, or even limited to a small locality. Pears are one of the fruits most in demand not only when fresh because of their flavor, the abundance of

Right, from the top: an Argentine William, which has a juicy and fragrant pulp, the widespread Kaiser variety, which is also suitable for cooking, and two Abate pears, which have a sugary and aromatic pulp.

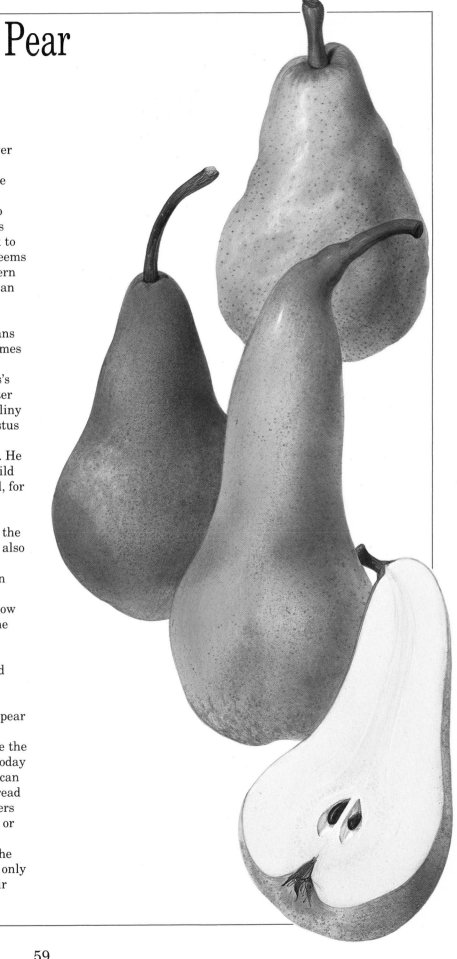

Pear

THE VERSATILE PEAR

Some smaller varieties of pear, with a compact and grainy pulp, are more suitable for cooking purposes. They are generally cooked whole, poached in a little water with sugar, cinnamon, and cloves and served with raspberry or chocolate sauce, or vanilla custard. They are also delicious served with a chocolate mousse or pudding. Commercially, they are canned or bottled in syrup, or used to make juice or liqueur. Pears go very well with cheese. They are less frequently used in appetizers and main courses, although they are equally delicious served in this savory way.

vitamins and the percentage of carbohydrates which make them so nourishing, but also as preserves, jelly, candied or canned fruit, etc. However, this fruit ripens and is harvested during an extremely short period of the year, so supplying the market for many months with fruit harvested long before is a problem to be overcome. It is a horticultural achievement that fresh pears are available during winter and even spring, when the trees have not even begun to bloom. The logical result of this desire for around-the-year consumption was the large-scale development of cold storage, requiring two well-defined stages: first, the harvesting of the pears when still unripe, then their storage under conditions that slow down the processes of maturation. The farmer's experience plays a decisive role during the first phase, since there are no instruments that can determine the degree of ripeness.

In the second stage it is necessary to provide a constant temperature during the long stay in the cold rooms, proper humidity level, so that there will be no weight loss in the stored product, and periodic ventilation and purification of the air. At the end of this waiting period in cold storage at a temperature of 30°–33°F (−1°–1°C), with a maximum of 35°F (2°–3°C), the pears that are not yet ripe undergo a supplementary maturation of 12 days in a temperature of approximately 65°F (18°C). This process should ensure that the pears will finally reach the consumer in perfect condition, with no trace of their early harvest showing in their appearance.

A considerable part of the fruit's production is used in the food industry for canning, either in syrup or in their own juice; preserves and jelly, candied or dried pears, etc. The fruits used for these purposes are harvested at a particular degree of maturity and carefully chosen. The varieties that are most suited to commercial purposes are the Bartlett and the William, because of their remarkable aroma and delicious white pulp

A Max Red Bartlett and a Butter William. The William varieties are the best for use in canning, juice, and preserves, thanks mainly to their strong aroma. The pear tree is easily cultivated in an ordinary garden, taking up little space but yielding excellent results.

Pear

without granulation. Other valued varieties are the Butter Hardy, which is very good for fruit salads, and Bolsc, Clapp Favorite, Dorset, Gorham, Kieffer, and Seckel. An Italian specialty, *mostarda cremonese*, a relish made with semi-candied fruits in a sugary syrup flavored with mustard, calls for pears of small size, whole and colored red or green. Like other fruits, pears have a certain importance from a nutritional and dietetic standpoint because of the vitamins they contain. They are also a good source of energy, supplying nearly 40 calories per 3½ oz (100 g), and a considerable amount of mineral salts. The usable carbohydrates can total up to 11% and the three principal vitamins present are, in decreasing order, vitamins A, B, and C respectively. Another element they contain is iodine which helps to keep the thyroid healthy in its function of relating the oxidation processes and the metabolism of the body. It is believed that pears may also be eaten by persons with severe kidney malfunctions because of the very low amount of sodium they contain. A pure complexion and shiny hair are thought likely to be the result of a regular consumption of pears.

The early Butter Morettini is an excellent choice for summer fruit salads. Early pears are generally defined as those that ripen before the end of July.

The passa crassana is a winter pear, with yellow-green mottled skin, and a juicy, white pulp which is sometimes grainy.

Quince · Loquat or Japanese medlar

The loquat or Japanese medlar is usually eaten fresh, although it also makes excellent preserves and confectionery.

The many varieties of quince (*Cydonia oblonga* or *C. vulgaris*) obtained over the centuries appear to be derived from a form native to the Caspian regions, where it is still found in the wild state. This theory is supported by the fact that the cultivated plants growing there have a moderately edible fruit with a sweetish flavor. In spite of the most advanced techniques of modern agriculture, in those areas where the quince is cultivated it is still not edible fresh but must be cooked for a fairly long time. The cultivated varieties can be divided into two groups: to the first belong the cultivars producing round fruits; to the second, those producing oblong fruits. The varieties belonging to the first group are generally chosen for commercial purposes such as confectionery, preserves, and jams because they are better suited for processing.

The loquat, also called Japanese or Chinese medlar (*Eriobotrya japonica*), imported from Japan at the end of the eighteenth century, was for a long time grown in France purely as an ornamental. It was not until the middle of the nineteenth century that horticulturists became interested in the fruit, because it ripened so early. This is why the loquat became so popular, despite the fact that it is not a particularly flavorsome fruit. It should be picked when perfectly ripe, so that the sugary content and juicy and refreshing pulp are at their best. Generally it is eaten fresh, but it can be used to make delicious preserves and many types of confectionery. It can also be put, like some candied fruit, into various relishes. As a whole the loquat is poor in nutritive qualities, although it is thirst-quenching and easily digestible.

Advance, Premier, Tanaka, Olivier, and Pineapple are cultivars of the loquat, which is grown extensively in the southern states of America, in Australia, and in southern Europe.

The golden-yellow flesh of the quince is acid, hard, and unpalatable, but when cooked and sweetened it can be made into various kinds of preserves and jams, on its own or mixed with other fruits such as apples and pears.

Pomegranate · Mulberry

The pomegranate (*Punica granatum*) is undoubtedly known to many people who have tasted it, if only out of curiosity, at least once. Probably native to Persia, this tree has always been connected with religious ceremonies or rites, during which both the flowers and fruits were used, because of their rather mysterious qualities. This was originally the custom among the Phoenicians, and later among the Greeks and Romans. Today it is grown more as an ornamental plant than as a fruit tree although the fruits have a pleasantly acid taste and can be eaten fresh, or used in the preparation of syrups, especially grenadine, and an alcoholic drink, as well as a jelly.

The black mulberry (*Morus nigra*) appears to have originated either in the southern part of the Caucasus, or in the mountains of Nepal. The white mulberry (*M. alba*) originated in China, where it is thought to have been cultivated for at least 5,000 years for the rearing of the silkworm. They were both known to the Greco-Roman world, but only the black mulberry, having a better fruit, was spread and cultivated, while the other species, although having edible fruit but of a poorer quality, was used exclusively for silkworm culture. Mulberries have a pleasant flavor, and are generally eaten fresh. The juice is sometimes used to color wines.

Above left: a pomegranate flower. Right: the pomegranate fruit. Below: the mulberry.

Whortleberry · Red and black currant · Gooseberry

Whortleberries. Right: red and black currants. Above: gooseberries. Fresh whortleberries are delicious served simply with sugar and lemon, or with cream. Their flavor is enhanced by the addition of a little red wine, orange juice, gin or vodka.

In the temperate regions of the northern hemisphere, in pastures and woods, it is common to find the whortleberry or bilberry (*Vaccinium myrtillus*), called blueberry or huckleberry in the United States. The fruits are believed to have been used for human consumption since prehistoric times, even, perhaps, up to 30 centuries before Christ. The berries of this shrub are used alone or, in north European countries, especially Germany, as a side dish for game or meat, or as a dessert. They are, however, most suitable in the preparation of sweets, preserves, and confectionery. In central Europe a whortleberry wine is made which is pleasant to taste and also recommended as an astringent and antiseptic for the intestinal tract. Besides the black whortleberry, there are other species of *Vaccinium* in the United States and Canada. They produce large fruits, which are used not only in their native countries, but in recent years have also been exported to Europe, especially to Britain.

The red currant (*Ribes rubrum*) is native to northeastern Europe as far as the Arctic Sea, and the steppes of northern Asia as far as Siberia and eastern Manchuria. It produces red, semitransparent berries with a pleasantly sour taste. Part of the production is eaten as fresh fruits; the rest is used commercially in the preparation of jelly, preserves, syrups, and currant wine. The berries contain citric, malic, and ascorbic acid, equal parts dextrose and levulose, and are therefore considered a refreshing medicinal essence. They have also been recommended for cases of dysentery. The jelly and syrups, which are particularly

Whortleberry · Red and black currant · Gooseberry

Red currants (left) can be easily cultivated in the garden. The bushes are grown on a support, such as a frame or wall. They thrive in sunlight or light shade, and produce fruit from June to end September.

Below: the red gooseberry, a variety of red currant. It has an acid flavor and is mainly eaten fresh, in fruit salads.

refreshing in the summer, also have an emollient action. Besides many varieties with more or less red fruit, many forms obtained by cultivation have colors ranging from yellowish to white. Prominent among the latter is the delicious Holland White which is very good for desserts. At Bar-le-Duc in France, red and white currants are used to make a famous preserve.
The black currant (*R. nigrum*) is a species closer to the gooseberry than to the red currant. The fruit is black and the flesh reddish and sweetish and not particularly good. It is used in France to make a very good liqueur, called Cassis. The therapeutic properties of this plant are thought by some to be great in cases of arthritis, gout, dropsy, and many other complaints. They are not limited to the fruit, but are also common to the stem and the leaves.
The gooseberry (*R. Grossularia*) is a species native to Europe, western Asia, and northern Africa. It is a spiny shrub that produces sourer fruits than

those of the currant, of variable size, green, yellow, white or red, with a juicy flesh. It is hairy or smooth depending on the variety. The gooseberry is becoming less and less common in parts of Europe and the United States, where it is losing its popularity. In France and especially in England, it is very much in demand. European

varieties have very large fruits that are excellent for jams and preserves. Gooseberry wine can be made by fermentation of the fruits of *R. grossularia*, and often has a high alcoholic content. The most important American species is *R. hirtellum*. Gooseberry sauce is traditionally served with mackerel.

SWEET AND SOUR RED CURRANT SAUCE

3 lb/1.5 kg red currants; 1½ lb/700 g sugar; 1¾ cups/14 fl oz/400 ml white wine vinegar; ½ tsp cinnamon; 2 cloves, minced; 1 lemon; salt.

Wash and hull the red currants. Mix together in a bowl the vinegar, a few strips

of lemon peel, the cinnamon, and cloves. Cover and leave for 2–3 hours. Add the red currants, pour into a saucepan, and bring quickly to a boil. Skim and simmer over low heat for approx. 15

minutes, stirring continuously. Add the sugar and cook for a further 15–20 minutes. Season with a little salt. Pour the sauce, while still hot, into sterilized glass jars, and seal. Serve with roast meats, particularly lamb or game.

Raspberry · Blackberry

Both raspberries (top) and blackberries (above and right) are fruits of the Rubus *plant. In antiquity, the Greeks and Romans gave them the same name. The red raspberry is the most popular, but thanks to hybridization, there are also yellow, white, and black varieties. Generally, raspberries tend to be cultivated more than blackberries. A typical fruit of colder climates, the raspberry is much used in central and northern European cuisine.*

The raspberry grows wild throughout most of Europe, in eastern Asia, and in North America. Some fossils found in Swiss lake dwellings indicate that it was known several centuries before Christ. More recent information, apart from a single testimony from Propertius, comes from England where the raspberry was cultivated by the middle of the sixteenth century, and where it was also called hindberry. The British species, *Rubus idaeus*, was later introduced from England to the United States, but as it could not adapt to the new climatic conditions it was soon replaced by a more productive and hardy native species. The raspberry has the same vitamin properties as oranges and lemons and a higher energy value than the latter. The available carbohydrates are about 12–13%, while the vitamin content is 25 mg per 3½ oz (100 g) for vitamin B_1, and 30 mg per 3½ oz (100 g) for vitamin C. Also present are calcium, magnesium, and iron salts. The raspberry is also a good laxative with considerable diuretic properties. It is rich in pectin and is therefore one of the best fruits for jams and jelly. Raspberries can be eaten fresh, or with sugar and plain or whipped cream. It is used in a number of desserts.

The blackberry (*Rubus fruticosus*) is a shrub commonly found along hedges, in woods and in untilled fields of most of the northern hemisphere and also in South Africa. Its fruits can be picked in late summer and in the fall. They were undoubtedly eaten

If you are picking blackberries for jelly, a tart, or just to serve with cream or soaked in wine, wear gloves and use a stick, taking care not to stain your clothing with the indelible purple juice.

RASPBERRY CHAMPAGNE COCKTAIL

Pour a glass three quarters full with champagne or sparkling dry white wine. Add a splash of vodka and 2 tsp raspberry purée. Mix gently. Slice 1 strawberry almost in half and perch on the rim of the glass for decoration. Serves 1.

Raspberry · Blackberry

BLACKBERRY JELLY

Wash ripe blackberries and extract all the juice into a bowl by squeezing them in a damp cloth. Measure the juice obtained and cook in a saucepan with an equal amount of sugar, stirring and skimming until a setting consistency is achieved. Add some clear lemon juice, allow to cool a little, and pour into sterilized jars. Leave until cold, then leave to stand for 24 hours before sealing.

Above: blackberries. The tender spring leaves are edible and, according to Culpeper, boiled with lye can provide a rinse that "maketh the hair black."

by the first inhabitants of this planet, according to paleontological findings. Historical evidence is provided by Aeschylus and Hippocrates, 400–500 years before Christ. Today the blackberry is cultivated as a fruit plant. It is represented by different species and varieties that have been shown to be better adapted to the local climate and soils. The blackberry is a nourishing and refreshing fruit, containing about 85% water and 10% carbohydrates. The human body benefits from eating blackberries because of their content of vitamin B_1, and mineral salts, especially calcium, which is present in a higher percentage than in other fruits. Besides being eaten fresh, plain, or with sugar and cream or wine, blackberries can be used in jams, pies, preserves, and syrups. According to popular medicine they are also a good remedy for diseases of the mouth and throat. This belief goes back many years. Culpeper recommended them for quinsy, snake bites, kidney stones, and various other ailments.

67

Strawberry

One of the most popular fruits in the world perhaps, for its flavor and its scent, is the red wood or wild strawberry which can be found in the shade of pine or beech woods, hidden among other wild plants. The wood strawberry (*Fragaria vesca*) in its wild form is unequaled for its flavor. The commercial demands of modern living require far greater amounts than the limited quantities of this excellent fruit that can be collected growing wild. Today the strawberry has to be large, uniform, and able to withstand transportation, storage, and freezing. It must also be on the market for some months. Therefore new varieties have been cultivated from the original five or six species. However, they are rarely as good as the wild species. There seems to be a difference even in color between cultivated and wild forms. This difference between the two types is supposedly caused by a different ratio of two important pigments. Strawberries contain various types of sugars, fructose and sucrose being the most abundant. Also present are citric, tartaric, and salicylic acids, vitamins B_1 and B_2 and, above all, vitamin C. Strawberries represent a rich source of ascorbic acid (vitamin C) whose production is stimulated by sunlight. It has been ascertained that the quantity of vitamin C in the ripe fruits is increased in relation to the length of time in which the plant has been in the sun during the last few days before picking. Strawberries should be eaten as soon after picking as possible. The considerable vitamin properties are mostly lost in cooking, so that strawberry jelly, jams, and preserves, although good, have only a fraction of the natural vitamins.

It was only in the thirteenth century that the strawberry began to be grown in gardens. It was supposedly brought into France by a sailor named Freziers, from whom it received its French name, *fraise*.

Some strawberry varieties. Right: wild strawberries. To preserve strawberries, place in a jar, and fill with sugar syrup. Seal and sterilize the jars by boiling for 10 minutes.

68

Service tree or Sorb apple · Strawberry tree

The service tree (*Sorbus domestica*) is not of great importance since its fruits, the sorb apples, do not compare with those of the many other plants of the extensively cultivated rose family. There are two cultivated subspecies of service tree: the apple form (*malifera*), with roundish fruits whose shape resembles the apple's, and the pear shape (*pyrifera*), whose fruits are morphologically the same as those of the pear. Sorb apples, as they are sometimes known, cannot be eaten immediately after picking as they have a sour taste and a firm and hard pulp. They must therefore undergo a period of after-ripening until the beginning of decomposition changes their color and gives them a more agreeable flavor. The strawberry tree (*Arbutus unedo*) is one of the most typical plants of the Mediterranean landscape. It has been known at least since Greek and Roman times.

Theophrastus, Theocritus, Virgil, Ovid, and Pliny have left a wealth of information about this plant, which is also called cane apple or dogwood. The fruits, arbutus berries, are tasteless but slightly sour. They are used for preserves, in the preparation of a drink similar to cider, and for the extraction of alcohol.

Above: a service tree (sorb apple). Left: arbutus berries, fruits of the wild strawberry tree. These fruits can be used for preserves and jellies and to make a drink similar to cider, reputed to be beneficial to the digestive system.

69

Cherry

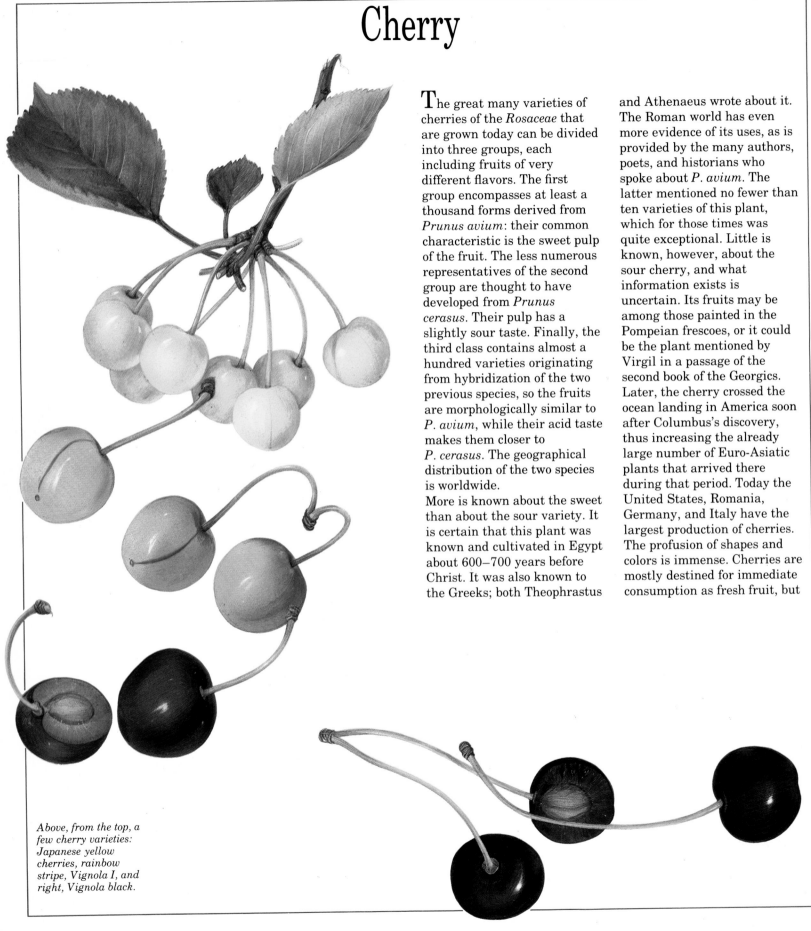

The great many varieties of cherries of the *Rosaceae* that are grown today can be divided into three groups, each including fruits of very different flavors. The first group encompasses at least a thousand forms derived from *Prunus avium*: their common characteristic is the sweet pulp of the fruit. The less numerous representatives of the second group are thought to have developed from *Prunus cerasus*. Their pulp has a slightly sour taste. Finally, the third class contains almost a hundred varieties originating from hybridization of the two previous species, so the fruits are morphologically similar to *P. avium*, while their acid taste makes them closer to *P. cerasus*. The geographical distribution of the two species is worldwide.

More is known about the sweet than about the sour variety. It is certain that this plant was known and cultivated in Egypt about 600–700 years before Christ. It was also known to the Greeks; both Theophrastus and Athenaeus wrote about it. The Roman world has even more evidence of its uses, as is provided by the many authors, poets, and historians who spoke about *P. avium*. The latter mentioned no fewer than ten varieties of this plant, which for those times was quite exceptional. Little is known, however, about the sour cherry, and what information exists is uncertain. Its fruits may be among those painted in the Pompeian frescoes, or it could be the plant mentioned by Virgil in a passage of the second book of the Georgics. Later, the cherry crossed the ocean landing in America soon after Columbus's discovery, thus increasing the already large number of Euro-Asiatic plants that arrived there during that period. Today the United States, Romania, Germany, and Italy have the largest production of cherries. The profusion of shapes and colors is immense. Cherries are mostly destined for immediate consumption as fresh fruit, but

Above, from the top, a few cherry varieties: Japanese yellow cherries, rainbow stripe, Vignola I, and right, Vignola black.

Cherry

Left: red and black morellos. Sour, morello cherries can be placed in a glass pot, dredged with sugar, and left in the sun for a few weeks. Serve with ice cream. Morello cherries can also be preserved in alcohol, unpitted and with part of the stalk left on. Leave for 2 months before eating.

a fair amount is used in the canning industry and in distilleries for the making of liqueurs and brandies. For preserves, confections and similar products, the sour cherries are preferred, especially when they are not too ripe. Cherries are very important in the spirits industry. The most famous products are various cherry brandies: Maraschino, Kirsch, and Ratafia. Kirsch is a characteristic liqueur smelling of bitter almonds. The nutritional value of cherries is relatively low. However, some varieties contain a large amount of sugar, an average of about 10%.

Wild cherries. A delicious liqueur is made by infusing 100 or so wild cherry leaves with a little spirit (eg brandy) and 4½ cups/1¾ pints/ 1 liter good red wine. Strain after 1 week and add sugar syrup to the mixture.

Plum

Apricots, cherries, plums, peaches, and almonds are names with different etymologies; but the genus name *Prunus*, given by Linnaeus, is common to all these trees that produce some of the most prized types of fruit. Although in Roman times *Prunus* probably indicated only the plum tree, with the passing of time it became usual to include in the same genus many species found mostly in temperate regions. Some representatives of this genus also grow in South America in the Andes. Today the plum is cultivated to some extent everywhere in Europe and in the United States. The biggest producers are the east European countries. Among the thousands of cultivars throughout the world are found the characteristic mirabelles with very small fruits: the Florentia and the Shiro, both juicy and sweet, but with slightly tart skin; the Reine Claude (or "greengage"); and the Santa Rosa. There are many American varieties such as Damson Beauty, Italian Prune, Burbank, Sugar, and Stanley. Plums are eaten fresh or dried (prunes), but a large part of the harvest is used by the canning industry for preserves, jams, and sweet

pickles. Some varieties are also distilled to make brandy such as the Balkan Slivovitz. Prunes preserved in brandy, and kept for several months, are excellent. Plums are harvested when their characteristic fragrance is strongest; the first fruits to be collected are those that are going to be preserved or candied. The late varieties are used for drying: the fruits are laid in the sun and then baked in special ovens at a particular temperature. The skins acquire the beautiful brownish color and sheen which make them so valued commercially.

The mirabelle is a small, golden-yellow plum with a very penetrating perfume. It has a sweet flavor and is used stewed or to make jam, and commercially in the manufacture of spirits. The sloe is another species of the *Prunus* family, but is hardly edible, being extremely sour. There are two regions in France where it is celebrated: in Angers where it is distilled to make a famous liqueur, and in the Haute-Saône where it is grown for jam and distilling. The laxative action of prunes is well known. Culpeper spoke highly of plums as fruits belonging to Venus. As well as recommending the fruits "both in health and sickness, to

Above: Ruth Gastetter plums. Right, from top to bottom: Mirabelle, Florentia, and Saint Peter. Cooking plums in sweet dessert wine and a little sugar greatly enhances their flavor: boil sugar to taste in a mixture of dessert wine and water until a syrup is obtained. Add a few whole plums to the liquid. Remove from the heat and leave the plums to soak for about 15 minutes. Drain the wine syrup vigorously to thicken then pour over the plums. Serve hot, with cream.

Plum

Far right: Stanley plum. Right: Shiro plum. Below: Sugar plum. The laxative effect of plums, both fresh and dried, is well known, particularly if the fruit is consumed in the morning on an empty stomach.

relish the mouth and stomach . . ." he also wrote that "plum-tree leaves boiled in wine, are good to wash and gargle the mouth and throat" and that the leaves boiled in vinegar would also cure ringworm! Taken in excess, however, the versatile plum could cause colic. Because of the organic acids in plums, they have been recommended for those with gout and uricemia. They are high in carbohydrates but their vitamin content is negligible.

Each species of *Prunus* contains a large number of cultivars. Throughout the centuries, man has always placed great importance on the nutritional and commercial value of plants, and has also succeeded in obtaining particular varieties valued for their flowers or leaves and therefore used as outdoor ornamentals. Early in their cultivation it was probably almost exclusively the sugar content of the ripe fruit that led gardeners to think of its

high energy value. When man began to analyze chemically the various components of the single species, however, he discovered numerous mineral salts and, more recently, vitamins. This discovery brought both hope and dissension. Today, science tries to show each kind of food, including fruit, in an impartial light, emphasizing the calorific or mineral or vitamin properties, which can be present at various levels simultaneously. It is

PRUNES

Plums for drying should be unblemished, ripe (but not too soft), and as large as possible. Plunge in boiling water and boil for a few minutes. Lift out with a slotted ladle, then spread out on a cooling rack. Leave in the sun, and turn every day. The time required to dry the plums will be approx. one week. Store in a cool, dry place, in cloth bags or waxed paper bags. Soak in water before serving cold or cooked. Prunes go well in both sweet and savory dishes.

Plum

The juicy and fragrant Reine Claude, with greenish skin and pulp.

impossible to discuss the precise composition of fruit in a general way. The sugar content of a cherry differs considerably, for example, from that of a peach. A fairly accurate average can, however, be obtained. It can be seen that fresh fruit contains more water than anything else, 80–90%; the amount of assimilable carbohydrates is also high, about 12%. Mineral salts, protein and lipids have approximately the same values, 1% or less. The rest of the weight is made up of nonassimilable substances (2–3%) and various vitamins which, however, are not always present. With the exception of a few very rich fruits, they are not generally found in great quantity. The vitamins of the B complex are often scarce or even absent, while a satisfying amount can be provided of the groups A and C. Contrary to general belief it is not true that fruit is an inexhaustible source of vitamins. Mineral salts which are present in small amounts cannot be compared in quantity with those provided by, for example, milk, meat, and cheese. Fruit does, however, have a beneficial effect on the human body, because of its assimilable sugars and the number of calories produced. Another important factor is the presence in fresh fruit of some organic acids, such as tartaric, citric, and oxalic. Some fresh fruits are considered by some to be useful for cases of acidosis and rheumatic disorders.

Above: the Burbank variety. Right: the Santa Rosa plum, with crimson skin and pulp and a fragrance that ranges from Muscat to banana. Prunes are picked when their characteristic fragrance is at its strongest.

Peach · Apricot

Peaches can be eaten either fresh or dried, used to make preserves and jelly or canned. The peach tree (*Prunus persica vulgaris*) is believed to have originated in China, where it still grows in the wild state, and to have come to Europe through Persia (now Iran). In China the peach was known 2,000 years before Christ. From Persia it was introduced to the Greco-Roman world, perhaps by Alexander the Great. The Spanish introduced it into Latin America during the sixteenth century and in

the next century it came to California. In the nineteenth century the plant reached Australia, but it was not until early in the twentieth century that it arrived in southern Africa. Today the peach is one of the most widely cultivated fruit trees throughout the world, wherever the soil and climate are suitable. The two countries with the highest peach production are the United States and Italy. There are many cultivated varieties. The sugar content of the peach is not normally higher than 9%, while the amount of mineral salts is considerable. The vitamin value is far greater than in other fruits, especially of vitamins A and C. Peaches make many excellent desserts; baked and stuffed with almonds, butter, and ground macaroons, or stewed with wine or lemon, in pies, flans or shortcakes, and in the famous Peach Melba. It is said that once, when Madame Récamier, the great French beauty of the early nineteenth

A large and yellow-fleshed Hale peach and the Lugo beautiful variety, with a highly scented white flesh.

Two Loadel peaches. It is best to store peaches on a rack in a dry, well-ventilated place, so air may circulate freely around them.

Peach · Apricot

PEACHES IN SYRUP

The most suitable varieties for this treatment are yellow peaches. Peel, halve, and remove the pit. Place the peach halves in a large, wide jar, arranging them neatly next to one another with a wooden spoon. Boil enough sugar and water to make a sugar syrup to cover the peaches: 2 lb/1 kg peaches will take 2 lb/1 kg sugar and 4½ cups/1 liter/1¾ pints water. Cool the syrup and pour over the fruit, ensuring it seeps between all the peach halves. Seal and sterilize the jar for 20 minutes. Leave for 2 months before eating.

Above: an Armking nectarine. Below, from the left, a Jalon white nectarine, a nugget apricot, a caninos apricot, and two Imola royal apricots. These fruits ripen very quickly and should only be stored for a very short time.

century, was ill, and refusing all food, her life was saved by a dish of peaches in syrup and cream, which brought back not only her appetite, but the will to live.

A particular group of the peach family is that of the nectarine. These fruits were already known in England at the end of the sixteenth century. The name is believed to be derived from "nectar," the drink of the gods, to which this fruit was compared because of its superb flavor. Nectarines (*Prunus persica* var. *nectarina*) are classed as fuzzless peaches with an even richer flavor than the *P. persica*. There is an old, but inaccurate, country belief that the nectarine evolved from a peach, which was crossed with a plum.

Contrary to what the Latin scientific name, *Prunus armeniaca*, might suggest, the apricot is not originally from Armenia. The apricot has been found in China as a wild plant for at least 4,000 years. It was the Arabs who spread the cultivation of the apricot throughout the Mediterranean, although it was not until the fifteenth century that it became popular in Europe. Only in the eighteenth century did the plant become part of the cultivated flora of the United States and South Africa. Today the apricot is recognized, in its many varieties, as an excellent fruit, especially because of its vitamin content and mineral salts. The usable sugars do not go over 6–7%. The level of potassium, however, is high. It is essential to eat this fruit when it is fully ripe in order to get the most out of its high content of vitamin A.

Citrus fruits

Citrus fruits, which are in the
Rutaceae or rue family, include
oranges, tangerines, lemons,
grapefruits, limes, and citrons.
The genus *Citrus* contains
woody perennial plants with
evergreen leaves of varying
size from shrubs to small trees.
They do best in the mild
climates of southern Italy,
Sicily, Spain, Greece, Brazil,
Mexico and, in the United
States, Florida and southern
California. The fruit of plants
of the genus *Citrus* is a special
kind of berry called a
hesperidium, a term derived
from Greek mythology.
Traditionally, oranges were
identified with the golden
apples that grew in the mythical
garden of the Hesperides (in
actual fact, probably the
Canaries). The classification of
the citrus is complex, and
controversial. It seems right to
speak of an "orange type" and
a "citron type."
The sweet orange is native to
the Far East: India, China
(where it is considered to be a

ORANGE AND ONION SALAD

4 large oranges; 1
small onion, chopped;
½ cup/3½ oz/100 g
pitted black olives;
olive oil; salt and
pepper.

Peel the oranges,
remove the bitter
white pith, and slice.
Arrange on a serving
plate and season.
Cover with the
chopped onion and

the olives. Dress with
a little olive oil and
leave to stand at
room temperature for
a short while before
serving.

Citrus fruits

The strongly scented lemon blossom. Its pollen produces one of the most highly prized varieties of honey.

The citron (above) is seldom consumed in its natural state. It is an ingredient for a number of refreshing beverages, and its candied peel can add flavor or decoration to a dessert. Right and below far right: the lemon, perhaps the most widely used fruit in cooking. Both juice and rind act as ingredients, flavoring, and decoration.

wild fruit), and Indochina. Its introduction to the Mediterranean region was relatively late; it probably became known to the Romans around the first century A.D., following the conquest of Oriental territories by the Roman Empire. During the expansion of Arab domination the cultivation of the sweet orange became a heritage of the Mediterranean. Vasco da Gama is said to have brought a

root to Portugal. According to some authorities the word "orange" derives from the Arabic *narandj*, which comes from the Sanskrit *nagarunga*, meaning "fruit favoured by the elephants." The cultivars of the sweet orange are now very numerous. Among them are many important American cultivars, notably Valencia, Washington Navel, Hamlin, Pineapple, and Homosassa. Oranges are extensively grown in Florida and California. In Italy they are distinguished commercially as "blondes" and "blood," while in the United States they are classed as normal, blood, and navel. Among the former, the most usual is the "common blonde," the "Calabrese" or "oval," the "vanilla," "sweet" or "Maltese." Among the blood oranges grown in Europe the best known are the *tarocco*, the *sanguinello*, and the *moro*. Oranges are commonly used fresh, or as a refreshing drink. They can also be made into a salad: the orange segments are seasoned with oil, vinegar, and pepper and a little curry powder (if wished), and served with watercress. Oranges have a high vitamin value, especially vitamin C: 60 mg per 3½ oz (100 g) of fruit. The solid residue is 10%; protein less than 1%; sugars are between 7% and 8%; no lipids are present; 3½ oz (100 g) of fruit supply 35 calories. The fruits of the bitter orange have no food interest. But the flowers and leaves are highly prized in the cosmetic industry for essences and perfumes. The rind is used for the extraction of an essential oil for liqueurs such as curaçao.

Citrus fruits

The grapefruit tree, which originated in Malaysia, is now cultivated worldwide. The fruits grow in clusters, like grapes, giving the grapefruit its name. Like the orange, it is a very versatile fruit.

GRAPEFRUIT FIZZ

Slice the top off a grapefruit, extract all the pulp, and place the empty grapefruit "shell" in the freezer. Extract all the juice from the pulp and chill in the refrigerator. Mix 3 tsp chilled peach-flavored brandy or liqueur, a splash of lemonade, and the grapefruit juice. Pour into the grapefruit shell to serve. Drink through a straw.

The mandarin or tangerine (*C. reticulata*), native to southern China (Yunnan) and Laos, is eaten almost exclusively as a fresh fruit, but can also be candied or glazed, or used in the preparation of a delicate liqueur. It is grown in the southern United States (where excellent cultivars include Satsuma, Dancy, Clementine, Kara, Frua, Sweet, and King Orange), and in parts of France. Those of Nice and Algeria are the most prized. The "temple orange" is a hybrid between mandarin and orange, with large fruits, soft skin, and a pleasing taste. The vitamin value of the tangerine, expressed in vitamin C, is approximately one third of that of the orange, and the calorific value is also lower: 7–8 calories per 3½ oz (100 g) of fruit. The tangerine contains more water than the orange, and the percentage of carbohydrates is lower. The lime (*C. aurantifolia*), a small fruit tasting rather like the citron or the lemon, is mostly used candied or for summer drinks. The bergamot is inedible and grown for the essence extracted from the rind, which is the basis for many perfumes. Tahiti and Key are two outstanding American cultivars. Grapefruit grows extensively in the United States. The fruit is spherical or globose. The pulp is juicy with an agreeable tart taste. It can be eaten fresh, or used in the preparation of an excellent juice. In Europe and America grapefruit is often served at the start of a meal. The species or variety name of the citron, *Medica*, does not indicate medicinal qualities; it means "coming from Media."

Grapefruit and clementine. There is also a pink-fleshed variety of grapefruit, which is more sweet-tasting. The clementine is a hybrid derived from crossing orange and tangerine. It is preferable to the tangerine because it is juicier and frequently seedless.

Citrus fruits

Above: the kumquat, a fruit of Oriental origin. Below: two tangerines. Kumquats and tangerines are easily grown; in cold weather, bring inside and stand in a well-lit spot.

Diamante, Corsican, and Etron are common American varieties. An essential oil used for liqueurs, perfumes, and medicines is obtained by distillation of the rind.
The Mediterranean regions provide the best conditions for growth of the lemon, which is originally from the Far East. In the United States lemons are grown extensively in Florida, Texas, and California. Among the best known cultivars are the very popular "common," the *monachello* or "little monk," the *spadafora*, and, as a curiosity, the "Turk's Head" with very large fruits, the size of a man's head, having sweet pulp and juice. American cultivars are Eureka, Lisbon, Meyer, and Villa Franca. There are many culinary uses for the lemon, of which both the peel and the juice are used. The high amount of vitamin C, 60 mg per 3½ oz (100 g) of fruit, is also a known fact. Lemons are also used in lemonade, sherbets, ice cream, and to enhance the flavor of seafood. The kumquat (*Citrus japonica* or *Fortunella margarita* in honor of Robert Fortune, who introduced it to Europe) has not been found in the wild state; it is said to be native to China, and has been cultivated for a long time in China,

Japan, Indochina, and Java, while it was only later that it was introduced into the Mediterranean basin, America, and Australia. Its rind is very aromatic, sweet and edible, and the fruits are eaten whole, fresh or candied or preserved in alcohol like cucumbers or pickles. It is a perfect garnish for roast duck.
In the "citron type," *C. Medica* (*C. cedra*) is the type species or prototype. Also grouped within

this category is the true lemon, *C. limon* (*C. medica acida*, *C. medica limon*) and the pear or sweet lemon, *C. medica limia*. Among other citrus fruits there are the hybrids: temple (sweet orange and mandarin), tangelo (mandarin × grapefruit: pomelo), citrange (sweet orange × trifoliate orange, *Poncirus trifoliata*) and, lastly, the kumquat (*Fortunella Margarite* or *C. japonica*).

Indian fig or Prickly pear

The Indian fig (*Opuntia ficus-indica* of the *Cactaceae* or cactus family) has been part of the European flora since around the sixteenth century. The Spanish imported it from Mexico to Europe soon after the discovery of America. It is therefore of American origin, and spread rapidly in the temperate and warm regions of southern Europe and Africa. It is not to be found in the northern regions of Europe and only a few specimens which, in fact, never produce fruits can be found along the Tyrrhenian coasts. Instead, around the Mediterranean, the Indian fig has become very much part of the countryside, often making a magnificent display. The fruit is about the size of a slightly elongate apple; the color is first green, then, while it ripens, yellow and red. The internal part consists of a very sweet pulp, pale pink or whitish, depending on the different varieties, which enclose many hard seeds. There are also varieties completely without, or with only a few, seeds, and fruits of smaller size (Indian fig *ariddari*).

To pick and eat Indian figs can literally be a "thorny" problem. A stick is used for harvesting, at the tip of which a tin can is attached with the opening upward. The sharp edge of the can cuts the fruit from the plant and makes it fall inside. Eating the fig is a little more complicated. It is necessary to use a knife and fork. The skin is cut lengthwise so that it separates from the delicious juicy pulp. The seeds are eaten by some people, but others discard them.

Indian figs are eaten raw when very ripe but can also be stewed or preserved for domestic use. Some of the varieties more commonly cultivated are: the yellowish Indian fig; the violet-red Indian or "bloody" fig of small size; the late *bastarduni* Indian fig, large with a sweet pulp and excellent for prolonged storage.

Prickly pears are prized for their fragrant, sweet pulp, which varies in color from yellow to red.

PRICKLY PEAR JAM

2 lb/1 kg peeled prickly pears; 9 oz/250 g sugar; grated peel of 1 lemon.

Chop the prickly pears, dredge with the sugar, and leave overnight to macerate. Cook over low heat for 1 hour. Sieve, then mix in the lemon peel. Cook until thick. Transfer to jars and seal.

Fig

Black figs with, below, a white fig. These ripen in late summer. Opposite: breba figs, which ripen in early summer on biferous plants, i.e. those that produce two crops of fruit.

The area of growth of the wild fig (*Ficus carica* of the *Moraceae* or mulberry family) is much larger now than in the past. The fig is to be found in a vast uninterrupted area stretching from eastern Iran to the Canary Isles, through the Mediterranean countries. It is believed to have come from Syria. Later, especially through the Phoenicians, it spread to China and India, and, relatively recently, was introduced to America and South Africa. Its cultivation goes back to very early times. Drawings of figs, dating back to several centuries before Christ, were found in the Gizeh Pyramid; the plant was undoubtedly known in Babylon, and is mentioned three times in the *Odyssey*. Aristotle, Theophrastus, and Dioscorides speak of the fig as a plant cultivated for a long time, whose fruits, especially when dried, were highly prized. Pliny writes that in his day there was a square where the Romans assembled, in which grew a fig tree in memory of the one under which, according to legend, Romulus and Remus were found suckling milk from the she-wolf. He adds that

FIGS WITH CUSTARD

8 ripe figs; 2 glasses brandy; 2¼ cups/ ½ liter/12 fl oz milk; peel of 1 lemon; 4 egg yolks; ½ cup/ 125 g/4 oz sugar; 1 tsp vanilla essence.

Slice the figs in half and soak overnight in the brandy. Bring the milk to a boil with the lemon peel, then remove the peel. Beat the egg yolks with the sugar and vanilla until pale; gradually add the hot milk. Cook the resulting mixture in a double boiler until thick, but take care not to boil. Remove from the heat and allow to cool. Serve the custard in a crystal bowl, topped with the drained figs.

Fig

FIG PASTRIES

8 oz/200 g puff pastry;
14 oz/400 g figs;
3½ oz/100 g seedless
white raisins
(sultanas); 1–2 tsp
cinnamon; 2 oz/50 g
sugar.

Roll out the pastry
and leave to stand for
10 minutes. Slice it
into 4–6-in/11–15-cm
squares. For the
filling, peel and chop
the figs. Combine
with the seedless
white raisins
(sultanas) and
cinnamon. Mix well.
Place 1 tbsp of the
filling onto the
squares and seal
the pastry parcels.
Dredge with sugar
and bake at
350°F/180°C/mark 4
for 15 minutes. Serve
lukewarm or cold.
These pastries may
also be filled with fig
and lemon jam.

whenever the tree died of old age, the priests would be careful to plant another of the same race.

Today the cultivation of the fig is extensive, particularly in Spain, Turkey, and Italy, but more limited in the United States. There are at least 700 varieties which basically derive from a single species, *F. carica*, and from the subspecies *sativa*, which is commonly called domestic fig. There is also a wild species or caprifig, whose fruits are not edible, being dry and stringy. The fig produces only one (uniferous figs) or two crops (biferous figs); in the latter case the figs of the first crop, early figs, mature at the beginning of summer; second-crop figs appear toward August or September.

Depending on the color of the skin, there are white, purple and red figs. They are usually eaten fresh, and have a pleasant taste, but are less nutritious than is commonly believed (80% water, 12% sugars). Part of the fresh fruit crop is canned for preserves, or used in spicy relishes. The greater amount of figs is sold as dried fruits which increases their nutritional value considerably, as the sugar content becomes five times greater than in the fresh fruit, and the amount of water is reduced to a quarter. Dried figs are an important commercial product as they can be exported to countries with unsuitable climates for their cultivation. The dried product is very good when stuffed with walnuts or almonds, and small pieces of orange or citron. Figs can be baked after being covered with confectioner's sugar or honey, and can also be used to make an alcoholic drink and, after roasting, as a coffee substitute. All apricot recipes are suitable for figs.

Figs can be combined with salami or cured ham as a delicious appetizer. They can also be made into jam, desserts, and sweet fritters. Dried, stuffed with almonds or walnuts, or added to anise-flavored cakes, they are a good source of energy thanks to their high sugar content.

Grape

The lambrusco or Northern Fox grape, produced in the Emilia Romagna region of Italy. Like all wine grape varieties, this grape is also good for eating.

Viticulture had its beginnings somewhere around the Caspian Sea in the area generally considered the place of origin of *Vitis vinifera*, our most common grape. It goes so far back in time that the vine is thought to have been already established throughout the world even before the coming of man.

Its cultivation suffered a decline after the fall of the Roman Empire, around the second century A.D., until the rise of the city-states (e.g. Florence, Siena, Pisa, etc.) in the later Middle Ages. After the discovery of America, wild species were imported from the new continent and from them new varieties were obtained.

GRAPE AND GOAT'S CHEESE SALAD

2 hearts escarole or endive; 4 small bunches grapes; 10 oz/300 g goat's cheese; 2 tbsp skinned almonds; sweet paprika; tabasco; cider vinegar; olive oil; salt and pepper.

Work the goat's cheese with a spoon and mix in salt, pepper, and a few drops of tabasco. Form the mixture into grape-sized balls and dust with paprika. Shred the salad. Roast the almonds under the broiler. Mix 2 tbsp cider vinegar with 4 tbsp oil and season with salt and pepper. Pour this dressing over the shredded lettuce. Arrange a bunch of grapes on each of 4 plates, add a few cheese balls, and sprinkle some roasted almonds on top.

Grapes are now widely available throughout the year although this is largely due to chemical intervention. It is therefore preferable to enjoy this fruit during the fall, which is its natural ripening season.

Grape

Some centuries later these wild species saved the European grape industry which was then ravaged by disease. Viticulture has so progressed during the twentieth century that it is now one of the most prominent harvests in existence. Throughout the world Europe clearly occupies first place with an area of about 17–18 million acres reserved for viticulture, in a total world figure of 75 million acres. In Europe, Italy leads in acreage followed by Spain and France.

The cultivated varieties are very numerous, and there are also many characteristics that bring them into one or the other of the two groups into which they have been subdivided: table or dessert grapes and wine grapes. Both types are, however, good for eating. Grapes also have

HOW TO DRY GRAPES

Hang bunches of grapes in a dry and well-ventilated place (e.g. in a room with a window that may be closed overnight), taking care that they do not touch each other. After a few days, when all the moisture has gone, pit carefully and place in a jar with a handful of sugar. Shake the jar well so the sugar penetrates between all the seedless white raisins (sultanas). Leave for one month before using.

Two prized wine varieties: sangiovese (left) and trebbiano of Empoli. Because of their high sugar content, grapes are a good source of energy. They are refreshing and have diuretic properties.

Grape

GRAPES IN SPIRIT

2 lb/1 kg white grapes; 5 oz/150 g sugar; 2¼ cups/½ liter/18fl oz pure spirit (e.g. vodka); 1 tsp cinnamon; 1 tsp vanilla extract; 2 cloves.

Clean the grapes and pierce with a pin. Place in sterilized jars. Melt the sugar in the spirit over gentle heat. When cold, stir in the cinnamon, vanilla, and cloves. Fill the jars with this. Seal and keep in a dry, well-ventilated place for approx 1 month, shaking the jars occasionally to ensure all the grapes are flavored by the spirit.

digestive and therapeutic properties which are rare in other types of fruit, and are considered to be very nourishing. A grape is formed by the pulp, which is the most important part, enclosed by a thin, membranous skin, and enclosing seeds (grapestones). Water, in which all the various substances are dissolved, is the greatest component of the pulp. A good percentage of carbohydrates is present, 18–20%, in the form of glucose and fructose, both of which are easily assimilable and provide many calories, which explains why grapes, although poor in protein and lipids, are considered to be so nutritious. They also contain potassium, iron, sodium, calcium, magnesium, and phosphorus, which have a refreshing action maintaining the balance of the kidney's functions and helping the elimination of waste and excess acids. Grapes are also fairly rich in vitamin C, while

the B complex is present in larger amounts in the white or lighter-colored grapes. Wine is the result of the alcoholic fermentation of the must, the juice pressed from fresh, or even partly dried, grapes. Wines differ vastly according to the different varieties of grapes, the composition of the soil, the climatic conditions, and the various treatments to which the must and the grapes themselves are subjected. According to their color, wines are classified as red, rosé, and white, while according to their use they are called "table" or "dessert" wines, "sparkling wines," etc. Wine has been known since very early times, and is considered a high-energy food. It has been claimed by some medical authorities that people who drink a little red wine every day have a longer lifespan. In certain remote districts grapes are still crushed by the feet, but it is now more usual

Grape

Opposite: cornicella grapes, which have an unusual, elongated shape, and a variety of black or dessert grape.

Left: muscatel grapes, which are sweet, juicy, and strongly scented. Muscat wine is served chilled with desserts.

for mechanical presses to be employed. The harvest time varies according to the variety, but usually takes place during a spell of warm, dry weather. Very good vintages are stored for about three years in heavy wooden casks (although in hot countries, such as Algeria, the casks are lighter), but lesser vintages are put into metal or japanned casks.

Wine should always be handled with respect. A cheap or young wine is vastly improved if the cork is completely removed from the bottle at least three to four hours before it is to be drunk. This "softens" the wine and takes away any acidity. Never be afraid of extravagance in using a good wine in cooking. Good food is worth good wine.

FROSTED GRAPES

Sift confectioner's sugar into a bowl. Gradually pour in sufficient hot water until a thick but smooth pouring consistency is obtained. Add 1–2 tbsp liqueur of choice. Dip grapes in the mixture and leave until set.

Melon

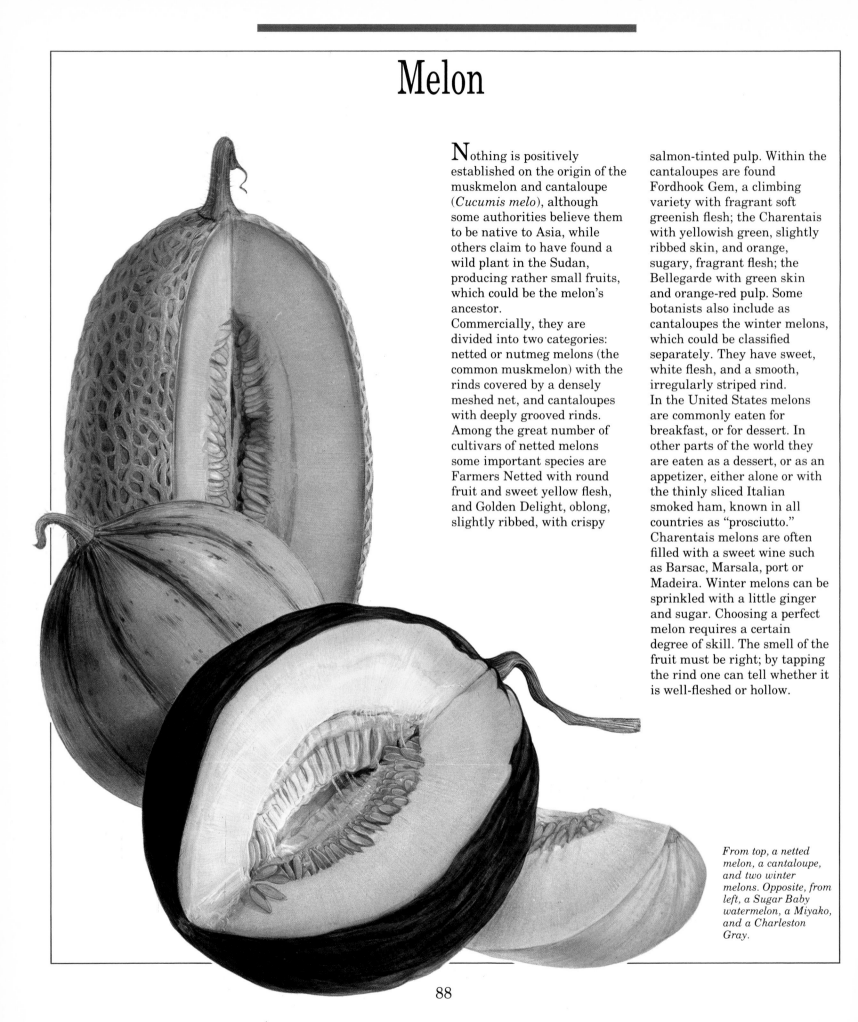

Nothing is positively established on the origin of the muskmelon and cantaloupe (*Cucumis melo*), although some authorities believe them to be native to Asia, while others claim to have found a wild plant in the Sudan, producing rather small fruits, which could be the melon's ancestor.

Commercially, they are divided into two categories: netted or nutmeg melons (the common muskmelon) with the rinds covered by a densely meshed net, and cantaloupes with deeply grooved rinds. Among the great number of cultivars of netted melons some important species are Farmers Netted with round fruit and sweet yellow flesh, and Golden Delight, oblong, slightly ribbed, with crispy salmon-tinted pulp. Within the cantaloupes are found Fordhook Gem, a climbing variety with fragrant soft greenish flesh; the Charentais with yellowish green, slightly ribbed skin, and orange, sugary, fragrant flesh; the Bellegarde with green skin and orange-red pulp. Some botanists also include as cantaloupes the winter melons, which could be classified separately. They have sweet, white flesh, and a smooth, irregularly striped rind.

In the United States melons are commonly eaten for breakfast, or for dessert. In other parts of the world they are eaten as a dessert, or as an appetizer, either alone or with the thinly sliced Italian smoked ham, known in all countries as "prosciutto." Charentais melons are often filled with a sweet wine such as Barsac, Marsala, port or Madeira. Winter melons can be sprinkled with a little ginger and sugar. Choosing a perfect melon requires a certain degree of skill. The smell of the fruit must be right; by tapping the rind one can tell whether it is well-fleshed or hollow.

From top, a netted melon, a cantaloupe, and two winter melons. Opposite, from left, a Sugar Baby watermelon, a Miyako, and a Charleston Gray.

Watermelon

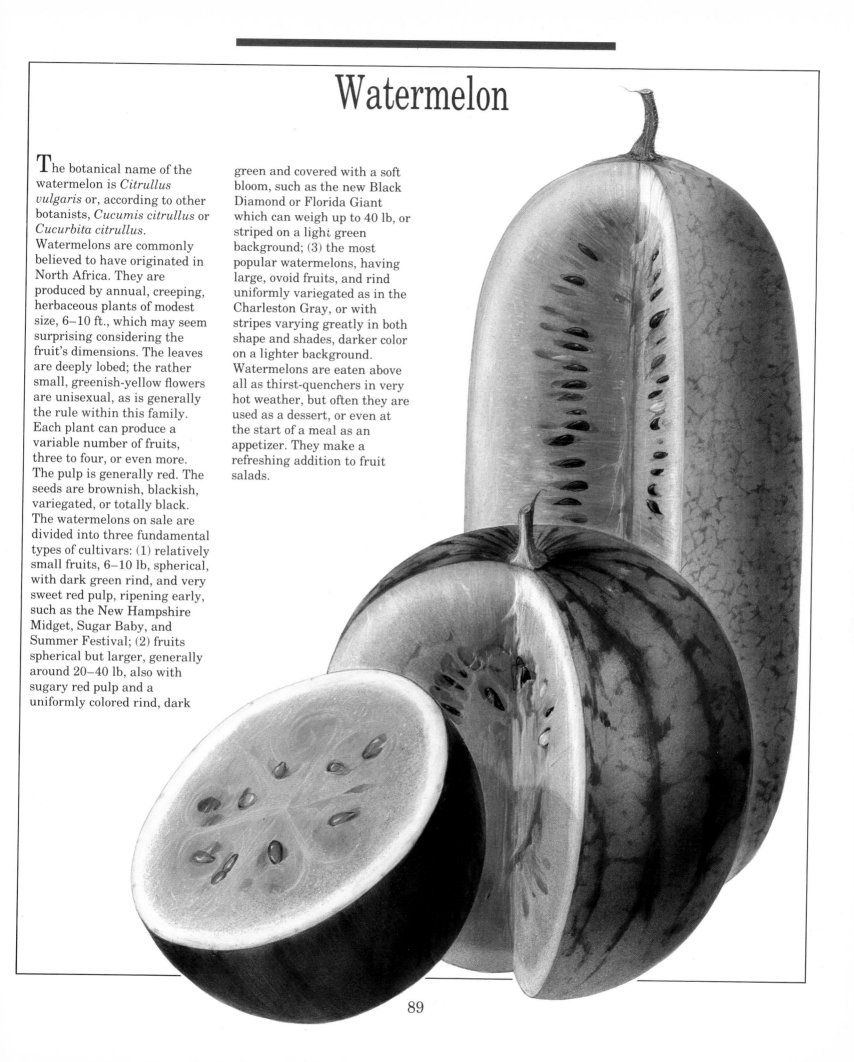

The botanical name of the watermelon is *Citrullus vulgaris* or, according to other botanists, *Cucumis citrullus* or *Cucurbita citrullus*. Watermelons are commonly believed to have originated in North Africa. They are produced by annual, creeping, herbaceous plants of modest size, 6–10 ft., which may seem surprising considering the fruit's dimensions. The leaves are deeply lobed; the rather small, greenish-yellow flowers are unisexual, as is generally the rule within this family. Each plant can produce a variable number of fruits, three to four, or even more. The pulp is generally red. The seeds are brownish, blackish, variegated, or totally black. The watermelons on sale are divided into three fundamental types of cultivars: (1) relatively small fruits, 6–10 lb, spherical, with dark green rind, and very sweet red pulp, ripening early, such as the New Hampshire Midget, Sugar Baby, and Summer Festival; (2) fruits spherical but larger, generally around 20–40 lb, also with sugary red pulp and a uniformly colored rind, dark green and covered with a soft bloom, such as the new Black Diamond or Florida Giant which can weigh up to 40 lb, or striped on a light green background; (3) the most popular watermelons, having large, ovoid fruits, and rind uniformly variegated as in the Charleston Gray, or with stripes varying greatly in both shape and shades, darker color on a lighter background. Watermelons are eaten above all as thirst-quenchers in very hot weather, but often they are used as a dessert, or even at the start of a meal as an appetizer. They make a refreshing addition to fruit salads.

Banana · Alkekengi

Bananas are generally eaten raw, although there are many recipes for cooked bananas. They should be eaten when the skin becomes slightly streaked and softer. It is at this point that the starch in the flesh turns to sugar, making the fruit easy to digest.

The most important species of the large group of edible plants belonging to the genus *Musa* can be limited to *M. paradisiaca* and *M. nana*, although almost 30 species are known. The banana tree and its fruits, bananas, have been known since ancient times, even before the beginning of the cultivation of rice. Their place of origin is thought to be in east Asia and Oceania, from where they spread throughout the world. In Africa they were undoubtedly introduced by the Arabs. The Spanish and Portuguese brought this valued plant to America, first to the Antilles, then Santo Domingo, later to the Guianas and Brazil. A flourishing industry has now developed around the banana which is one of the most profitable agricultural resources of many countries situated along the tropical belt. Four South American countries export the largest tonnage of bananas: Honduras, Ecuador, Costa Rica, and Panama. To grow well, the banana needs a constantly warm climate. Some thousands of years ago, before man came to appreciate this plant, it produced almost tasteless fruits with black and bitter seeds. Through cultivation and genetic improvement it has now reached its remarkable flavor and fragrance. The banana is almost as rich as tomatoes and oranges in vitamins B and C, and so has antiscorbutic qualities. It also contains iron, phosphorus, potassium, and calcium, but it is mostly for its high content (almost 20%) of easily assimilable sugars that it is considered so nutritious. The considerable amount of vitamin A also promotes the secretion of gastric juices, helping the digestion. Bananas can be eaten fresh, or flambéed with brown sugar, brandy or rum, or served with dates. American and Canary bananas are the most abundant.

The Alkekengi (*Physalis pubescens* of the *Solanaceae* or nightshade family) is an unusual plant. The berry is covered with a papery husk. It is native to Mexico and is related to the tomato, the eggplant, and the pepper. The fruits are agreeable to eat, slightly acid, and vaguely similar to the tomato, although they are not highly regarded. They can be eaten raw or preserved and contain a fair amount of vitamins. They are sometimes called Cape gooseberry, strawberry tomato or winter cherry.

Some alkekengi with their papery husk. An old recipe suggests fermenting these fruits with grapes at harvest time to make a wine which is a good remedy for kidney stones. More often alkekengi are used to make jams and decorate tarts and flans. They also make delicious little chocolates when dipped in melted chocolate and left to set.

Pineapple

When eaten fresh as a dessert, the pineapple is delicious sliced and sprinkled with kirsch, which complements its flavor. The pulp can also be scooped out and, after the hard core has been discarded, mixed with ice cream and stuffed back into the shell, to be frozen until it is to be eaten. If the ice cream is flavored with a sweet white wine it is even better.

One of the earliest stories concerning the introduction of the pineapple to Europe concerns the Emperor Charles V of Spain, who, seeing for the first time this strange fruit brought from America by Columbus, was so fearful of its oddity that he refused to taste it, in spite of his courtiers' assurances of its delicacy and fragrance. The Spaniards called it *pina* because it resembled the pinecone, and the same term soon appeared in the English language: pineapple.

The pineapple has over 15% sugar, malic and citric acids, water, and a ferment called bromeline which is very similar to pepsin. In Anglo-Saxon countries, especially in the United States and Canada, pineapples are used as a garnish for roast meats, especially ham. The pineapple was also cultivated in hothouses for a certain time in Europe. This method proved unprofitable and was discontinued. The most common European species is the white pineapple with ovoid fruits, and almost white pulp. The "yellow pineapple," pyramidical fruit with golden flesh, is better tasting than the white; the "sugar loaf pineapple," with very large fruit, has a most delicate flavor.

Pineapples are best sliced lengthwise, as they lose less juice in this way. After slicing, peel, then sprinkle with kirsch to serve.

Persimmon or Kaki

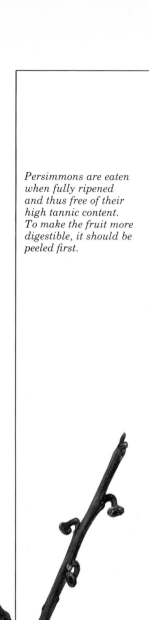

Persimmons are eaten when fully ripened and thus free of their high tannic content. To make the fruit more digestible, it should be peeled first.

The persimmon or kaki tree (*Diospyros kaki*) is found in the wild state in some mountainous regions of central and eastern China. Its cultivation is ancient in both China and Japan. The introduction of the persimmon as a fruit tree in the western world dates back only to the nineteenth century, first in the United States, then France, as late as 1884. But in less than a century this beautiful autumnal fruit has spread everywhere. Although persimmons become ripe almost at the end of fall, they retain all the characteristics of the most typical summer fruits: sugary, juicy, and colorful. It seems a quirk of nature that, while other plants are disappearing at the approach of winter, the persimmons with their beautiful bright colors can still be seen hanging from the already leafless branches. In some areas, however, the fruit cannot complete the ripening cycle on the plant, so the farmer has to use artificial means to turn the still greenish pulp into its golden perfection.

Persimmons have considerable food value, due to their high percentage of glucose and protein. In order to fully appreciate the taste of the fruit, it must be eaten when fully ripe, when all traces of tannic substances have disappeared. It is this that gives the fruit its typically sour taste. Persimmons are eaten raw or stewed, and are only rarely used in the canning industry. They are commercially cultivated in the southern United States, France, Spain, Italy, and generally around the Mediterranean. They are also known, more poetically, as the "fruit of Jove."

Opposite: the two main types of date: hard and soft. Soft dates are more highly prized than hard dates in that they retain their moisture for a long time, even after drying. The best quality is the Deglet Ennour or Sunray, typical of the oases.

Date

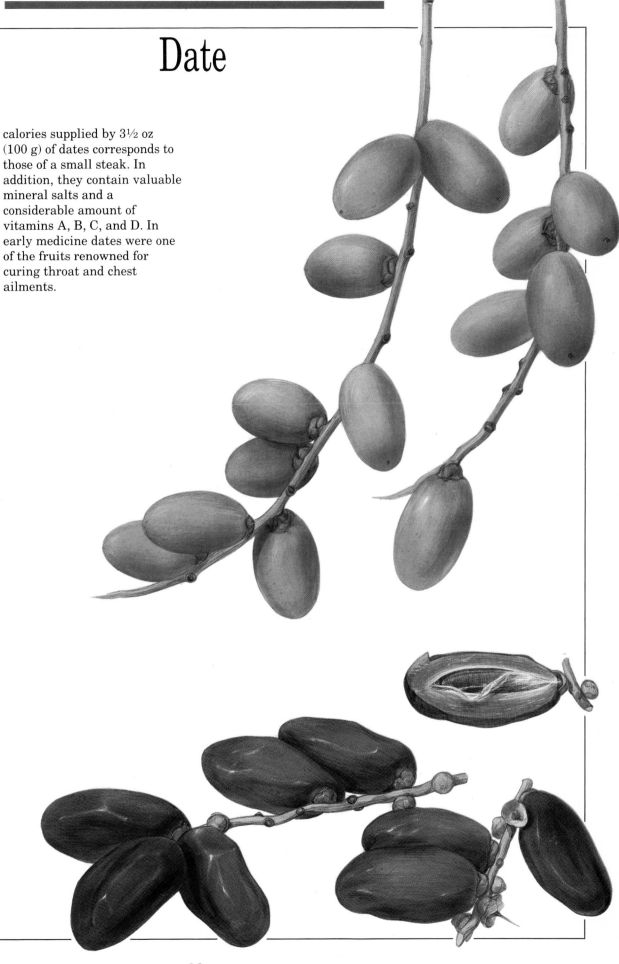

The date is thought of as a highly esteemed food for the African and Middle Eastern populations, and as a dessert for the tables of Western countries. There are people for whom the date represents almost the only available and abundant food; in Arabia, Egypt, and in general all the countries of North Africa, this fruit is the staple fruit of the poor. The cultivation of dates goes back to antiquity; records show that they were known to the Chaldeans. Dates are the fruits produced by a particular group of palm trees, the "date palms" which botanically belong to the species *Phoenix dactylifera*. The date palm is almost worshiped by the local inhabitants for its fruits and the many other uses that can be made of other parts of the plant. The terminal, upper part of the trunk, where the inflorescence and the new leaf-shoots are borne, provides a juice that, after fermentation, yields a "palm wine," and also a spirit. The stems and leaves are used for building huts, while the fibers of the leaves are used to manufacture baskets, ropes, hats, mats, and many other everyday objects. The wood of the tree is fairly combustible, and, in some areas, is the only wood product available to make fires.

The many varieties of the date palm can be divided into two main groups: hard and soft dates. The date can be considered a concentrate of nutritious and calorific substances: the percentage of sugars makes up 70% of the weight. To prove the high calorific potential, the 300 calories supplied by 3½ oz (100 g) of dates corresponds to those of a small steak. In addition, they contain valuable mineral salts and a considerable amount of vitamins A, B, C, and D. In early medicine dates were one of the fruits renowned for curing throat and chest ailments.

Avocado

AVOCADOS WITH SALMON ROE

2 avocados; 2 lemons;
2 hard-boiled egg
yolks; tabasco sauce;
3 tbsp salmon roe;
2 tbsp whipped
cream; salt.

Split the avocados in
half and remove the
pit. Sprinkle with

lemon juice to
prevent
discoloration.
Remove most of the
pulp with a teaspoon,
but leave a thin layer
in place. Purée the
pulp, lemon juice, egg
yolks, a few drops of
tabasco, and 2 tbsp

salmon roe. Season
with salt then add the
grated peel of
1 lemon and the
whipped cream. Fill
the avocado shells
with the mixture and
garnish with lemon
and the remaining
roe.

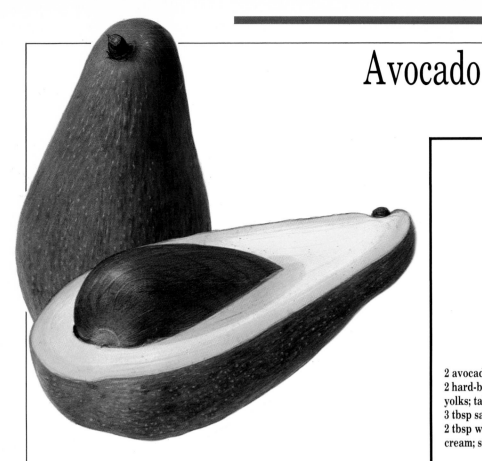

*The avocado is eaten
mainly as an
appetizer, although it
can also form the basis
of a very good sauce
and is the perfect
partner for shellfish.
To prevent
discoloration of the
pulp, the avocado
should only be
prepared just before
serving, and sprinkled
with a little lemon
juice.*

The avocado (*Persea
americana* of the *Lauraceae* or
laurel family) is originally
from Central America and is
widespread in Peru, Costa
Rica, Guatemala, and the
southern states of America,
where numerous varieties of
different color and fragrance
are grown. The fruit is shaped
like an elongate pear, with a
yellowish white pulp tending
to green, of a semifirm
consistency; in the lower part
there is a single large seed.
The chemical composition of
the avocado shows that the
percentage of water, about
60%, is relatively low
compared to the average of
other fruits, so consequently
there is a higher percentage of
other components, increasing
the nutritional value of the

fruit. Lipids are present in
large amounts, 30%. The
digestible carbohydrates are
only 3–10%. As well as protein
and mineral salts, there are
many vitamins, from A to K,
including B_1, essential for
normal metabolism, and B_2
which stimulates growth; also
vitamin C (antiscorbutic) and
pantothenic acid. The avocado
is therefore highly nutritious,
supplying about 250 calories
per 3½ oz (100 g) of pulp. It is
eaten fresh and, because of the
low percentage of sugars, can
be used as an appetizer and in
salads. If it is prepared some
time before it is to be eaten,
the stone should be left in the
dish with the pulp, as
otherwise the avocado will
turn black and look very
unappetizing.

*The avocado is ready
for eating when the
skin (smooth or
wrinkled) yields
slightly to the touch.*

Cherimoya · Lychee

The cherimoya (*Annona cherimola* of the custard-apple or *Annonaceae*) is a species typical of the Colombian and Peruvian Andes where it grows up to altitudes of 6,000 ft. It is also cultivated largely in the Antilles, Venezuela, and the Guianas. After discarding the outer greenish part, the fruit is eaten raw without sugar. The pulp is very digestible. In its native countries, it is considered one of the most delicate tropical fruits. Its flavor, between the pineapple and the strawberry, is, however, a little unusual for European palates, which may be why it is not very popular in Europe. Also, to develop all its most valued qualities, the fruit must reach perfect ripeness, which can only take place while it is still on the plant, or very soon afterward.

The lychee (*Litchi chinensis*) or lichee, whose origin is evident from the Latin name, is a strange fruit, similar to a large walnut, of 1–1½ in (25–35 mm) in diameter, with an involucre covered by a shiny, scaly shell which contains the edible part, composed of a fleshy white mass completely covering the seed. It is grown domestically in the southern states of America.

Passion flower · Kiwi or Chinese gooseberry

A passion flower. The fruit may be used to make juice or added to fruit salads. Choose fruits that are not too wrinkled, or the pulp may be dry.

The name of the *passiflora* or passion flower is known far and wide, even by those who have never tasted the fruit. This plant has always aroused some interest, especially the flowers, each part of which has been interpreted, in an imaginative way, as relating to the Passion of Christ. The three styles represent the three nails with which Christ was crucified; the ovary is the sponge soaked in vinegar; the stamens represent the wounds on the hands, feet, and in the side; the crown, which is located above the petals, stands for the crown of thorns; and the petals and sepals indicate the Apostles. Botanically, the genus *Passiflora* includes species typical of warm or warm-temperate regions, found particularly in America. The majority of these species are grown as ornamentals, and a few have a certain nutritional importance for their edible fruit. *Passiflora edulis* is undoubtedly the best among the latter species. It is a climbing perennial, native to Brazil, and widely cultivated in tropical regions. It is also grown today around the Mediterranean. The fruit, which is called passion fruit, becomes, when ripe, the size of an egg and purple-red in color. It contains a sweet and juicy pulp into which the small seeds are so tightly enclosed that it is difficult to eliminate them when eating the fresh fruit. Through particular processes eliminating the seeds, a juice can be extracted from the fruit, which is bottled and widely used in the countries where it is grown. The fruits are also made into various confections and jellies. A plant of Chinese origin, *Actinidia sinensis*, usually called kiwi, Chinese gooseberry or Actinidia, has recently aroused much interest for its fruits which, according to recent studies, are thought to have considerable medicinal properties. The kiwi contains protein, iron, calcium, and phosphorus salts, and also a large amount of vitamin C, as much as is found in ten lemons. The fruit ripens at the beginning of winter and can be stored until spring. It should be peeled before eating, and when sliced, reveals a beautiful green and black pattern. The taste is pleasantly sour, but those who do not like such a flavor can improve it with some sugar or a few drops of liqueur.

A passion fruit. The kiwi (below) is a fruit rich in vitamins. It provides an effective garnish for pies, jellies, and puddings. It keeps very well and gains in sweetness and fragrance the longer it is stored.

Mango · Papaya

The mango comes from the East Indies, Malaysia, southern Florida, and California. It vaguely resembles a kidney-shaped peach, tapering at the top, with a juicy and fragrant pulp and a distinctive flavor, something between the apricot and the pineapple. The mango tree, *Mangifera indica* of the *Anarcardiaceae* or cashew family, is one of the most productive plants of the tropical regions. Mangoes are normally eaten fresh, but can also be used in sweet chutneys and various jams.

The papaya (*Carica papaya*), of the small *Caricaceae* or pawpaw family, is native to the warm, tropical regions of America, India, the Malay Archipelago, and Tahiti. Its reputation derives from its fruit, a large berry, almost the size and shape of a melon. The pulp is abundant, soft, and orange-yellow in color. The flavor and texture are also similar to the melon's. Papayas are used as an appetizer, and as fresh fruit and juice. Because of their digestive enzyme, they are used in meat tenderizers.

PAPAYA AND KIWI CUPS

Cut two papayas lengthwise in half. Scoop out and discard the black seeds in the middle. Spoon out the flesh and cut into medium-sized pieces. Put the empty skins in the freezer. Peel 3 kiwi fruit and chop. Place all the fruit in a bowl, sprinkle with rum and leave to stand for 1 hour. Spoon the fruit and a little of the juice into the reserved papaya skins, decorate with whipped cream, and serve.

Top: papayas. Above: mangoes. The mango is ripe when it yields to light pressure from your fingers. The papaya is known for its digestive properties. It is therefore excellent served at the end of a meal, sprinkled with a little lemon juice.

Peanut

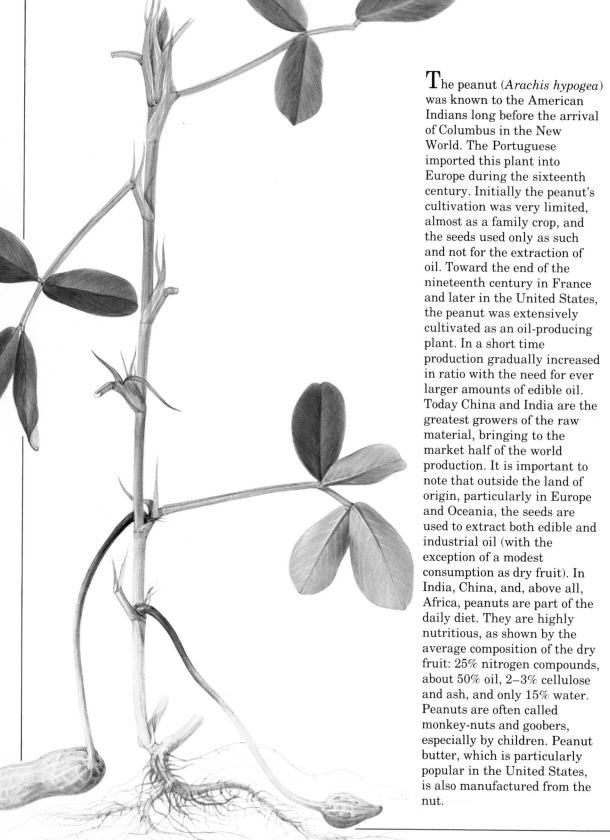

The peanut (*Arachis hypogea*) was known to the American Indians long before the arrival of Columbus in the New World. The Portuguese imported this plant into Europe during the sixteenth century. Initially the peanut's cultivation was very limited, almost as a family crop, and the seeds used only as such and not for the extraction of oil. Toward the end of the nineteenth century in France and later in the United States, the peanut was extensively cultivated as an oil-producing plant. In a short time production gradually increased in ratio with the need for ever larger amounts of edible oil. Today China and India are the greatest growers of the raw material, bringing to the market half of the world production. It is important to note that outside the land of origin, particularly in Europe and Oceania, the seeds are used to extract both edible and industrial oil (with the exception of a modest consumption as dry fruit). In India, China, and, above all, Africa, peanuts are part of the daily diet. They are highly nutritious, as shown by the average composition of the dry fruit: 25% nitrogen compounds, about 50% oil, 2–3% cellulose and ash, and only 15% water. Peanuts are often called monkey-nuts and goobers, especially by children. Peanut butter, which is particularly popular in the United States, is also manufactured from the nut.

PEANUT CRUNCH

½ cup + 3 tbsp/5 oz/150 g sugar; juice of 1 lemon; 7 oz/200 g shucked peanuts; 1 tbsp peanut oil.

Spread the shucked and skinned peanuts on a baking tray and roast for 10 minutes. Meanwhile, melt the sugar with the lemon juice in a saucepan, stirring continuously with a wooden spoon. As soon as the sugar turns color, add the roasted peanuts and allow the mixture to darken a little. Mix well. Grease a working surface with the peanut oil and spread the mixture out onto this into a rectangle approx ¾ in/2 cm thick. Cut the peanut crunch into portions before it cools and sets, using an oiled knife.

Left: a peanut plant. The peanut is a nutritious, energy-rich food. It can be used in many sweet and savory preparations, and goes well with cheeses, cereals, and vegetables.

Coconut

The coconut palm (*Cocos nucifera* fam. *Palmaceae*) is considered to be "king" of the plants in tropical and subtropical regions by the local inhabitants, because for many of them these plants are their only cash crop and primary source of food. All parts of the plant can be used in various ways. In Sanskrit this palm is called *kalpa vriksha*, which means "tree which gives all that is necessary for living." This is an apt name as the trunk provides excellent wood, the leaves are used by the natives for roofing their huts, and the young terminal buds are eaten under the name of "palm cabbages."

The most important products are obtained from the fruit, the coconut (a drupe). Abundant oil is extracted from the endosperm of the fruits; the kernels, freed of the shell and dried, constitute the "copra" which, by pressing, will produce up to 60–65% of an oil that is refined and transformed into a vegetable butter good for human nourishment, especially in vegetarian cookery, and for those who find that ordinary butter has too much cholesterol for their well-being. Today there is a great demand for coconut oil. At room temperature this oil is solid or semifluid; it is white or slightly yellowish and has a pleasing flavor when it is fresh. As well as its uses in the production of margarine and butter, coconut oil is made into soaps, hair lotions, perfumes, cosmetics, cakes, and confectionery. The fruit contains a sweetish liquid, while the flesh, grated and pressed with a small amount of water, will yield coconut milk. Dietetically, coconuts contain a considerable amount of lipids, around 36%; the percentage of usable protein is 4%, much lower than that of other dry fruits, which range between 9% and 20%. The principal salts are compounds of calcium, sodium, phosphorus, potassium, magnesium, iron, and copper, while vitamins are scarce. Coconut flesh is a good source of energy and easier to digest than other dry fruits.

Coconuts may be eaten raw, in segments. The peeled and grated pulp may be used in a variety of cakes, puddings, and cookies.

Pistachio · Almond · Hazelnut · Brazil nut

The pistachio (*Pistacia vera*) plant probably originated in the Levant, and spread through Palestine, Persia, Iraq, and into certain areas of India and Russian Central Asia. It is mentioned in the Bible. Much valued for its fruits, and even more for the seeds contained in them, the pistachio is made up of about 17% sugars and a considerable number of lipids, up to 54%. The shelled pistachio nut is used as a flavoring for sauces, cakes, and ice creams.

The almond (*Prunus Amygdalus* or *Amygdalus communis* of the *Rosaceae*) probably originated in some areas of Asian Russia, China, and Japan. As a cultivated plant it was known to the Hebrews several centuries before Christ, and is mentioned in the Book of Genesis. The almond tree is grown all over the Mediterranean, from Provence to Algeria, favoring arid and rocky soils. Depending on the hardness of the shell and flavor of the seed, two types of almond are distinguished: sweet with soft, semisoft, and hard shells, and bitter, with hard shells. Bitter almonds are

HAZELNUT AND RUM ICE CREAM

3 egg yolks; 6 tbsp/3½ oz/100 g sugar; 1 cup/9 fl oz/250 ml milk; 2 glasses light cream; vanilla essence; 1 liqueur glass rum; 2½ oz/70 g chopped, roasted hazelnuts.

Beat the egg yolks with the sugar. Heat the milk until lukewarm, and add to the egg mixture. Heat, stirring continuously, in a double boiler, until thickened. Add the cream and vanilla essence, stir well, and leave to cool. Add the rum, and pour the mixture into the ice cream maker. When the ice cream is nearly ready, add the hazelnuts.

poisonous and must not be eaten raw. Almonds are used in confectionery for the preparation of nougats, candied almonds (i.e. sugar-coated), macaroons, and flour. Over half the almond's weight is oil, which is used by the pharmaceutical and perfume industries.

Many fossil remains of cultivated hazelnuts or filberts (*Corylus avellana* or *C. maxima*) have been found, proving their cultivation to be very old. Filberts are used in confectionery for making chocolate and nougat candies. When subjected to a pressing process, they yield an oil which is often used in the preparation of cosmetics and perfumes.

The species of the genus *Bertholletia* characterizes the Brazilian flora. They are large trees, with sizeable, leathery leaves, whose large fruits open at maturity to show about 20 kidney-shaped seeds with woody and wrinkled shells, enclosed inside. These seeds are called Brazil nuts or Para nuts, and contain a kernel similar to the almond or coconut in taste. The nuts are popular all over the world, and grow mostly in South America, especially Brazil.

Cashew · Walnut · Pecan

In the cashew (*Anarcardium occidentale*) the part constituting the false fruit (cashew apple) is tasty and juicy and, when fully ripe, can be eaten raw, or sliced and sweetened with sugar. The dry fruit called the "nut," which is the true fruit, must be freed from the shell, which contains a very caustic oil, and it can then be eaten either raw or roasted.

The common walnut is believed to originate in northern Persia, Armenia, and areas around the Caspian Sea. Like all fruit trees that have been cultivated for a long time, the walnut is represented by a considerable number of varieties much prized for their seeds. Walnut oil is sweet, and characteristically aromatic, but turns rancid if it is not used quickly. The young seeds are used in confectionery.

The pecan (*Carya illinoensis*) is of North American origin. It is a large tree, belonging to the *Juglandaceae* or walnut family. The fruit, like that of the walnut, is enveloped in a hard and woody husk, which opens when ripe, releasing four nuts with edible, oily kernels of excellent flavor. One of the most famous and irresistible North American desserts is the pecan pie, made with maple syrup.

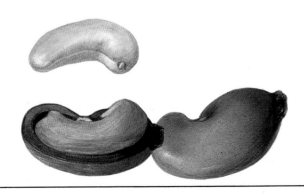

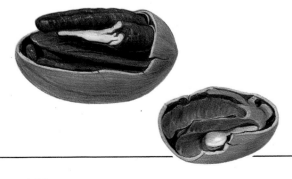

Opposite, top left: pistachios and, below, almonds and Brazil nuts. Above: a walnut branch and a few walnuts. Left: pecan nuts and cashews.

Italian stone pine · Chestnut

The Italian stone pine (*Pinus pinea*), probably a native of Asia Minor, has been grown around the Mediterranean for a very long time, having been established there because of its climatic needs. The fruits do not appear on the plant until their fifteenth year of growth and yield their greatest production only after half a century of life. Pignolia nuts, as the seeds are called in the United States, are provided by the pinecones, and used in the confectionery industry to make various kinds of sweets and cakes. The pignolias are white, fleshy, and resemble almonds in flavor. They can also be eaten raw, or as a garnish for cookies, or in macaroons. In cookery they are known as pine nuts or pine kernels. They cannot be stored for long because the fats which they contain spoil easily.

The street vendors selling roasted, and roasting, chestnuts are one of the most nostalgic characteristics of approaching winter in the streets of many American and European cities in late autumn.

For commerce, and also because the knowledge of the systematics of the species is rather scarce, there is a tendency to divide the chestnut into two large groups: marrons and domestic chestnuts. The marrons are heart-shaped, with triangular bases; shiny, reddish-brown shells with darker stripes, sweet and fleshy pulp completely detached from the inside pellicles. The domestic chestnuts, which are generally larger, are flattened on one side and have very dark brown shells; the internal skin, or pellicle, is attached to the flesh, which, although less sweet than that of the marron, has a very pleasant flavor. Chestnuts have a high food value: when fresh they contain somewhat less than 60% water and as much as 37% sugar and starches. The rest is provided by nitrogen compounds, cellulose, ash, lipids, and mineral salts. So there is a large amount of carbohydrates, while the protein is present only in traces.

Chestnuts can be used in a number of dishes. The famous Mont Blanc, for example, is a dessert of meringue, whipped cream, and chestnut purée. Chestnuts can also be made into a flour, used to make the Italian specialty, castagnaccio, or into preserves. Candied as marrons glacés, they are an internationally renowned delicacy.

HERBS AND SPICES

Basil · Balm

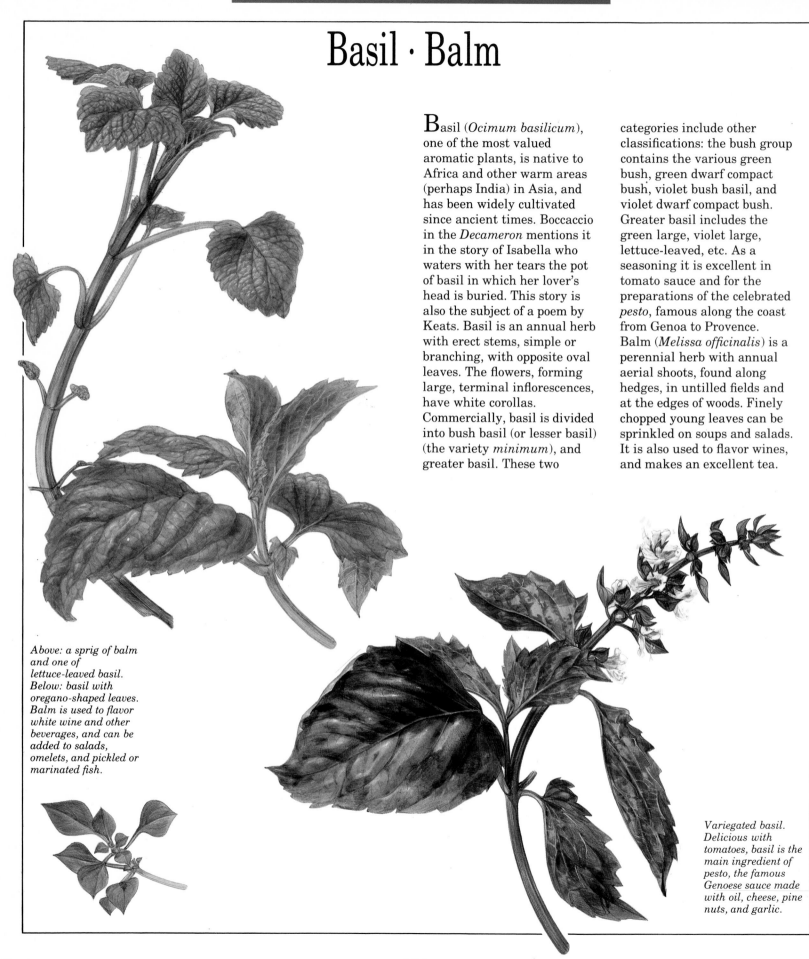

Basil (*Ocimum basilicum*), one of the most valued aromatic plants, is native to Africa and other warm areas (perhaps India) in Asia, and has been widely cultivated since ancient times. Boccaccio in the *Decameron* mentions it in the story of Isabella who waters with her tears the pot of basil in which her lover's head is buried. This story is also the subject of a poem by Keats. Basil is an annual herb with erect stems, simple or branching, with opposite oval leaves. The flowers, forming large, terminal inflorescences, have white corollas. Commercially, basil is divided into bush basil (or lesser basil) (the variety *minimum*), and greater basil. These two categories include other classifications: the bush group contains the various green bush, green dwarf compact bush, violet bush basil, and violet dwarf compact bush. Greater basil includes the green large, violet large, lettuce-leaved, etc. As a seasoning it is excellent in tomato sauce and for the preparations of the celebrated *pesto*, famous along the coast from Genoa to Provence. Balm (*Melissa officinalis*) is a perennial herb with annual aerial shoots, found along hedges, in untilled fields and at the edges of woods. Finely chopped young leaves can be sprinkled on soups and salads. It is also used to flavor wines, and makes an excellent tea.

Above: a sprig of balm and one of lettuce-leaved basil. Below: basil with oregano-shaped leaves. Balm is used to flavor white wine and other beverages, and can be added to salads, omelets, and pickled or marinated fish.

Variegated basil. Delicious with tomatoes, basil is the main ingredient of pesto, the famous Genoese sauce made with oil, cheese, pine nuts, and garlic.

Parsley · Garden thyme · Wild thyme

Parsley is a herb, known to the ancient Romans as is clearly indicated by its Latin genus name *Petroselinum*. During past centuries parsley was used more as a medicinal plant than as a garden vegetable. Today it is considered primarily as a seasoning or garnish for soups, salads, and sauces. It is rich in minerals, primarily iron salts, and, in a smaller degree, sulfur salts; also it is rich in vitamin C. Its most important properties, besides its functions as a seasoning, are its appetite-stimulating qualities. In medieval times parsley was thought to belong especially to the devil, and Good Friday was said to be the only day of the year on which it could be sown successfully, and then only if the moon was rising. There is an old country saying in England: "Only the wicked can grow parsley."

Garden thyme (*Thymus vulgaris*), a small shrub with gray-green leaves, of the *Labiatae*, has a strong aromatic scent and a pungent flavor.

The whole plant, especially the lateral branches which are gathered at the flowering stage, constitutes a versatile drug with a tonic effect. It is used in cases of anaemia, bronchial and intestinal disorders, and as an antiseptic against tooth decay. It gives relief from catarrh and coughs, and also provides an essence which is used in the liqueur and perfume industries. It is one of the most popular herbs in cooking.

Wild thyme has been valued by herbalists for many centuries. According to the *Doctrine of Signatures* it was under the dominion of Venus, and therefore good for helping nervous disorders. A tisane was drunk to allay giddiness and headaches. It was said by Culpeper to be "a certain remedy for that troublesome complaint, the nightmare." Even earlier it was used as a kind of incense or insecticide to fumigate rooms and keep away troublesome insects. Its name is derived from a Greek word meaning to fumigate. Today, because of its valuable oil, thymol, it is used in medicine to help bronchial and intestinal disorders, and as an antiseptic and expectorant. It is also one of the most popular domestic herbs for flavoring.

Below: thyme is an excellent flavoring for veal, pork, lamb, and many wine-based stews. It also goes well with vegetables and in soups, marinades, and stuffings.

Above: wild thyme. Below: parsley. Indispensable in cooking, chopped parsley may be used to flavor sauces, soups, meat, fish, shellfish, eggs, and vegetables.

Marjoram · Oregano

Marjoram or sweet marjoram (*Origanum majorana* or *M. hortensis*) is a perennial and suffruticose herb, woody at the base and herbaceous above. It is native to Asia and is frequently grown in gardens, and in pots in kitchens. The herbaceous tops are the parts used. They contain the active principles of the *Labiatae*, essential oils, and have a stimulating and antiseptic action on the body. Sweet marjoram is used to season many dishes from omelets to meat or fish casseroles. Oregano or wild marjoram (*Origanum vulgare*) is a perennial herb with annual aerial shoots. The parts used are the flowering tops that are sold in small, fragrant bunches. Wild marjoram contains essential oils and has aromatic, antiseptic and antispasmodic properties. In cooking, oregano is the typical and indispensable flavoring of the Neapolitan pizza. Sprinkled lightly on tomato salad it enhances the flavor.

Oregano (above) is best picked at the end of August, when it is in full flower. Hang the sprigs upside down to dry. To use, crumble flowers and leaves and discard the tough stems. Such a mixture will produce a much stronger fragrance than commercially dried oregano, which usually contains only the leaves. Marjoram (right) is a typical ingredient in Mediterranean cookery, and goes well with vegetables, rich dishes, stews, mushrooms, and potatoes. It can be used dried or frozen, although it loses much of its aroma this way. Marjoram should always be added toward the end of cooking.

MARJORAM SAUCE

2–3 tbsp/1½ oz/30 g butter; 2 tbsp flour; 1¼ cups/½ pint/275 ml milk; chicken broth; few sprigs majoram or 1 tsp dried marjoram; salt and pepper.

Melt the butter in a saucepan and add the flour. Cook the resulting roux for a few minutes, then gradually add the milk, stirring continuously between additions. Add sufficient chicken broth until a creamy but pouring consistency is achieved. Add the marjoram, stir well, and turn off the heat. Season.
This sauce goes well with boiled vegetables or fish.

Caper

The caper (*Capparis spinosa* of the *Capparidaceae*) is a perennial plant. The leaves are fleshy and shiny, and the flowers are particularly beautiful with four large white petals and numerous long stamens. The ovary is supported by a long peduncle called "gynophore." The fruit is a dry, spongy berry containing numerous blackish, kidney-shaped seeds. Within the vast species *C. spinosa* three varieties can be distinguished: *aculeata* and *inermis*, both completely or almost glabrous, and *sicula*, typical of the southern Mediterranean regions. They are all characterized by the white and tomentose vegetative parts and the presence of thorns. This last variety, besides growing on rocky terrain, is also found on stony and clay-loam soils. The young floral buds, not yet open, the young fruits, as soon as they form, as well as in some areas the young branches with the tenderest leaves, are the parts of the plant which are used. Preserved or pickled capers are used to garnish hors-d'œuvres, in sauces and stuffings, and to flavor meats. They contain a bitter and irritant glucoside, having tonic and diuretic properties. The smaller and firmer "nonesuch" capers which grow in France are better than the English variety.

A flowering caper sprig. Below, a caper bud. The capers that are used in cooking, preserved in salt or vinegar, are the buds, which are picked before they open.

MEDITERRANEAN SALAD

5 oz/150 g mixed salad leaves; 1 buffalo mozzarella weighing 1 lb/500 g; ½ red bell pepper; 1 zucchini; 2 tbsp pickled capers; 2 ripe tomatoes; 1 tbsp dried oregano; red wine vinegar; oil; salt and pepper.

Rinse and dry the salad leaves and spread out on a serving plate. Lay the sliced mozzarella, shredded pepper, and zucchini on top.

Sprinkle the capers all over. Coarsely chop the tomatoes. Mix 3 tbsp red wine vinegar with 7 tbsp oil, season with salt and pepper, add the chopped tomatoes and oregano, and pour the dressing over the salad.

Rosemary

Rosemary is an excellent flavoring for roasts, stews, sauces, soups, and savory butters. A sprig of rosemary kept in a bottle of olive oil with 2 minced cloves of garlic will provide an aromatic dressing for boiled fish or broiled meats.

ROSEMARY BREAD

1 lb/450 g strong white flour; ½ oz/15 g yeast; 1 cup/9 fl oz/ 250 ml lukewarm milk; 1 tsp salt; 2 tsp dried rosemary; 2 oz/50 g margarine or shortening; 1 egg, beaten. *To glaze:* 1 egg, beaten.

Sieve ½ cup/5 oz/ 150 g of the flour into a large basin. Blend the yeast and the milk and add to the flour. Stir well, and leave for ½ hour. Sieve the remaining flour and the salt into another basin, add the rosemary, and quickly rub in the margarine or shortening. Stir in the beaten egg, and add this mixture to the dough in the other basin. Knead thoroughly until the dough leaves the sides of the bowl clean. Place the dough on a floured work surface and knead for a few minutes until smooth and elastic. Place in a greased bowl, cover with a cloth, and leave to rise until doubled in bulk. Knead for a further 2–3 minutes, divide into 3 sections, and shape each into a long sausage. Place on a buttered baking tray and form into a plait. Brush with beaten egg, and bake at 375°F/190°C/mark 5 for 1 hour, until golden.

Rosemary (*Rosmarinus officinalis*) is a perennial evergreen. It contains principles similar to those of sage and thyme, essential oil composed of borneol, pinene, and camphene, and bitter principles, tannic acid (tannin) and resins. Because of these components rosemary has some properties of pharmacological interest, and its tonic, stimulant and digestive actions, as well as its flavor account for its widespread use in the kitchen. Rosemary is considered by many gourmets to be the best herb of all for roasts and barbecued meat, and it is also good for boiled meats and sauces.

This plant was known in ancient times, and was woven into heroes' crowns with myrtle and laurel. It was also used in orgies and banquets because of its aromatic perfume.

Various medicinal properties were attributed to it and it was widely used by Arab physicians in the early centuries A.D. It is mentioned in Charlemagne's Capitularies and by many early herbalists including Gerard, who records that "there is such plenty thereof in Languedocke, that the inhabitants burne scarce any other fuell." He adds that "The distilled water of the floures of Rosemary being drunke at morning and evening first and last, taketh away the stench of the mouth and breath, and maketh it very sweet . . ." Today the herb is known for its tonic, eupeptic, carminative and emmenagogic properties and is also thought to be beneficial in modifying bronchial secretions. It is used to treat dyspepsia and stomach pains. The drug comes from the leaves, which should be gathered during the flowering stage, preferably in spring, with or without the twigs. Rosemary has many culinary uses; the leaves and young branches are particularly full of flavor; and it is also used in the cosmetic industry.

Bay or Laurel · Juniper

The laurel (right, a branch with fruits) is used to flavor roasts, stews, fish dishes, and pâtés, as well as to make them more digestible.

True laurel or bay (*Laurus nobilis* of the *Laureaceae*) is a dioecious plant, that is, with masculine and feminine flower structures on separate plants. The latter are easily recognizable at the time of fruiting as they bear the fruits. Besides being an aromatic plant used in the *bouquet garni* for cooking, bay is a truly medicinal herb, and all parts of the plant are used, including the fruits. The laurel is historically an illustrious, symbolic plant. Wreaths to crown heroes and scholars were made with its leaves; the term "laureate" derives from this tradition. In the Middle Ages and even up to the eighteenth century, bay, apart from being a cure-all, also "resisteth witchcraft very potently" according to Culpeper's *The English*

Physician Enlarged, or the Herbal, 1653.
The juniper (*Juniperus communis* of the *Cupressaceae*) is also a healing plant. For culinary uses (the flavoring of meats, especially game) and in the spirits industry, for the manufacture of gin, only the berries are needed, while the medicinal action (anticatarrhal, soothing, diuretic) is present in both the berries and the branches. These contain pinene, camphene, borneol, a bitter principle called juniperin, wax, and resins. As well as gin, a medicinal wine called Juniper Hippocras is made from the berries.

Juniper berries are used to flavor marinades for game, and are good in many meat dishes. They are the main flavoring ingredient of gin.

Mint · Myrtle

Below: a sprig of calamint (left) and one of peppermint (right). Mint marries well with a wide variety of other flavors, from chocolate to mayonnaise; it can be used in salads, soups, vegetables, drinks, and ice creams.

Peppermint (*Mentha piperita*) is one of the best known aromatic herbs, particularly for its importance in the confectionery and spirits industries. It is probably a hybrid between *M. viridis* (gentle or green mint) and *M. aquatica* (water mint). It is a perennial herb with square stems characteristic of the mint family, *Labiatae*. Its opposite leaves are either dark red (black mint) or green (white mint), heart-shaped at the base and oval elongate or lanceolate. The inflorescence is a spike of whorled flowers. Peppermint is a stimulant of gastric secretions and movements, and is therefore good for the digestion. Besides its use in confectionery and distilling, it is also used to flavor toothpastes and as a component of analgesic and disinfectant remedies. In some countries it is used to season meats, particularly mutton and lamb, and vegetable dishes, while elsewhere it is used as an infusion for tea. Calamint (*Satureja calamintha* or *C. officinalis*) is also a perennial herb with annual shoots. It has specialized uses in the kitchen, mostly in the preparation of zucchini, and other vegetables. It is also known by the names of catnip and catmint (both, obviously, irresistible to cats).

Myrtle (*Myrtus communis*) is dedicated to Venus who rose out of the waves, because it flourishes better near the sea than anywhere else. It is still the custom in many European countries for brides to wear wreaths of myrtle, symbolizing love and constancy. After its later dedication to Mars it became debased and the symbol of unchaste desire. Wine in which myrtle leaves had been steeped was said to become more potent and to encourage sensuality. It is chiefly the leaves, but also the fruit, which is a many-seeded blue-black berry, that are used in pharmacy, their content of tannin, essential oil, resin, and a bitter principle giving them an astringent, antiseptic, and haemostatic action.

Below: a sprig of myrtle. This is a typical plant of the Mediterranean, although it is also found in western Asia. In cooking, the leaves, flowers, and fruits are used to flavor syrups and liqueurs. Myrtle leaves can be used to add flavor to roast meats, particularly poultry and game.

Sage

Sage (*Salvia officinalis*) is among the most common aromatic and seasoning herbs. It owes its generic name to the Latin word *salvere*, to heal, evidence of the high regard in which it was held in ancient times. Its popularity continued throughout the Middle Ages. Charlemagne advised its cultivation, and contributed to the herb's diffusion across northern and central Europe. It is quite rightly considered a medicinal plant. Its leaves, which are picked in late spring just before the flowers open, contain essential oil formed by various components: salviol, salvene, pinene, and borneol (camphol). These are bitter substances and resins, and they are said to have tonic-digestive, antispasmodic, antiseptic, and antiperspirant properties. Its popular uses justify this belief: compresses or simple rubbings of the leaves have been said to have a beneficial action on rashes or eczema, as has their application to ailing teeth and gums.

Better known than the pharmaceutical applications are the gastronomic uses of sage in the cooking of certain types of fish, such as trout with butter and sage, as a seasoning for marinated fish or a stuffing for poultry or pork, and in many other recipes.

There are about 500 different species of sage, all with a pleasant scent and a slightly bitter, aromatic flavor. In the United States there are only small cultivations of the garden sage and the white sage, so each year large amounts are imported. Sage is also used in the cosmetic industry in place of certain animal products. An old English saying advises: "Eat sage in May and you'll live for aye." It was reputed to flourish only where there was a domineering wife.

Right: a sprig of sage in flower. Above: a sprig of clary (Salvia sclarea), a herb very similar to sage.

HERB LIQUEUR

Herbs and fruit are often used to flavor spirits.
The method is simple. Place fresh, unblemished herbs or fruit into a clean bottle and fill with vodka, brandy or grappa. Seal and leave for 6 months before drinking. Sage, wild fennel, and thyme are all suitable for this treatment. The photograph shows grappa flavored with sage and lemon peel.

Cinnamon · Nutmeg

CINNAMON PUDDING

1 cup/7 oz/200 g sugar; 2 eggs, separated; ½ cup/3½ oz/100 g butter; 1¾ cups/7 oz/200 g all-purpose flour; 1 tsp baking soda; 1 tsp powdered cinnamon; pinch of salt; 1 cup/9 fl oz/250 ml milk.

Beat the sugar and eggs until creamy and white. Add, a little at a time, the softened butter, the sifted flour and baking soda, the cinnamon, and the salt, alternating with gradual additions of the milk. Beat the egg whites until stiff peaks form and fold gently into the mixture. Pour into a buttered and floured 9½-in/26-cm pudding or pie dish and bake at 350°F/180°C/mark 4 for approx. 50 minutes.

The scientific name of cinnamon (*Cinnamomum zeylanicum*) means "fragrant plant of China." This name was, in fact, first given to another cinnamon, China cinnamon, cultivated for thousands of years, while the much-prized and only medicinal cinnamon, Ceylon cinnamon, did not become known in Europe until the sixteenth century. Cinnamon is cultivated extensively in Ceylon, and in the Seychelles, Guiana, Jamaica, and Brazil. It contains an essential volatile oil which gives it general stimulant properties and, in particular, digestive functions.

Nutmeg (*Myristica fragrans*) has always been highly prized. The plant providing this fruit is an evergreen tree, native to the Moluccas, but now also cultivated in other tropical regions. The part of the nutmeg used as a spice is provided by the seed. The fruits are harvested when ripe and their fleshy pericarp is discarded; what is left is a large oval seed with a woody involucre and enveloped by a peculiar structure, the aril, which is bright red and divided into narrow ridges. The seeds are freed from the aril and allowed to dry. The aril, reddish-yellow during drying, is sold under the name of mace, and used to flavor curries and meat dishes. When the seeds are perfectly dried, the shell is broken and the seed is extracted. The commercial nutmeg has a whitish coating because the nuts have a cover of milk of lime. Nutmeg has various uses, as a seasoning for a vast range of foods, from meat stuffings and vegetables to desserts. It must be used sparingly because of its strong aroma and also because in larger doses it could become poisonous. In bygone times it was known as an abortifacient.

Saffron · Clove

Right: a crocus. It is the dried stamens of the crocus that produce saffron, one of the most highly prized spices of all.

Saffron (*Crocus sativus*), originally from Asia Minor, has been used in the Orient since ancient times. It was spread throughout the Mediterranean by the Arabs, and in the rest of southern Europe by the Crusaders. In Europe, Spain, France, Italy, and Austria are the leading producers. Saffron is also grown in Iran, Afghanistan, China, and in Pennsylvania in the United States. The cultivation is easy, but the harvest is burdensome. The "drug" is provided by the dried stamens of crocus flowers. If they are mixed with the styles the spice loses its value and is known commercially as "female saffron." The loss of weight of the product is huge: from 176 lb (79 kg) of flowers the farmer collects only about 2.2 lb (1 kg) of fresh saffron which, after drying, is reduced to about 2½ oz (50 g). Saffron has a characteristic bitterish-aromatic smell and flavor. It contains a coloring substance and a volatile oil. Besides the pharmacological uses due to its sedative properties, the principal use of saffron is in cooking. It is used to color rice in both Oriental and European dishes, especially in risotto and the Mediterranean fish soup, known in France as *bouillabaisse*.

The aromatic and antiseptic properties of the clove are well known. Cloves are the flowers, in bud, of *Eugenia caryophyllata* of the *Myrtaceae* or myrtle family. In cookery they are used in the preparation of fruits cooked in wine, or in pies (apple, etc.), in the preparation of winter drinks such as mulled wine, and to season meats, especially ham. Cloves are believed to have originated in China. In olden times cloves were used to make pomanders, which were carried around as a protection against infection. To make these, an orange must be completely stuck all over with cloves, so that no part of the rind shows. It should then be wrapped in tissue paper and left in a warm place to dry out thoroughly. This will take only two or three weeks in a warm closet, and about five weeks in an ordinary cupboard or drawer.

Hop · Dill · Cumin

Hop shoots (above) can be cooked in the same way as asparagus. They are good in omelets. They must be boiled prior to use, however, to eliminate their characteristically pungent taste. If not used as soon as they are picked, hop shoots will wilt. To revive them if this should occur, plunge the stems into iced water and cover with plastic.

Hop (*Humulus lupulus*) is a very common plant, found wild or cultivated, in Europe, Asia, and North America. Its commercial importance is in the making of beer, for which the cones of the female plant are used. The hop has an estrogenic action, feminizing and anaphrodisiac, so that, besides serving as a sedative, it is believed by some to be the cause of the disorders (obesity, sterility, hepatic degeneration) afflicting hard beer-drinkers. The hop shoots, that is, the edible shoots of the panicle, are eaten in some parts of Europe as a vegetable. They are boiled in salted water with a little lemon juice, and then served with butter or cream, or added to omelets. In Britain they are used only in brewing, and in the United States they are not to be bought commercially, but are sometimes used as a vegetable in remote country areas.

Dill (*Anetum graveolens*) is one of the plants used in both medicine and cooking since ancient times. Its seeds are used for seasoning pickles and vinegar; they can also flavor cakes, sauces, soups, and various other dishes. The young leaves and the tenderest shoots are used in the same way and also to add zest to salads and cooked dishes. The young stems can be eaten raw, seasoned with oil, salt, and pepper.

The seeds of cumin (*Cumin cyminum*), as well as other aromatic *Umbelliferae*, have been used for many centuries. They are mentioned in St Mark's Gospel, but their golden age was probably during the Middle Ages when they were highly valued as a spice for flavoring cakes and breads, especially among the Germanic peoples. In the Netherlands, they are still used to give a characteristic flavor to some typical cheeses. Cumin is also a fundamental ingredient of certain liqueurs and a seasoning for several types of pickled vegetables.

Above: a sprig of cumin. Below, a few dill seeds and a sprig of caraway. Dill is much used in northern European and Russian dishes. It can flavor vegetable salads and fish dishes.

114

Coriander · Corn poppy

Above and below: coriander. As it has a very pronounced flavor, coriander marries well with strong-tasting dishes. The ground seeds are used in Indian cookery, in conjunction with other spices, to make curry flavoring. Fresh coriander leaves are good in salads and sprinkled over boiled vegetables.

Coriander (*Coriandum sativum*) is an aromatic herb belonging to the parsley family (*Umbelliferae*). Its name, used by Pliny, comes from the Greek and means bedbug. It was given to this plant because of the odor produced by it when struck or broken. The coriander is grown for its seeds which must be dried out before use in order to lose the nauseating smell. These seeds, like those of the anise, can be used as an aromatic seasoning, and for the extraction of an essence for making liqueurs. The tender leaves give a pleasant aroma to certain types of salad, although care must be taken not to use too many.

A field of wheat scattered profusely with scarlet poppies evokes all the heat and stillness of a summer's day. The field or corn poppy (*Papaver rhoeas*) is widely diffused across the temperate zones of Europe and Asia, and North Africa. Although it does not contain morphine as does *P. somniferum*, it has nevertheless been used for many centuries as a mild sedative. Etymologically *papaver* comes from the Celtic word *papa*, meaning pap or porridge, and refers to the Celtic custom of mixing poppy juice with gruel to make crying babies go to sleep. The ancient Egyptians, as long ago as 1500 B.C., are recorded as using poppy seeds in baking for their aromatic flavor, and this practice survives today. The poppy was also used as a flavoring in ancient Roman cooking.

Bottom: The poppy is a mainly medicinal plant and is hardly ever used in cooking.

POTATOES AND SPINACH WITH CORIANDER

14 oz/400 g potatoes; 14 oz/400 g spinach; 1 onion, peeled; oil; ½ tsp ground coriander; ½ tsp paprika; salt.

Peel and boil the potatoes, then dice.

Chop the spinach and onion. Heat some oil in a skillet and fry all the vegetables for approx. 10 minutes, adding the coriander and paprika. Season to taste with salt and serve.

Fennel

A Mediterranean plant that grows along coastlines, fennel leaves are good added to mixed salads. Top: wild fennel.

PASTA WITH SARDINES

10 oz/300 g fresh sardines;
8 sprigs fennel leaves; 1 tbsp
seedless white raisins; 1 onion;
½ cup/4 fl oz/125 ml oil; 1 tbsp
tomato paste; 1 tbsp pine nuts;
10 oz/300 g macaroni; salt and
pepper.

Clean and gut the sardines,
removing the heads. Boil the
fennel leaves briefly then drain,
reserving the water, and chop.
Soak the raisins in lukewarm
water. Chop the onion and fry in
the oil. Add the tomato paste, a
little water, the drained raisins,
pine nuts, and the sardines.
Cover with the fennel leaves,
season, and cook over low heat
for approx. 10 minutes. Cook the
macaroni in the fennel-flavored
water until tender, drain, and
mix with the sardine sauce.

"Crabs, salmon, lobsters are
with Fennel spread/That never
touched the herb till they were
dead," said *The Art of Cooking*
in 1700. To most people fennel
(*Foeniculum vulgare*) is better
known as the finest herb for
flavoring fish dishes than as a
medicinal plant. Yet it has
been used for its curative
properties since ancient times,
being especially valued as a
restorer of lost eyesight, and,
so it was believed, having the
power to remove cataracts.
Fennel is believed to have
originated in Syria and the
Azores, but it will grow in
almost any soil, especially
where there is plenty of sun.
The ancient Greeks gave it to
their Olympic competitors to
increase their strength while
preventing them from putting
on weight. Culpeper,
centuries later, wrote: "It is
much used in drink to make
people more lean that are too
fat," and in some countries
where herbal medicine is still
practised, fennel is made into
soups, or eaten as a vegetable,
by people trying to slim. In the
eighteenth century the peeled
stalks were eaten like celery,
to induce sleep. It is thought to
impart strength and courage.
In the Middle Ages
supernatural powers were
attributed to fennel which was
believed to drive away evil
spirits. In early times
therapeutic doses of fennel oil
had been observed to cause
hallucinations and a form of
madness resembling epilepsy.

Pepper

Pepper (*Piper nigrum*), a member of the *Piperaceae*, originated in India and is cultivated in other tropical countries. The drug is derived from the fruits, which are small drupes. Three forms of pepper are available commercially, black, white, and green. The first comes from fruits gathered while still immature, and dried. White pepper is obtained from the mature fruits, which are red. These are fermented in heaps or macerated in water for several days. The fruits are rubbed to detach the skin and fleshy part leaving the white pepper, which is less pungent than black pepper. Green pepper is also gathered when immature and stored in boxes. In small doses pepper has tonic and appetite-stimulating properties, but its principal use is in cooking. It is one of the earliest known spices in Europe, and came from Arabia via the Red Sea which was the old spice route used before the destruction of Rome. Hippocrates (*c.* 460–*c.* 377 B.C.), the Father of Medicine, made great use of pepper in his prescriptions.

Below: the pepper plant, with its characteristic inflorescences. Right: the different kinds of pepper: white, black, green, and pink. Green and pink pepper are used chiefly in the form of peppercorns. They have a sharper aroma than white or black pepper.

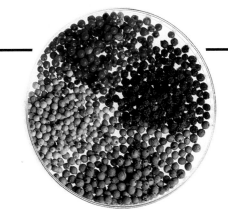

PEPPER IN COOKING

Pepper should be bought in the form of peppercorns, to be freshly ground as required. It is advisable to keep two separate pepper mills, one for black pepper, which is sharply flavored, and one for white, which is less pungent. The addition of whole peppercorns to food during cooking produces an intensely aromatic overall effect but without the piquancy of freshly ground pepper. Coarsely crushed peppercorns go well with rare meat dishes that are cooked with wine and other spices (e.g. steak "au poivre"). The peppercorns should be lightly crushed using a pestle and mortar.

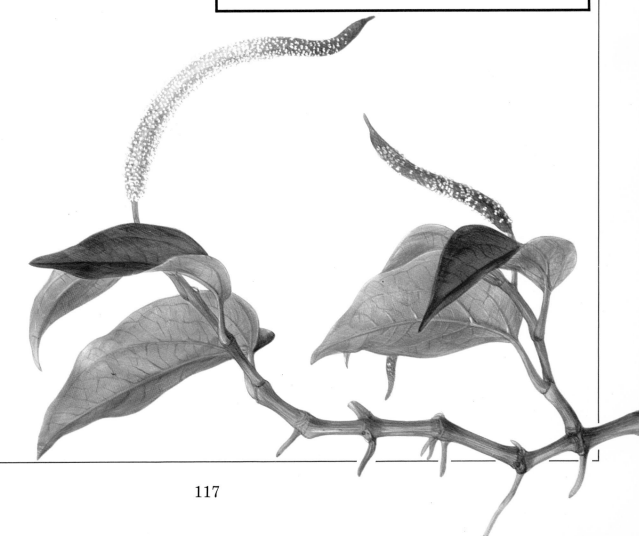

Aniseed · Star anise · Lemon verbena · Cardamom

Above: a cardamom seed. Below: aniseed and a sprig of lemon verbena. Right: a star anise, which derives its name from its characteristic shape.

ANISE CORDIAL

Mince 2 oz/50 g star anise with a piece of vanilla bean and a piece of cinnamon bark. Place the spices in a jar. Pour in 4½ cups/1¾ pints/1 liter 90° proof spirit. Leave to infuse for 20 days. Make a sugar syrup with 4½ cups/1¾ pints/1 liter water and 2¼ lb/1 kg sugar. Leave to cool. Mix with the flavored spirit. Seal and leave for one month before sampling.

Aniseed, or anise, is one of the valued oil-bearing seed plants of the *Umbelliferae* or parsley family. It is cultivated for the presence of a volatile oil consisting largely of anethole. It is used in dispensary for its carminative and expectorant properties, and in the distilling and confectionery industries as a flavoring. It has been recognized for its therapeutic and commercial properties, and is mentioned in the New Testament: "For ye pay tithes of mint and anise and cumin." The aromatic Chinese or star anise (*Illicium verum*) must not be confused with the umbelliferous aniseed. It is named for the decorative shape of its fruit, which makes an agreeable tisane. It is also known as the yellow-flowered starry aniseed tree of China. The Chinese have been using it medicinally for centuries, especially for rheumatism and lumbago, and many Chinese dishes are seasoned with it. Lemon verbena (*Lippia citriodora*) has been highly regarded for its delicate refreshing scent since very ancient times. The cultivated verbena is probably derived from wild species found in

Brazil and Argentina, which found their way to North America and Europe. It is often grown as an ornamental pot herb, and the dried leaves may be used in the same way as lavender to give a pleasant fragrance to linen. The leaves are used in medicine. They contain an essential oil rich in citral, terpenes, and glycosides. Made into a tisane it aids the digestion.

Cardamom (*Elettaria cardamomum*), which belongs to the *Zingiberaceae*, possesses properties similar to those of the anise. It is grown in Ceylon and southern parts of India. Only the seeds are used, and contain a volatile oil with carminative properties. It is used as a flavoring agent both for medicines and in liqueurs, and also as a spice, particularly in curries.

118

Vanilla

Vanilla (*Vanilla planifolia* of the *Orchidaceae*) derives its name from the Spanish *vaina*, "sheath"; therefore *vainilla* = small sheath, with reference to the thinness of the fruit which is a black capsule. Vanilla is the only genus of the large orchid (*Orchidaceae*) family to have an economic use. The "drug," which is the part used commercially, is represented by the fruits called "sticks," beans or, improperly, "pods." The plant is native to Mexico and is grown in several tropical countries: Guiana, Tahiti, Madagascar, Mauritius, the Seychelles, Java, and several South American countries. Commercially there are three kinds of vanilla: "Fine vanilla," "cimarron" or "woody" vanilla, and "vanillon." "Fine" vanilla, which is the most valued, comes from Mexico and is black, smooth, and frosted, which accounts for its alternate name, "crystallized vanilla." The "cimarron" (Spanish, meaning "wild") is a woody plant growing in the wild state, with shorter fruits, less tapered, more solid, and much less frosted. "Vanillons," or "West Indies vanillons" with long, soft, viscous fruits, rather bitter and with a stronger scent than that of the true vanilla, rarely have a crystallized covering, and derive from another species: *V. pompona.*
Vanilla is used as flavoring in the confectionery and distilling industries, either as an extract, in powder form, or in its original state.

VANILLA PUDDING

6 leaves gelatin;
7 oz/200 g almonds;
6 tbsp/3½ oz/100 g sugar; 2¼ cups/
18 fl oz/500 ml milk;
1 vanilla bean; 2¼ cups/18 fl oz/500 ml heavy cream, whipped; 10 oz/300 g blueberries.

Soften the gelatin in cold water, following the manufacturer's instructions. Blanch the almonds in boiling water, peel them, and pulverize in a blender or food processor with 2 tbsp sugar and a little water. Bring the milk to a boil with the vanilla bean, add the softened gelatin and allow to dissolve. Remove from the heat and add the almond mixture. Leave to stand for 15 minutes. Remove the vanilla bean, and leave to cool. When cold, fold in the whipped cream. Dampen an 8½-in/ 22-cm mold with cold water, and pour the mixture into it. Refrigerate for a few hours until set. Unmold. Accompany by a sauce made by blending or sieving the blueberries with the remaining sugar.

Vanilla beans impart their distinctive flavor to liquid. After infusing them, they should be dried and stored until needed again. They can be used repeatedly, until their aroma fades. Stored in a jar of sugar they produce vanilla sugar.

Bitter orange · Bitter almond

BITTER ORANGE PRESERVES

Cook 3–3½ lb/1.5 kg whole bitter oranges in a generous quantity of water. Boil over moderate heat until fork-tender. Drain and cool then plunge into a bowl of cold water; leave for 2 days, changing the water twice a day. Peel the oranges (reserve the peel) and cut into segments, discarding the seeds. Make a thick sugar syrup with 3–3½ lb/1.5 kg sugar and half this weight in water. Place the orange segments in a colander over a bowl and pour the boiling syrup over them, taking care they are evenly coated and allowing the excess to drain off slowly. Transfer the syrup in the bowl to a saucepan and bring to a boil. Add the orange segments and the peel, cut into strips. Stir well, until a setting consistency is achieved. Pour into jars and leave to stand for a day before sealing.

The bitter orange (above) cannot be eaten raw and is used mainly in jams and preserves for its aromatic properties. Lengthy and time-consuming preparations are usually required in order to reduce the bitter flavor of these fruits.

The fruits of the bitter orange are of scarce food interest. The flowers and leaves, however, are highly prized in the cosmetic industry for essences and perfumes. The peel is used for the extraction of an essential oil used in liqueurs such as Curaçao.

The Greeks ate five or six bitter almonds (*Prunus amygdalus* var. *amara*) before dining, in the belief that their drying nature expels moisture and therefore provokes thirst. Sweet and bitter almonds grow on trees of the same species, but have very different properties; amygdalin is absent from the sweet almond (*P. amygdalus* var. *dulcis*). The almond belongs to the *Rosaceae* and is native to Barbary. Today it is extensively cultivated in California, North Africa, and around the Mediterranean. Both the sweet and the bitter almond provide a delicate oil. The bitter almond is more prized in medicine; it contains, besides the oil, emulsion, sugar, mucilage, and ash. The ash contains potassium, calcium, and magnesium phosphates. The almond's sedative and antispasmodic properties make it useful in the treatment of nervous coughs, insomnia, and diseases of the respiratory organs. Bitter almonds are toxic and must not be eaten raw.

Bitter almonds are very similar to sweet almonds. In baking, they can be used in conjunction with sweet almonds, as the combination yields a more pronounced flavor. Bitter almonds are poisonous, however, and should never be eaten raw or, indeed, consumed in large quantities.

Carob · Mustard

It is believed that the carob (*Ceratonia siliqua*) is native to the Orient, probably the Levant. Today it grows spontaneously throughout the Mediterranean. Carobs are harvested in September by shaking the branches of the tree with long sticks. They are then kept in well-ventilated storehouses where they are allowed to dry completely. The fruit is used partly for human consumption, especially in the Mediterranean where the pod is eaten as a form of candy bar by children. It is also used for animal feed. A good yield in alcohol can be obtained by fermentation of the pulp, because of the rich sugar content (up to 50%). The pharmaceutical industry uses carob in the preparation of cough linctus, and a particular syrup, called "carob molasses" which can be made at home. Health-food enthusiasts find the carob a very good substitute for chocolate. The carob is sometimes called "St John's Bread" as it is thought to be the locusts eaten by John the Baptist in the desert. The black mustard (*Brassica nigra* or *Sinapis nigra*) and the white mustard (*B. alba* or *S. alba*) are interesting aromatic and medicinal plants.

The black mustard (of the *Cruciferae* or mustard family) is common in central and southern Europe, western Asia, and North Africa. It is an annual herbaceous plant. The white mustard (of the *Cruciferae*) is a plant scattered all over the Mediterranean area, either wild or cultivated. Like the black mustard, the "drug" (i.e. the part used for medicinal purposes) is provided by the light yellowish seeds. Mustard gives food a typically pungent taste, and, from a culinary viewpoint, is well known for stimulating the digestion. Mustard is used for preparing sauces and may be served with boiled or roast meats. Some of the French commercial brands such as Dijon and Bordeaux are exported all over the world.

ARTICHOKE AND RADICCHIO SALAD WITH MUSTARD DRESSING

1 head radicchio; 4 fresh artichoke bottoms; juice of 1 lemon; 1 tbsp mustard; salt; pepper; tarragon vinegar; 2 tbsp heavy cream at room temperature; oil.

Clean and shred the radicchio. Soak the artichoke bottoms in water acidulated with lemon juice to prevent discoloration. Make the dressing. Mix the mustard with a little salt to taste in a bowl, add pepper and

1 tbsp vinegar. Add ½ cup/4 fl oz/125 ml oil in a thin stream, beating continuously. Add the cream. Mix well. Drain the artichokes, mix with the radicchio, and toss the salad in the mustard dressing.

Above: the mustard plant. The seeds are ground and may be mixed with other spices. Below: carob fruits.

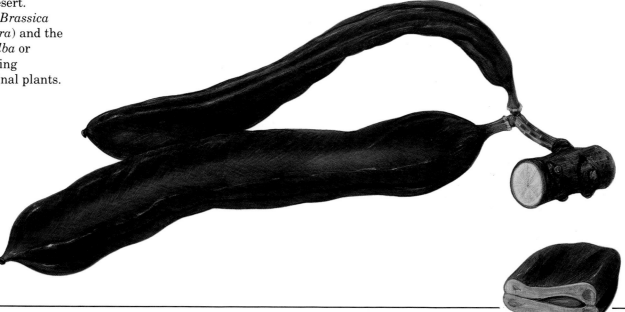

Licorice · Rue · Tamarind

The licorice plant. It is the seeds that yield the strong, characteristic aroma. Right: a tamarind seed and, below, a flowering sprig of rue.

The etymology of *Glycyrrhiza*, the botanical name of licorice, derives from the Greek words "glycor" which means sweet, and "rhizos" meaning root: hence, "sweet root." The medicinal qualities of licorice are many and varied. Its emollient and expectorant properties were known to the ancient Egyptians and Indians, and later it was used in Greek and Roman medicine. It is still considered excellent by many people, in cases of catarrh, hoarseness, coughs, and throat infections in general.

The use of rue (*Ruta graveolens* of the *Rutaceae*) is practically limited to the flavoring of *grappa*, a brandy typical of northern Italy. In the past, however, its reputation as a medicinal plant was very great. The ancients considered it a true panacea; Theophrastus, Dioscorides, Galen, and other great physicians of classical antiquity, used it in many cases to cure poisoning, gout, pimples, dropsy, nose-bleeding, and even hysterics. It was because of its anaphrodisiac qualities that this plant was grown in the Middle Ages in all monasteries and its use prescribed for monks who wished to preserve their purity.

The tamarind (*Tamarindus indica*) is a large tree, attaining a height of about 80 ft (20 m), belonging to the *Caesalpinioideae*. It originated in tropical Africa. In medieval times the Arabs brought it from India to Europe, where it is now grown extensively. Arab physicians were the first to recognize the emollient and laxative properties of the tamarind.

The drug comes from the acid pulp of the berries, and contains a high concentration of malic, citric, tartaric, and oxalic acids, as well as glucose, fructose, sucrose, potash, and pectin.

Ginger · Rhubarb

A rhubarb rhizome with stems and leaves. Below: ginger. Rhubarb leaves must not be eaten, only the vivid red stems.

Ginger (*Zingiber officinalis*) is a sturdy, perennial, herbaceous plant belonging to the *Zingiberaceae*, which originated in Malabar and parts of India, particularly Bengal. It is now grown in many regions with warm climates. It is thought that ginger came to southern Europe from the Orient, just prior to the time of the Romans. From Europe, ginger, through Spanish domination, arrived in the West Indies where its cultivation spread rapidly. In the Middle Ages it was believed to possess miraculous properties, for example, against cholera, but today it is used exclusively in the distilling industry and as a spice. It is, however, still listed in some pharmacopeias. In cooking it is much used in Oriental cuisine and in English cookery as well. Rhubarb (*Rheum rhaponticum* or *R. palmatum*) is native to Tibet and northern Asia, and came to Europe around the fourteenth century. Rhubarb is a large, perennial, herbaceous plant with a big, short-branched rhizome, and annual leaves having a thick, cylindrical and fleshy petiole and a large blade. The plants form the first flowers when they are three or four years old. The leaves should not be eaten, being poisonous. The rhizome contains anthraquinones, tannic acid, resinous substances, and its properties are of both pharmacological interest (laxative) and culinary importance. Rhubarb aids the digestion. The thick, pink petioles or stems can be eaten either stewed or baked in tarts. Plenty of sugar is needed. It is never eaten raw. It is a popular and fairly inexpensive fruit, but is not often served in restaurants.

FIGS WITH GINGER

14 oz/400 g fresh figs; 1 lemon; 1 piece root ginger; 6 tbsp/ 3½ oz/100 g sugar; 1 cup/ 9 fl oz/250 ml light cream.

Place the cleaned and trimmed figs in a saucepan. Add water to cover. Slice the lemon and add to the saucepan with the chopped ginger and sugar. Bring to a boil. Cook over low heat for 20 minutes. Drain the figs and cook the syrup for a few minutes more to thicken. Arrange the figs in a serving dish and pour over the ginger syrup. Chill for 2 hours. Serve with the cream.

Coffee

A sprig of coffee with four vivid red, that is fully ripe, berries and a green, unripe berry.

The history of the origin of coffee (*Coffea arabica*) is confused, although Abyssinia is considered to be its native land.

From Abyssinia coffee arrived in Arabia, Egypt, the Sudan, and Constantinople, and later, through the Venetians, who controlled the Mediterranean during the sixteenth century, it became known throughout Europe. But it is the Dutch who deserve recognition for having fully appreciated the aromatic and stimulant qualities of the new beverage, and for having realized the possibility of its extensive cultivation in their colonies, so coffee was introduced into South and Central America, where it found a better habitat than in its place of origin. Consequently, in a short time Brazil, Colombia, and Mexico had the largest production, and

still do today. The many grades of coffee generally take their name from their place of origin. Mocha is the port of Yemen from which mocha (moka) coffee, characterized by relatively small beans and the pronounced aroma, was originally exported. From the Antilles and Central America comes the Puerto Rico with large beans, and the Santo Domingo with medium-sized beans. The best grades are from South America which supplies about 80% of the world production. Brazilian coffees hold first place. Coffee infusion, or its active principle, caffeine, excites the nervous centers, especially the cortex of the brain, and the circulatory functions. In general, coffee is effective against drowsiness. In many countries coffee was a controversial subject. Some German doctors tried to get a law passed forbidding women to drink it as they believed it caused sterility. J. S. Bach wrote his *Coffee Cantata*, supposed to be women's reply in its defense. Coffee is widely drunk by people whose work is mental rather than physical, to relieve weariness and keep their minds alert. The best varieties come from Arabia, Martinique, and Réunion Island.

A sprig of the flowering coffee plant. One of the most popular beverages in the world, coffee numbers about 25 varieties. Coffee drinks may be prepared from ground beans or commercial coffee powder. Below: coffee beans.

Tea

The Dutch introduced tea into Europe early in the seventeenth century, and in 1644 the Earls of Arlington and Ossory brought it to England where their ladies showed other women of quality how to use it. Its price was sixty shillings a pound and it remained costly until about 1707 when it became possible for "the lower classes of people" to drink it. Culpeper spoke highly of it: "Green tea (*Thea viridis*) (*Camellia viridis*) is diuretic, and carries an agreeable roughness with it into the stomach, which gently astringes the fibers of that organ, and gives such a tone as is necessary for a good digestion: the Bohea (black tea) is softening and nutritious, and proper in all inward decays. Strong tea is prejudicial to weak nerves, but is salutary for violent headache and sickness occasioned by inebriation." Much has been written against tea and coffee, but the great physician Sir William Roberts (1830–1899) claimed that the drinking of tea, coffee, and cocoa produced an upward change in the mental caliber. Many intellectuals would seem to agree with this. Sydney Smith, Canon of St Paul's (1771–1845), speaks from the heart: "Thank God for tea! What would the world do without tea? How did it exist? I am glad I was not born before tea."

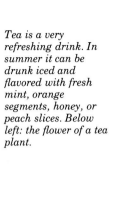

Tea is a very refreshing drink. In summer it can be drunk iced and flavored with fresh mint, orange segments, honey, or peach slices. Below left: the flower of a tea plant.

SPICED TEA

2¼ cups/18 fl oz/ 500 ml water; 1 small piece cinnamon bark; 8 cardamon seeds; 8 cloves; ⅔ cup/ 5 fl oz/150 ml milk; 6 tbsp black tea leaves (unscented).

Place the water in a saucepan, add the cinnamon, cardamom seeds, and cloves and bring to a boil. Cover and simmer for 10 minutes. Add the milk and sugar and bring to a boil again. Add the tea leaves, cover, and turn off the heat. Leave for 2 minutes then strain. Serve immediately.

Cocoa · Kola nuts

A kola nut and, below, two cocoa beans. Kola nuts are used primarily in the preparation of commercial carbonated drinks. Cocoa beans are reduced to a powder, then toasted before being blended with water and sugar.

Cocoa was introduced into Europe with the discovery of America, but some populations of Central and South America had probably known the plant and its products for centuries. The Emperor Montezuma and his courtiers are supposed to have drunk fifty jars a day. The cultivation of the cocoa tree (*Theobroma cacao*) extended rapidly in many areas, but not until around 1820 did the plant appear in Africa. The biggest buyers of cocoa are the countries of central and southern Europe and North America, where there is abundant milk production: a factor of primary importance for the development of the chocolate industry. Botanically, the cocoa tree is of medium size, similar to the cherry tree. The bark is the color of cinnamon, more or less dark; the wood white, fragile, and very light. The leaves are alternate, lanceolate, bright green, and the flowers, borne in small clusters along the stems and branches, have yellowish or pale pink petals. The fruits, called locally *cabosses*, are shaped like large cucumbers and are dark red speckled with yellow when fully ripe. Each fruit contains many "beans." The first chocolate factory in the United States was founded by Dr James Baker in 1780, and is still in existence today. Approximately 100 tonnes of kola nuts (*Cola nitida*) are imported into the United States each year to be used in cola drinks which are not considered by most people to be stimulants. *C. nitida*, however, contains 2% caffeine besides traces of tannin and theobromine.

CHOCOLATE MOUSSE

9 oz/250 g unsweetened chocolate; 2¼ cups/ 18 fl oz/500 ml milk; ¼ cup/2 oz/50 g sugar; 4 egg yolks; 5 egg whites.

Break the chocolate into pieces and melt slowly in a bowl with the milk over a saucepan of gently simmering water. Remove from the heat. Beat in the egg yolks and leave to cool for a few minutes. Meanwhile, beat the egg whites until stiff peaks form, then fold gently but thoroughly into the chocolate mixture. Pour the mousse into a glass serving bowl and chill.

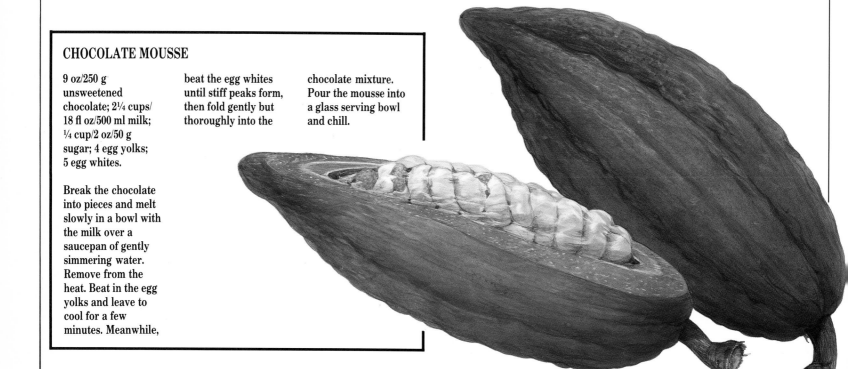

CEREALS, STARCH- AND OIL-PRODUCING PLANTS

Corn or Maize

Corn, Indian corn or maize (*Zea mays*) is a sturdy, annual plant of North American origin, belonging to the *Gramineae*, sub-family *Maydeae*. The male and female flowers are borne in separate inflorescences on the same plant. The male flowers are in a panicle, commonly known as a "tassel," at the top of the stalk. The female inflorescences are borne in spikes, commonly called "ears," which arise at the axils of the leaves, about halfway up the stalk. The ears are enclosed by thick bracts forming the husk, which were once used to make cheap mattresses. They also show long, silky strands called "silks" that some botanists consider as styles, others as stigmas. The kernels develop in the ears and are arranged in

POPCORN

Place a thin layer of olive oil and 3 tbsp popcorn kernels in a large, deep iron or copper skillet. Cover. Shake the skillet over high heat. After 15 seconds, when the popping noise has ceased, the popcorn is ready. Sprinkle with salt and eat while still hot and crisp.

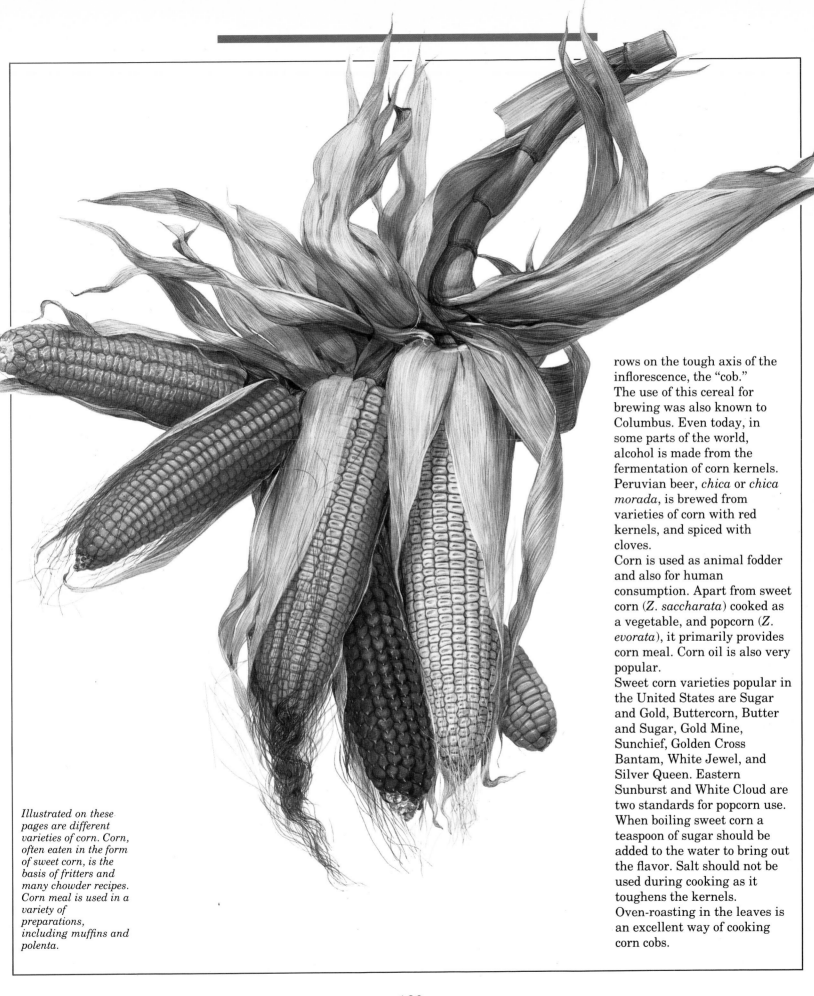

rows on the tough axis of the inflorescence, the "cob."
The use of this cereal for brewing was also known to Columbus. Even today, in some parts of the world, alcohol is made from the fermentation of corn kernels. Peruvian beer, *chica* or *chica morada*, is brewed from varieties of corn with red kernels, and spiced with cloves.

Corn is used as animal fodder and also for human consumption. Apart from sweet corn (*Z. saccharata*) cooked as a vegetable, and popcorn (*Z. evorata*), it primarily provides corn meal. Corn oil is also very popular.

Sweet corn varieties popular in the United States are Sugar and Gold, Buttercorn, Butter and Sugar, Gold Mine, Sunchief, Golden Cross Bantam, White Jewel, and Silver Queen. Eastern Sunburst and White Cloud are two standards for popcorn use. When boiling sweet corn a teaspoon of sugar should be added to the water to bring out the flavor. Salt should not be used during cooking as it toughens the kernels.
Oven-roasting in the leaves is an excellent way of cooking corn cobs.

Illustrated on these pages are different varieties of corn. Corn, often eaten in the form of sweet corn, is the basis of fritters and many chowder recipes. Corn meal is used in a variety of preparations, including muffins and polenta.

Wheat

Wheat is the most important of the cereals. It originated in the Eurasian continent and has probably been cultivated since prehistoric times, and man has spread it throughout the world. Today wheat is cultivated practically everywhere, with the exception of the coldest regions and the hot tropical zones. Like most of the plants commonly known as "cereals," wheat belongs to the *Gramineae*. All the various species of wheat are members of the genus *Triticum*. Depending on the consistency of the grain are distinguished "hard" or macaroni wheats with a horny texture, from "soft," that is, common bread wheats with a floury texture. The hard wheats are more suitable for the manufacture of spaghetti and pasta in general. The soft wheats are used exclusively for making bread. The endosperm of wheat grains are full of starch and contain a protein known as gluten. It is the gluten that imparts the elastic and tenacious consistency to dough and allows leavening naturally through the action of yeast, a process which is indispensable for making bread.

Although the main use of wheat is for bread, it is also important in the manufacture of spaghetti, pastry, cakes, and cookies.

Barley

Barley (*Hordeum vulgare*), an annual grass of moderate size, is a cereal belonging to the family of the *Gramineae*. It can be divided into three types: two-rowed, with kernels on two lines; four-rowed (kernels on four lines); and six-rowed (kernels on six lines). Barley may also be divided into three types based on the nature of the hulls. Some have none; some have loosely attached hulls and others have tightly attached ones. Barley is grown over large areas, in a variety of different climates from Norway to the Equator. Russia is the largest producer of barley (25 million tons), followed by Great Britain, France, the United States (around 10 million each), then Canada and other countries. Barley has a great variety of uses such as the manufacture of beer and whiskey; the grains can be milled into flour for breadmaking or the preparation of some soups; also for livestock feeding. These are only the uses made directly by man. For malting purposes (the first step of the brewing process to make beer) the preferred varieties are those of two-rowed barley of various cultivars such as Chevalier, Hanna, Probstein, Franken, and others. The barley used in the preparation of soups can be either simply "cleaned" barley, which has the grains freed from the hulls, or "pearl barley" in which the grains have been freed of hull and pericarp by a special polishing process.

Barley is used as grains and even flour. This is a nourishing cereal, often added to winter soups. In northern Europe and some Alpine valleys it is the basis of a local bread.

131

Rye · Oats

OAT COOKIES

¾ cup/6 oz/180 g butter;
6 tbsp/3 oz/60 g brown sugar;
¼ cup/3½ oz/120 g honey;
½ cup/4 oz/125 g chopped
peanuts and seedless white
raisins; 1 cup/9 oz/250 g
crumbled oat flakes.

Place the butter, sugar, and
honey in a saucepan over low
heat and stir until the sugar has
completely dissolved. Add the
peanuts, raisins, and oat flakes
and mix well. Butter a baking
tray and spread the mixture out
over it. Bake for 20 minutes at
400°F/200°C/mark 6 until golden,
then cut into square sticks. Cool
completely.

Rye (*Secale cereale*) is a large, herbaceous annual plant. Because of its height rye straw is greatly used to manufacture such things as handbags and straw hats. For centuries rye has been cultivated in Asia and central Europe; later it spread to southern Europe and the Mediterranean regions. The various cultivated varieties of rye do not show as many differences as those of wheat. From the cultural viewpoint they can be divided into autumn and spring cultivars. The countries with the largest outputs of rye are Russia (15 million tons), Poland (8 million), and Germany (5 million). Rye flour is used in human foodstuffs, and is mixed with wheat to make bread, which is characteristically dark, much appreciated for its flavor and recommended for certain diets. It is used mostly in central and northern Europe, some Alpine regions, and in the United States. In the United States whiskey is distilled from rye and maize, although in Britain it is made from malted barley. Oats are the basis of the famous Scottish breakfast food, porridge (oatmeal), which is eaten with milk and salt, although elsewhere, in the United States and even in England, it is more commonly eaten with sugar. Cultivated oats (several different botanical varieties are known) belong to the species *Avena sativa*, widely scattered in grassy and uncultivated fields of the northern hemisphere and naturalized in many other regions. Oats are an annual grass. They are used primarily as animal feed.

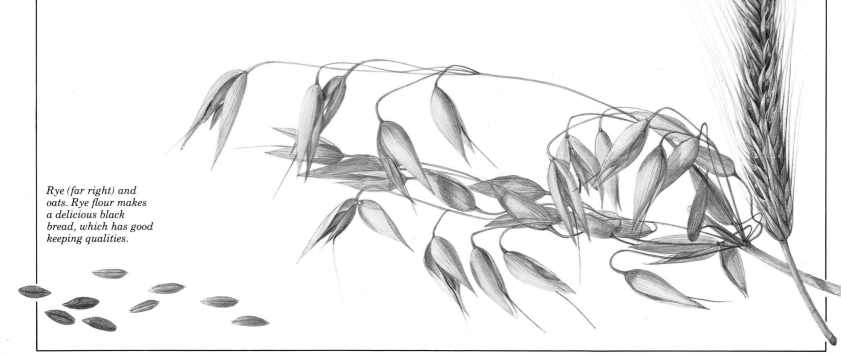

Rye (far right) and oats. Rye flour makes a delicious black bread, which has good keeping qualities.

Buckwheat

Buckwheat (*Fagopyrum sagittatum* or *F. esculentum*), commercially, is considered to be a cereal, although it does not belong to the *Gramineae*, as do true cereals, but to the *Polygonaceae* or buckwheat family. It is a plant for which, unlike so many others, the exact native area is known: a wide region extending from Lake Baikal in Siberia to Manchuria. From there the plant spread in very early times, through China, Japan, India, and later, in medieval times, to Europe. Scholars have proposed several different hypotheses concerning the routes followed by buckwheat in its penetration into Europe. The scientific name *Fagopyrum* is derived from "fagus," beech tree, and "pyrum," cereal, because of the resemblance between the buckwheat fruits and those of the beech tree. The plant first appeared in Germany in 1436 and in France in 1460. Buckwheat plantations give a characteristic air to the countryside. According to a nineteenth-century French history of European plants, "The fields of buckwheat look like a garden of white and pink flowers, or speckled with green, red, and white, all clustered at the top of the stems."

Buckwheat is used to make a flour suitable for pancakes, breads, and cookies.

Rice · Sorghum

Rice is widely cultivated throughout the world, in areas with warm climates and abundant water. If the general rule is observed that each continent has its specific cereal (Europe and north-central Asia being the wheat continents, America the corn continent, and Africa more or less the durra or sorghum continent), rice is, without doubt, the typical cereal of Southeast Asia. It is also largely cultivated in some parts of southern Europe. Rice, of the *Gramineae*, genus *Oryza*, subfamily *Orizeae*, is an annual grass of variable size, with rough and coarse tissues because of the presence of the element silicon. From the standpoint of cultivation "upland rice," with a low water requirement, can be distinguished from ordinary rice, and "floating (lowland) rice," which can reach a considerable height. The rice grains after threshing are still covered by the hulls consisting of glumes and glumellae. At this stage it is known as "paddy rice."

Before reaching the market the rice grains are put through a succession of operations, consisting first of the removal of the hulls, then removal of the bran layer and most of the embryo, bleaching, cleaning, and pearling (a polishing

Rice keeps well for a long time in a cool, dry place. It cannot be stored successfully in hot or damp conditions.
Good-quality rice should be shiny and uniform in color.

There are many different kinds of rice: smaller-grained varieties can be added to soups and broths, short-grain rice is best for risottos, and long-grain rice is used in salads or Oriental recipes. Rice may be boiled in water, broth, or milk.

WARM BROWN RICE SALAD

4 cups brown rice; 3½ oz/100 g cured ham; ½ avocado; 3½ oz/100 g Gruyère cheese; 2 tomatoes; 3½ oz/100 g cooked chicken meat; 1 lemon; oil; salt.

Boil the rice in salted water for 50 minutes then refresh under running cold water until lukewarm. Chop the ham, avocado, Gruyère, tomatoes, and chicken into even-sized dice, and add to the rice, stirring well. Make a dressing with oil, salt, and lemon juice and mix into the salad. Serve warm.

Rice · Sorghum

operation with talc), and eventually, oiling and coating. These various processes, of which only the first is necessary to make the grains edible, while making rice more appetizing to the consumer, deprive it of most of its nutritional qualities. During milling much of the vitamin B_1 (thiamine) is lost. Vitamin B deficiency can cause beriberi. Fats decrease from 1.6% to 0.25%; protein from 6.9% to 5.8%; carbohydrates increase from 90% to 93%. The calorific content of rice is approximately 350 calories per 3½ oz (100 g). Dietetically rice is extremely digestible and nourishing, recommended for infants, the elderly, convalescents, and those who suffer from gastroenteritic disorders. However, rice is good not only for special diets. It can be used in the preparation of many excellent dishes, including soups,

risottos, pilafs, and desserts. Rice flour is used for making bread only in emergencies, but semolina rice is very good. By contrast, the dietary interest in sorghum or millet (*Sorghum vulgare*) is very limited. In most countries it is cultivated almost exclusively for fodder and cut when still green. Even when the plants are allowed to reach full maturity the grains are used only for livestock feeding. Another use of sorghum (*S. vulgare technicum*) is in the manufacture of brooms for which the male panicles, freed of the grains, are employed. The variety *cernium* is cultivated in the warm highlands of Africa where it is known as durra. The grains are ground into a flour used to make bread.
Japanese or Sanwa millet, Barnyard, Proso, Pearl, and Ragi millets are some of the varieties currently in use.

TROPICAL RICE SALAD

9 oz/250 g Patna rice; 1 carambola (star fruit); 1 mango; 1 small papaya; 4 slices fresh pineapple; ½ cup/ 2 oz/50 g seedless white raisins (sultanas); ½ cup/ 2 oz/50 g skinned almonds; juice of 2 lemons; walnut oil; black pepper; salt; freshly ground pink pepper.

Rinse the rice under running cold water, dry, then cook in boiling salted water until done. Drain and cool. Peel and dice or chop the fruit. Toast the almonds under the broiler until golden. Mix all the ingredients on a serving plate. In a bowl, blend together the lemon juice, 2 tbsp oil, salt to taste, and freshly ground black and pink pepper. Pour the dressing over the salad and chill for 1 hour before serving.

Rice (bottom) and sorghum (below). The latter is used mainly for livestock feeding. In many African countries a variety of sorghum is cultivated to produce flour for breadmaking.

Sesame · Soybean

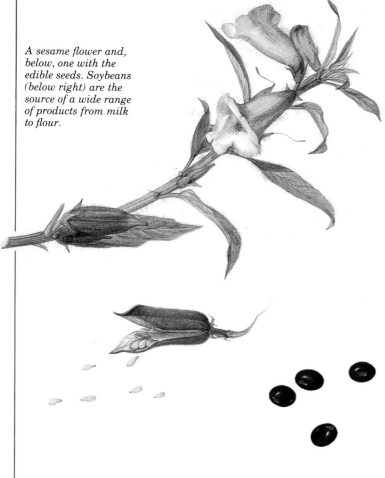

A sesame flower and, below, one with the edible seeds. Soybeans (below right) are the source of a wide range of products from milk to flour.

Sesame (*Sesamum indicum*) is perhaps one of the oldest cultivated plants, known to the Hebrews and ancient Greeks and Egyptians. Numerous historical references to sesame were made by Greek and Roman naturalists: Theophrastus in his *History of Plants* gives it a botanical description; Pliny in his *Historia Naturalis* writes that some populations, probably inhabitants of India, had been extracting large quantities of oil from sesame for a long period of time. Sesame seeds contain up to 55% oil. The enormous commercial importance of the sesame is evidenced by the extensive cultivations in Asia or Africa localized in tropical and subtropical areas, where the best sesame seeds are produced. They are known commercially as Indian sesame and African sesame. In the confectionery industry they are used to make *halva*, and added to cakes and cookies. They also produce an oil which is used to make soap and cosmetics.

The soybean (of the *Leguminosae*) is probably the most important legume among those cultivated in the Asian countries, for its high nutritive value and the varied industrial ways in which it is used. The soybean plant is rich in lipids and minerals, calcium, potassium, magnesium, and nitrogen compounds. The seeds have a high content of protein, among which is one similar to casein, of oil (soybean seeds are one of the major sources of vegetable oils), and of a sugar similar to lactose, as well as other carbohydrates. Soybeans are the cheapest source of vegetable protein, and are important in the daily diet of many Asiatic populations. The seeds provide milk, cheese, flour, bread, oil, and even coffee and cocoa substitutes. Soybeans can also be used to make soups, broths, salads, etc. Soy milk, which is obtained by grinding the seeds previously immersed in water for a day, has a composition similar to cows' milk; it froths when boiling, and in cooling forms a thick cream at the surface. Soy flour, besides being suitable for making bread, lends itself very well to the preparation of bread-sticks, cookies, and pasta. Oil, however, is the main product extracted from the seeds of this legume. It can be used in the manufacture of margarine and soaps.

BEAN SPROUT SALAD

1 lettuce; 4 carrots; 2 bunches radishes; 1 small tub soybean sprouts; 1 bunch fresh mint; 1 Japanese white radish (daikon); balsamic or wine vinegar; salt.

Wash all the vegetables. Trim and slice the radishes and carrots. Arrange on a bed of lettuce on a serving platter, with the bean sprouts in the middle. Peel and dice the daikon and mix with the chopped mint, 4 tbsp oil, and vinegar to taste. Pour this dressing over the salad and serve.

Colza · Rapeseed

The term colza, one of the many species of the genus *Brassica*, derives from the German *Kohlsaat*, meaning "cabbage seed." It is good fodder and also grown for pasture in parts of Europe. Colza (*Brassica napus* var. *oleifera*) is probably native to Africa and southern Europe, but is believed to have been known outside its center of origin a few millennia ago, in Russia and China. Information has been available since the seventeenth century when this plant became very important throughout most of Europe as the basis of one of the most important oil-seed cultures. Now, even though colza oil is still part of the numerous so-called vegetable oils, its cultivation has decreased. Recent studies now claim that the use of colza oil in cooking may be harmful.

Although known for several centuries, rapeseed (*Brassica rapa* var. *oleifera*), like colza, with which it is sometimes confused, began to be extensively cultivated as an oil-seed plant in central and northern Europe only around the beginning of the eighteenth century. However, with the exception of India and Romania where it is widely cultivated, in other countries where climatic conditions allow it, colza is preferred to rapeseed because of the higher oil content of the seeds.

Rapeseed and, below, colza. These are extensively cultivated as oil-seed plants.

Olive

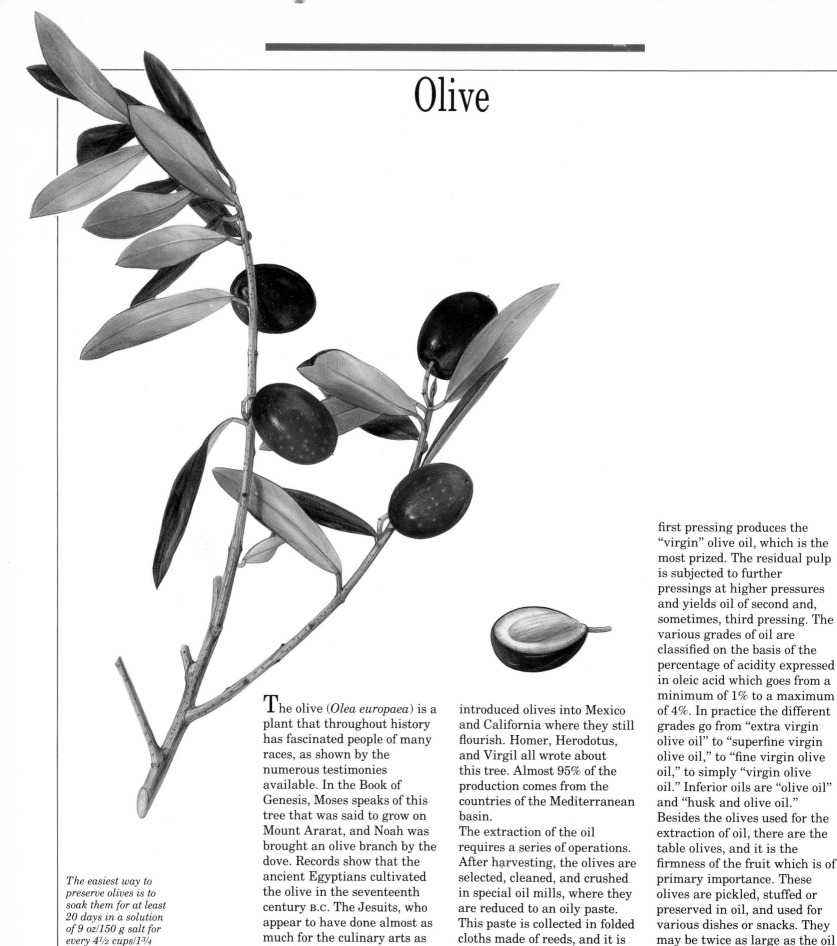

The easiest way to preserve olives is to soak them for at least 20 days in a solution of 9 oz/150 g salt for every 4½ cups/1¾ pints/1 liter water.

The olive (*Olea europaea*) is a plant that throughout history has fascinated people of many races, as shown by the numerous testimonies available. In the Book of Genesis, Moses speaks of this tree that was said to grow on Mount Ararat, and Noah was brought an olive branch by the dove. Records show that the ancient Egyptians cultivated the olive in the seventeenth century B.C. The Jesuits, who appear to have done almost as much for the culinary arts as they did for religion,

introduced olives into Mexico and California where they still flourish. Homer, Herodotus, and Virgil all wrote about this tree. Almost 95% of the production comes from the countries of the Mediterranean basin.

The extraction of the oil requires a series of operations. After harvesting, the olives are selected, cleaned, and crushed in special oil mills, where they are reduced to an oily paste. This paste is collected in folded cloths made of reeds, and it is then subjected to pressing. The

first pressing produces the "virgin" olive oil, which is the most prized. The residual pulp is subjected to further pressings at higher pressures and yields oil of second and, sometimes, third pressing. The various grades of oil are classified on the basis of the percentage of acidity expressed in oleic acid which goes from a minimum of 1% to a maximum of 4%. In practice the different grades go from "extra virgin olive oil" to "superfine virgin olive oil," to "fine virgin olive oil," to simply "virgin olive oil." Inferior oils are "olive oil" and "husk and olive oil." Besides the olives used for the extraction of oil, there are the table olives, and it is the firmness of the fruit which is of primary importance. These olives are pickled, stuffed or preserved in oil, and used for various dishes or snacks. They may be twice as large as the oil olives.

Sunflower

Sunflower seed oil is among the most suitable against cholesterol. It contains more than 90% polyunsaturated fats, as well as proteins, sugars, and cellulose. It is also used by the pharmaceutical or chemical industries.

Historic information about the sunflower (*Helianthus annus* fam. *Compositae*) and its place of origin is confused: some authorities believe that it is native to Peru, while others are equally certain that it originated in Mexico and some southern areas of the United States. The sunflower was cultivated in a primitive fashion in America by the Indians who used it as food. In France the tubers are still eaten between November and April, after being cooked like salsify. Today in several areas, from Russia to France, the United States to Mexico, China, India, and Australia, the sunflower is considered one of the most important

oleiferous plants because its oil can be used for human consumption. Sunflower oil is resistant to rancidity, can be used as an extender for more expensive oils and, mixed with other fats, either vegetable or animal, is used in the production of margarines, cooking fats, etc. Sunflower oil, which is extracted from the seeds, is also particularly suitable for the preservation of fish. Its seeds and those of *H. tuberosus* can be toasted for direct consumption and have a pleasant taste, similar to that of hazelnuts. The flowers always turn toward the sun, which, as much as for their large vivid yellow petals, accounts for their name.

SUNFLOWER SEED CANDY

14 oz/400 g cereal mix; 3½ oz/ 100 g chopped almonds and hazelnuts (untoasted); 3½ oz/ 100 g seedless white raisins; 4 tbsp mixed sunflower and sesame seeds, toasted; 8 tbsp honey; 2 tbsp sunflower seed oil.

Mix the cereal base, nuts, raisins, and seeds together then mix in the honey and oil. Cook in a medium oven (350°F/180°C/mark 4) for 20 minutes, then break into pieces and return to the oven briefly to brown evenly all over. This candy will keep for 1 month.

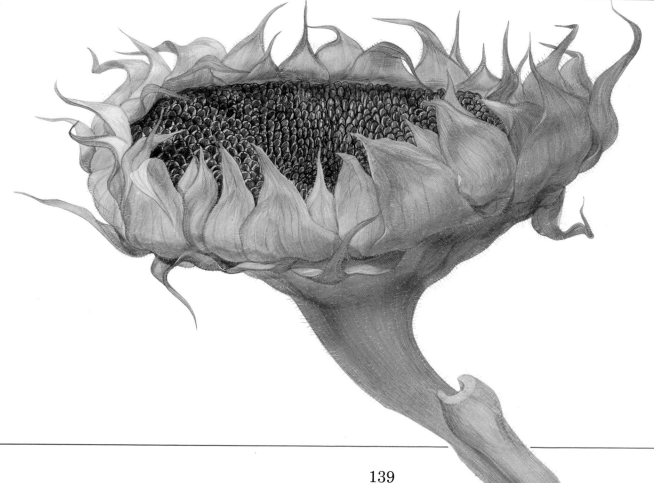

Sunflower seeds need full sunlight to mature. For this reason, the flower turns on itself, to follow the direction of the sun. The weight of the mature seeds makes the flowers bend in their characteristic manner.

Broad bean

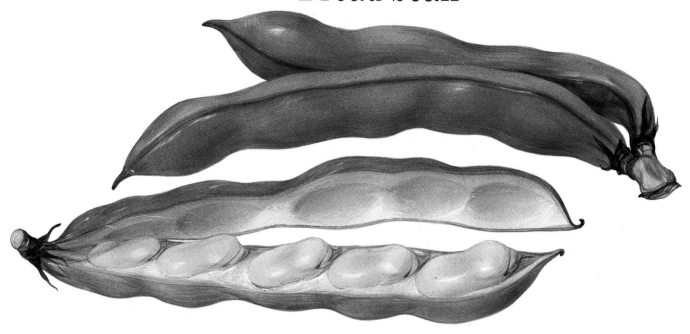

Young broad beans should be shelled and may be eaten raw, in a salad, with cubed cheese, olive oil, salt, and pepper.

The broad bean (*Vicia faba*) is considered native to the Mediterranean basin. In Egypt seeds have been found dating back to 2200–2400 B.C. In the Middle Ages broad beans were one of the staple foods. Today, they are cultivated in the Mediterranean regions, because of their resistance to drought. They are used as a fertilizer, as a rotation crop (that is, a crop which is grown alternately with others requiring great amounts of nitrogen fertilizers, such as various cereals), especially the small-seeded varieties which are also used for fodder. Fresh broad beans have 15–16% solid residue, 5% protein, 4% carbohydrates, and 40 calories per 3½ oz (100 g). Dry broad beans have a higher nutritive value: 87% solid residue, 21% protein, 53% carbohydrates, 3% lipids, 3% ash, and the highest calorific content after chick peas among leguminous plants: 332 calories per 3½ oz (100 g). Broad beans are known to be the cause of a strange illness, favism, with symptoms similar to those of common allergies, but that sometimes can produce coma and even death. This illness, caused by the consumption of the bean or by the inhalation of the scent which is given out by beans grown on marshy ground, cannot be considered a simple form of allergy; it appears only in individuals with a hereditary predisposition.

EGYPTIAN BROAD BEAN SALAD

8 hard-boiled eggs; 2¼ lb/1 kg broad beans; salt and black pepper; olive oil; 2 dried red chili peppers; 1 tsp ground cumin; coriander leaves.

Shell the beans and cook in boiling salted water for 10 minutes. Drain and peel off the thin outer skin. Mix together in a small bowl 6 tbsp oil, the finely sliced pepper, cumin, salt, and a little pepper. Leave to stand for at least 1 hour, then pour the dressing over the beans. Shell the eggs, cut them in half, and serve with the beans. Garnish with coriander leaves.

Lupine · Chick pea · Lentil

The Lupine originated in the Mediterranean basin and can still be found growing wild in Sicily and other Mediterranean regions. Since ancient times the lupine has been a staple food for the poor. It was grown in Egypt 2,000 years before Christ and was also widely cultivated by the Greeks and Romans for both humans and livestock. In ancient Rome cooked lupines were distributed to the people on holy days and at festivals. Although of high nutritive value, the lupine is of very little importance today as food; it is used more as a snack, like peanuts, salted almonds, and roasted pumpkin seeds, than as a main dish. The lupine is often grown as a fertilizer to enrich the soil because of its nitrogen-fixing bacterial root nodules. This is done also with other large *Leguminosae*, such as alfalfa (*Medicago sativa*) and lespedza. Some species and varieties are also grown as ornamental plants.

Chick peas (*Cicer arietinum*) have also been cultivated since ancient times. They were known in Greece at the time of Homer, and in Egypt and India even before that. Today they are widely cultivated around the Mediterranean. The commercial product is the dried seeds which are cooked before eating. They can be boiled, then seasoned with oil, or stewed, or, as in some regions in southern Italy, cooked under the embers. Lentils (*Lens esculenta* or *Ervum lens* or *Viceia lens*), unknown in the wild state, have been cultivated for a long time as confirmed by findings dating from the Bronze Age.

They were also known to the ancient Egyptians and in India around 2000 B.C. Lentils were also eaten by the ancient Jews, as the story of Esau, who renounced his birthright for a dish of lentils, shows. From the dietetic standpoint, lentils have the same merits and defects as other leguminous plants but they have a higher protein content (25%). They are used as a vegetable and in the preparation of soups.

Above: two varieties of lentil. The green sweet-tasting lentils can be used as side dishes; the small dark lentils have more flavor and are best in soups and vegetarian pâtés. Right: chick peas. Below: lupines.

CHICK PEA PÂTÉ

3 oz/80 g dry chick peas; 2 small onions; ½ tsp marjoram; 5 tbsp olive oil; salt and pepper.

Soak the chick peas for 12 hours, and drain. Cook them in a large amount of lightly salted water. When cooked, blend them in a food processor. Add the finely chopped onion, marjoram, and oil; mix well and season. Serve the pâté with wholemeal bread and crisp raw vegetables.

Beans

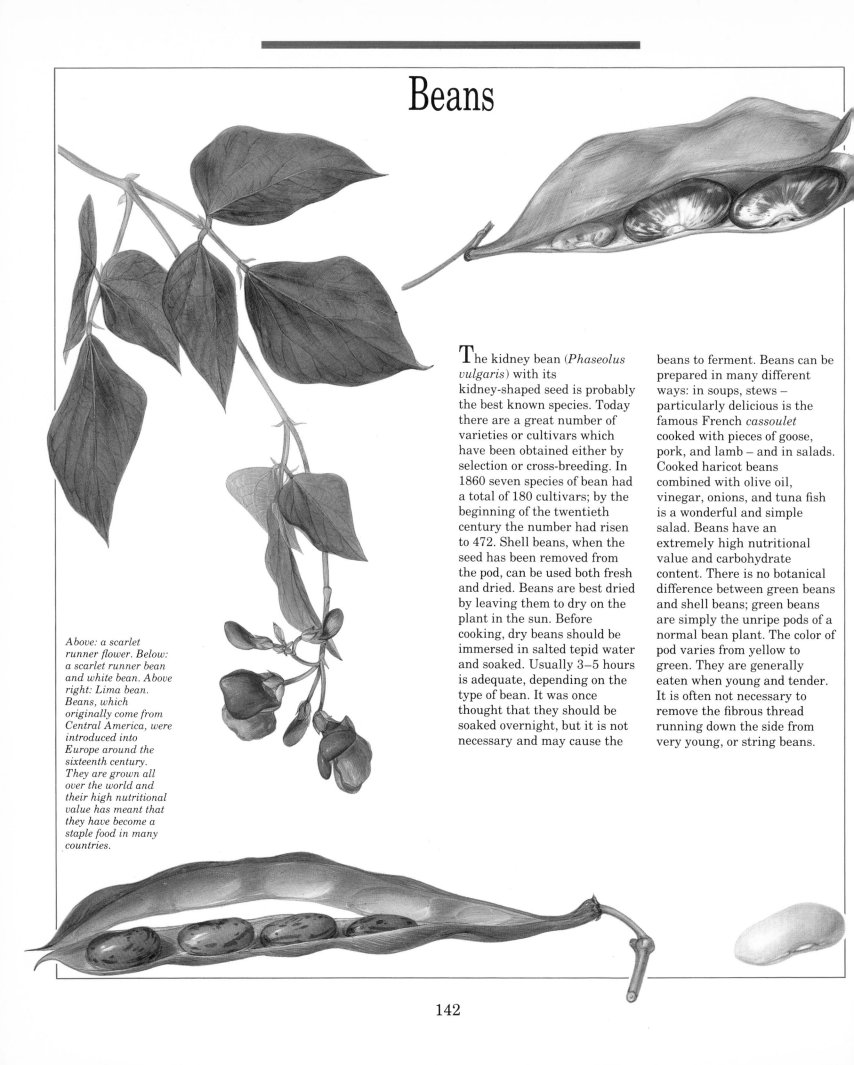

Above: a scarlet runner flower. Below: a scarlet runner bean and white bean. Above right: Lima bean. Beans, which originally come from Central America, were introduced into Europe around the sixteenth century. They are grown all over the world and their high nutritional value has meant that they have become a staple food in many countries.

The kidney bean (*Phaseolus vulgaris*) with its kidney-shaped seed is probably the best known species. Today there are a great number of varieties or cultivars which have been obtained either by selection or cross-breeding. In 1860 seven species of bean had a total of 180 cultivars; by the beginning of the twentieth century the number had risen to 472. Shell beans, when the seed has been removed from the pod, can be used both fresh and dried. Beans are best dried by leaving them to dry on the plant in the sun. Before cooking, dry beans should be immersed in salted tepid water and soaked. Usually 3–5 hours is adequate, depending on the type of bean. It was once thought that they should be soaked overnight, but it is not necessary and may cause the

beans to ferment. Beans can be prepared in many different ways: in soups, stews – particularly delicious is the famous French *cassoulet* cooked with pieces of goose, pork, and lamb – and in salads. Cooked haricot beans combined with olive oil, vinegar, onions, and tuna fish is a wonderful and simple salad. Beans have an extremely high nutritional value and carbohydrate content. There is no botanical difference between green beans and shell beans; green beans are simply the unripe pods of a normal bean plant. The color of pod varies from yellow to green. They are generally eaten when young and tender. It is often not necessary to remove the fibrous thread running down the side from very young, or string beans.

Beans

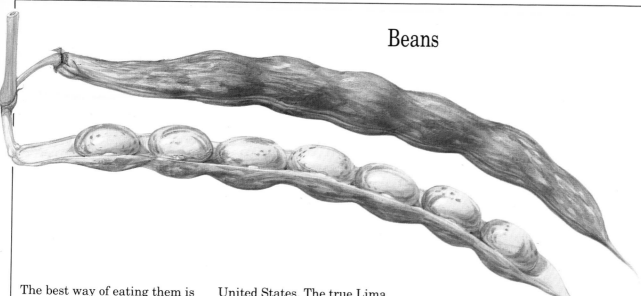

Illustrated on this page are a number of the more common European beans: kidney bean, Scotch bean, and cannellino.

The best way of eating them is either lightly boiled, or steamed, with butter, or in a salad dressed with garlic, oil, and vinegar. An alternative salad is made up of lightly cooked beans, chopped cold boiled potatoes, finely chopped parsley, garlic, oil, and vinegar. Young beans can also be pickled. The scarlet runner (*Phaseolus multiflorus*) can be used either fresh or dried. They are best eaten when young, as older runners tend to be rather tough and stringy. The white seeded variety (Spanish White) is the most common nowadays. It has white, large seeds with a soft skin and delicate flavor. The scarlet runner is used in soups, stews, and in salads. The Lima bean (*P. lunatus*) has a variety with small beans, known as Sieva or Carolina beans in the United States. The true Lima bean has much larger seeds which grow up to ¾ in in length. The Lima bean was used by the Incas and was introduced to Mauritius and Madagascar around the eighteenth century, where it became widely grown. It has become an important economic crop in tropical regions where it is grown in rotation with sugar cane. Lima beans are very popular in Great Britain and the United States where they are often known as "butter beans." Great Britain imports almost the entire production from Madagascar. Because of the delicate texture of the pulp of its seed and delicate flavor, the Lima bean is good both in soups and as a side dish. Both the Lima and scarlet runner have high nutritional values.

BEANS IN A FLASK

1 lb/500 g shelled fresh white (haricot) beans; ½ cup olive oil; 2 cloves garlic; 5–6 sage leaves; salt and freshly ground pepper.

Wash the shelled beans and place them in a wine flask. Add the oil, minced garlic, sage, pepper, and 2 cups/¾ pint/450 ml water. Cover the top of the flask with perforated foil (to allow air to escape), and place in a slow oven for 3 hours, or until the water is completely evaporated and the oil has been absorbed by the beans. Turn into a bowl and season with salt and freshly ground pepper.

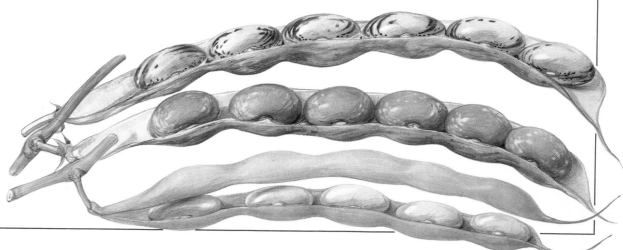

String bean

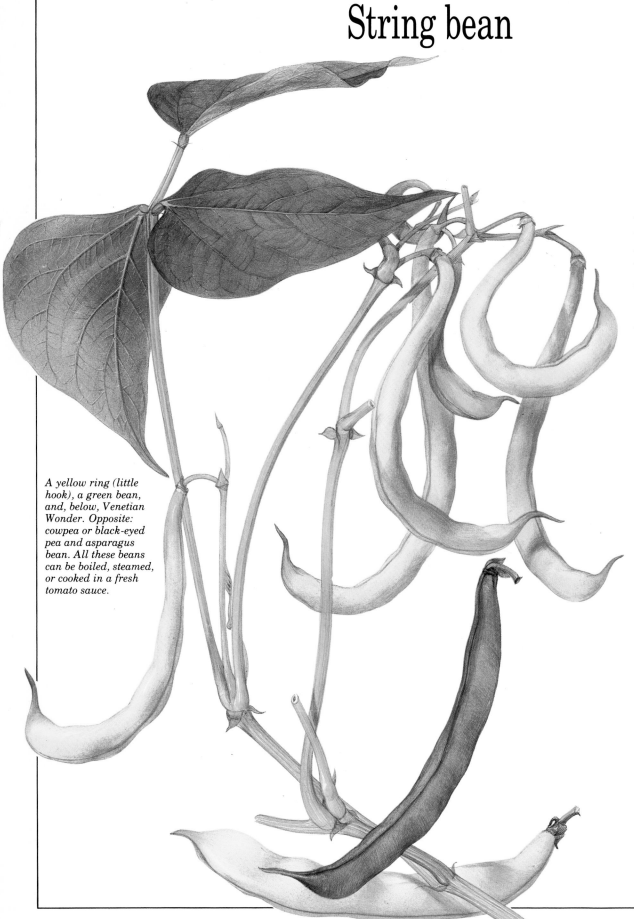

A yellow ring (little hook), a green bean, and, below, Venetian Wonder. Opposite: cowpea or black-eyed pea and asparagus bean. All these beans can be boiled, steamed, or cooked in a fresh tomato sauce.

String beans are produced by both tall climbing plants and low dwarf plants. The color of the unripe pods are generally bright green or yellow. Many of the differences among the abundant cultivars are almost impossible to define. Among the yellow dwarf varieties are: Brittle Wax, Goldencrop Wax, Surecrop Stringless Wax, Pencil Pod Wax, and Rustproof Golden Wax. The green dwarf varieties include: Tenderpod, Bountiful, Topcrop, Tendergreen, Contender, King of Belgium, and Bush Romano. Among the climbing yellow varieties particular mention should be made of Golden Pole, Kentucky Wonder Wax, and Burpee Golden which have large fleshy pods and different colored seeds. Another yellow climber is the peculiar "ring" or "hook bean" with curved hooklike pods. Among the climbing green varieties are: Kentucky Wonder, McCaslan, and Romano Italian Pole with fleshy flat pods and similar qualities to the yellow variety. There are also many cultivars with cylindrical-shaped pods. One of the most sought-after qualities in these types of bean is the absence of string – the tough and inedible fibrous strip along the side of the pod. The French are particularly good at growing beans and have achieved a wide variety of cultivars. These young thin beans should be cooked in a large pan of boiling water. (To

String Beans

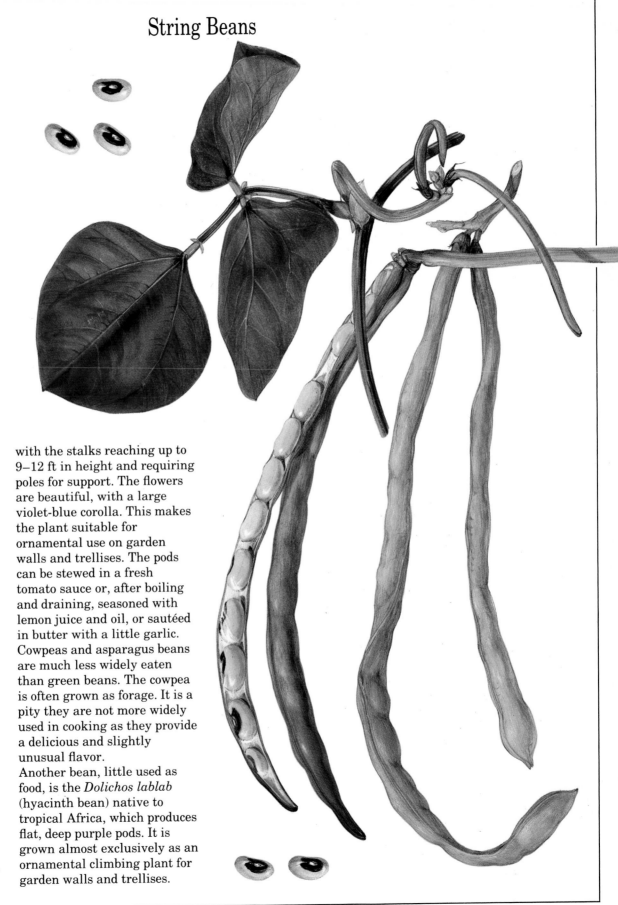

preserve the bright green color they should be cooked uncovered.) French beans are best eaten when still slightly crisp. Tiny thin beans are probably most delicious lightly steamed and served with a little butter.

The cowpea is native to South America and widely cultivated in warm and temperate regions. Botanically, it is known as *Vigna unguiculata*, *Dolichos unguiculatus*, or *V. sinensis*. There are several varieties which are grown in different countries, for example, the "cubia beledi" of Arab countries, the "dan tua" of the Far East, the African "niebe," the "pois chique" of the Antilles, and the American cowpea. Little is known of its introduction into Europe and of its distribution throughout the world. Cowpeas can be used shelled, either fresh or dried. The very young unripe pods are cooked in the same way as green beans. Cowpeas can be eaten either hot as a vegetable or cold in salads. They are not recommended for soups because of their strong flavor. The cowpea is similar to the kidney bean in nutritional value.

V. unguiculata var. *sesquipedalis* is known in many countries as asparagus bean or yard-long bean. The long immature pods can be eaten in the same way as green beans. This is an annual, climbing, herbaceous plant,

with the stalks reaching up to 9–12 ft in height and requiring poles for support. The flowers are beautiful, with a large violet-blue corolla. This makes the plant suitable for ornamental use on garden walls and trellises. The pods can be stewed in a fresh tomato sauce or, after boiling and draining, seasoned with lemon juice and oil, or sautéed in butter with a little garlic. Cowpeas and asparagus beans are much less widely eaten than green beans. The cowpea is often grown as forage. It is a pity they are not more widely used in cooking as they provide a delicious and slightly unusual flavor.

Another bean, little used as food, is the *Dolichos lablab* (hyacinth bean) native to tropical Africa, which produces flat, deep purple pods. It is grown almost exclusively as an ornamental climbing plant for garden walls and trellises.

145

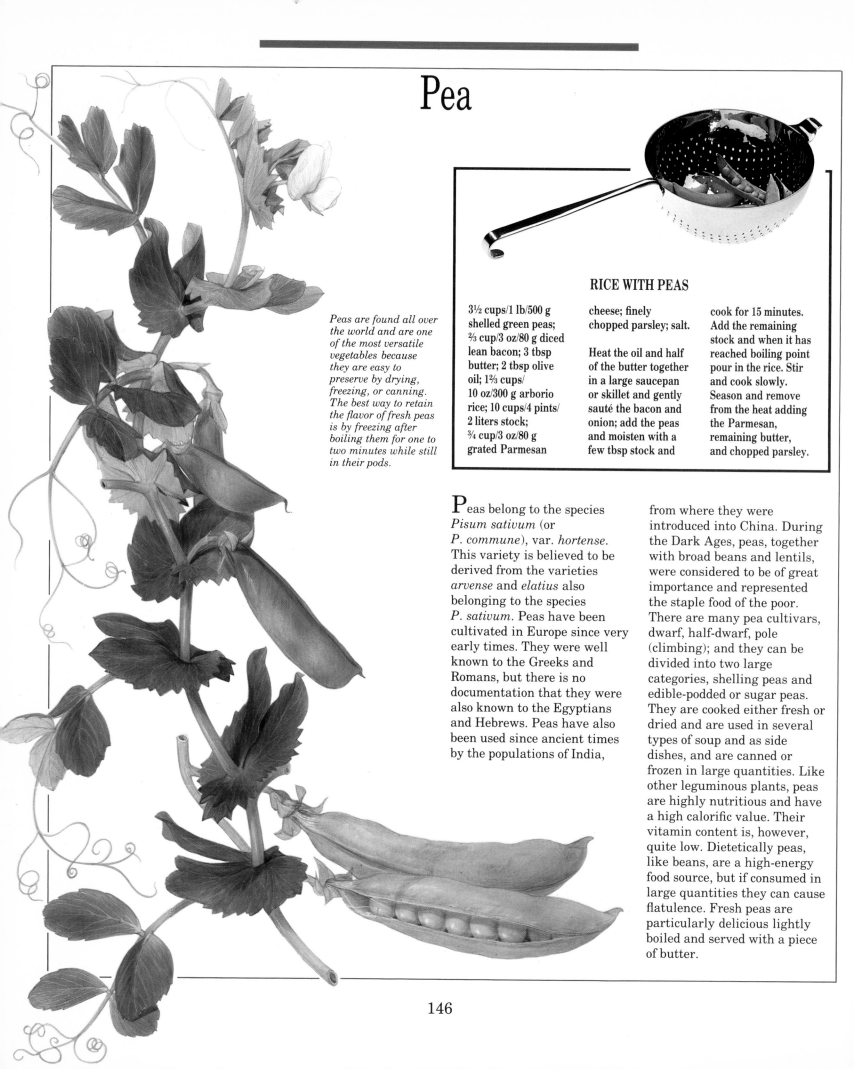

Pea

Peas are found all over the world and are one of the most versatile vegetables because they are easy to preserve by drying, freezing, or canning. The best way to retain the flavor of fresh peas is by freezing after boiling them for one to two minutes while still in their pods.

RICE WITH PEAS

3½ cups/1 lb/500 g shelled green peas; ⅔ cup/3 oz/80 g diced lean bacon; 3 tbsp butter; 2 tbsp olive oil; 1⅔ cups/ 10 oz/300 g arborio rice; 10 cups/4 pints/ 2 liters stock; ¾ cup/3 oz/80 g grated Parmesan cheese; finely chopped parsley; salt.

Heat the oil and half of the butter together in a large saucepan or skillet and gently sauté the bacon and onion; add the peas and moisten with a few tbsp stock and cook for 15 minutes. Add the remaining stock and when it has reached boiling point pour in the rice. Stir and cook slowly. Season and remove from the heat adding the Parmesan, remaining butter, and chopped parsley.

Peas belong to the species *Pisum sativum* (or *P. commune*), var. *hortense*. This variety is believed to be derived from the varieties *arvense* and *elatius* also belonging to the species *P. sativum*. Peas have been cultivated in Europe since very early times. They were well known to the Greeks and Romans, but there is no documentation that they were also known to the Egyptians and Hebrews. Peas have also been used since ancient times by the populations of India, from where they were introduced into China. During the Dark Ages, peas, together with broad beans and lentils, were considered to be of great importance and represented the staple food of the poor. There are many pea cultivars, dwarf, half-dwarf, pole (climbing); and they can be divided into two large categories, shelling peas and edible-podded or sugar peas. They are cooked either fresh or dried and are used in several types of soup and as side dishes, and are canned or frozen in large quantities. Like other leguminous plants, peas are highly nutritious and have a high calorific value. Their vitamin content is, however, quite low. Dietetically peas, like beans, are a high-energy food source, but if consumed in large quantities they can cause flatulence. Fresh peas are particularly delicious lightly boiled and served with a piece of butter.

MEDICINAL PLANTS

Mullein · Lime

Mullein (*Verbascum thapsus*) has always been known by many names, and there are several species. The tall, straight stems of the plant with their long spikes of golden yellow flowers have earned it the names of candleflower and candlewick. Mullein has been used by man since ancient times. Pliny recorded that "figs do not putrifie at all that are wrapped in the leaves of mullein." In the Middle Ages, possibly because of the ghostly appearance of the whitish gray leaves, the plant was believed to be a protection against demons, and monks grew mullein in large quantities in their herb gardens for many medicinal purposes. Culpeper employed black mullein (*V. nigrum*) for colic, coughs, all chest ailments and hemorrhoids, and used white mullein (*V. lychnitis*) as a cure for such diverse afflictions as gout and warts. For many years it was official in the *British Pharmacopoeia*.

The drug is derived from the leaves and flowers which are gathered in July and August. They contain a saponin, saccharose, essential oil, and mucilaginous substances. The leaves also have bitter principles, waxes, and resins. In certain country districts the flowers are still made into an infusion to bring relief from gout, and into poultices for neuralgia.

The lime tree or linden has been appreciated for its kindly and beneficial action for hundreds of years, as shown by the testimonies of Theophrastus, Pliny, and Galen, and it still enjoys the same reputation today. The bark, sap, and foliage were all thought to be good for the treatment of leprosy, abscesses, and thinning hair, but today the active ingredients are obtained only from the flower.

The generic name *Tilia* includes several species which are divided into two groups: those with single flowers and double-flowered limes. The active ingredients contained in the flower consist mainly of mucilage; carotene; the glycoside tiliacin; an essential oil; malic, tartaric, and acetic acids; and some vitamin C. The lime is useful for its diaphoretic and antispasmodic properties, but is more widely known as a soothing herb tea.

Left: mullein flower. The medicinal drug is obtained from the leaves and flowers. Below: lime flowers.

LIME TISANE

Lime flowers are used in the preparation of lime tisane. They should be gathered in late spring, dried, and stored in a wooden box. Place 1 tsp dried flowers into a cup and pour over boiling water. Cover with a clean cloth and leave to infuse. Strain the liquid and sweeten with honey. Tisanes should be drunk hot. They are very good for colds and for relieving tension. One cup of lime tisane each day is a very good substitute for tea and coffee.

Camomile

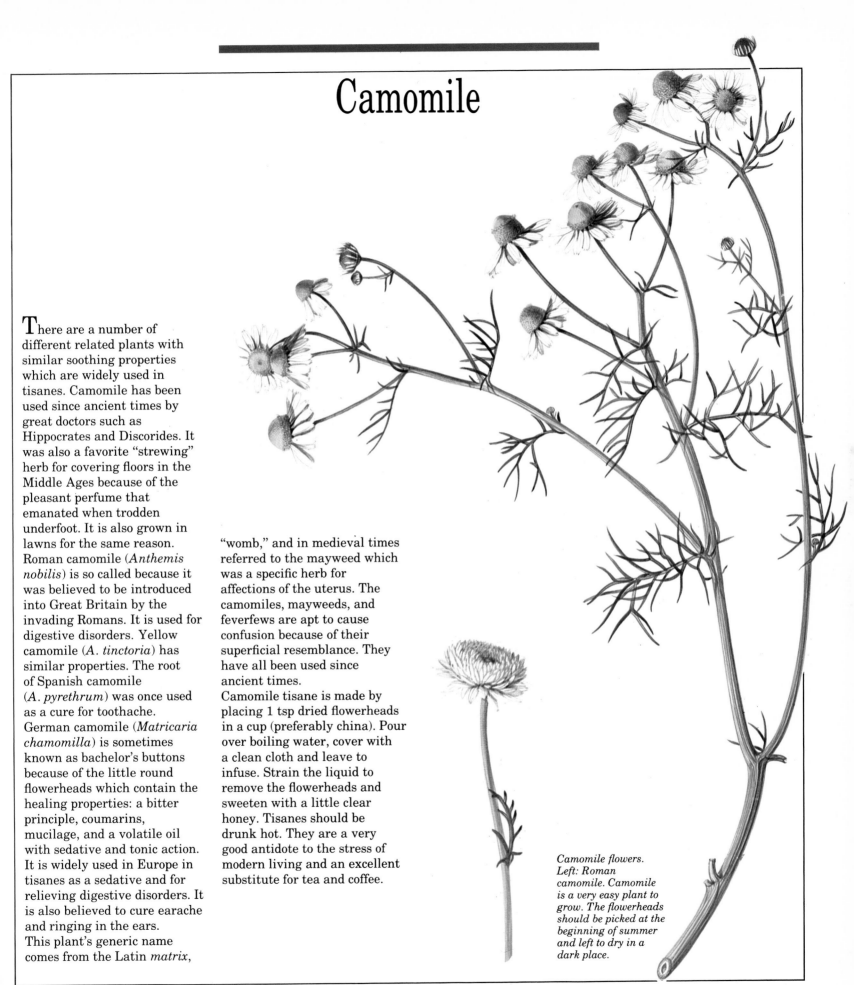

There are a number of different related plants with similar soothing properties which are widely used in tisanes. Camomile has been used since ancient times by great doctors such as Hippocrates and Discorides. It was also a favorite "strewing" herb for covering floors in the Middle Ages because of the pleasant perfume that emanated when trodden underfoot. It is also grown in lawns for the same reason. Roman camomile (*Anthemis nobilis*) is so called because it was believed to be introduced into Great Britain by the invading Romans. It is used for digestive disorders. Yellow camomile (*A. tinctoria*) has similar properties. The root of Spanish camomile (*A. pyrethrum*) was once used as a cure for toothache. German camomile (*Matricaria chamomilla*) is sometimes known as bachelor's buttons because of the little round flowerheads which contain the healing properties: a bitter principle, coumarins, mucilage, and a volatile oil with sedative and tonic action. It is widely used in Europe in tisanes as a sedative and for relieving digestive disorders. It is also believed to cure earache and ringing in the ears. This plant's generic name comes from the Latin *matrix*,

"womb," and in medieval times referred to the mayweed which was a specific herb for affections of the uterus. The camomiles, mayweeds, and feverfews are apt to cause confusion because of their superficial resemblance. They have all been used since ancient times.

Camomile tisane is made by placing 1 tsp dried flowerheads in a cup (preferably china). Pour over boiling water, cover with a clean cloth and leave to infuse. Strain the liquid to remove the flowerheads and sweeten with a little clear honey. Tisanes should be drunk hot. They are a very good antidote to the stress of modern living and an excellent substitute for tea and coffee.

Camomile flowers. Left: Roman camomile. Camomile is a very easy plant to grow. The flowerheads should be picked at the beginning of summer and left to dry in a dark place.

Marigold · Coltsfoot

The beautiful golden marigold flower (left) is rich in soothing properties. It is used in teas and tisanes or in beauty treatments for irritated skin or to smoothe away wrinkles.
The fresh flower petals add a distinctive flavor and splash of color to spring salads.
Below: coltsfoot, a soothing remedy for coughs.

"The Marigold floureth from Aprill or May even untill Winter, and in Winter also, if it bee warme": thus John Gerard, the sixteenth-century English botanist, explained the botanical name of marigold (*Calendula officinalis*), which came from the belief that it could be seen on the Calends, or first day, of every month throughout the year. The prefix "mary" comes from the belief that they adorned the Virgin Mary.

This herb is full of goodness: medicinal properties are found in the entire plant, particularly in the petals, which are made into ointments for cuts, burns, and bruises. Marigold, in the form of an infusion, soothes red, watery eyes, gives relief in bronchial ailments, helps combat anemia, and is prescribed in cases of amenorrhea. Fresh petals, sprinkled on salads, give a piquant flavor.

Coltsfoot (*Tussilago farfara*) has many local names which refer to the unusual formation of the scape: horse-hoof; bull's foot; foal's wort. The name Son before Father reflects the way the brilliant yellow flowers bloom much earlier than the leaves. The plant's botanical name comes from the Latin *tussis*, a cough. For hundreds of years herbalists used the leaves for coughs, and called the herb coughwort. Culpeper wrote that "the fresh leaves, or juice, or syrup thereof, is good for a hot, dry cough, or wheezing or shortness of breath." Coltsfoot is widely found in Europe, Asia, and North Africa in all kinds of waste places wherever the soil is heavy and damp. The leaves are covered on the underside with a thick, soft white down. After the leaves have been collected, usually in June or July, this down is stripped off and the leaves are then dried. They are tonic and soothing because of their mucilage. Coltsfoot is also good for skin blemishes. At one time Syrup of Coltsfoot was included in the *British Pharmacopoeia*.

Gentian

The etymological derivation of the generic name of the gentian plant is from the discovery of the Illyrian King, Genthius, of the yellow gentian (*Gentiana lutea*), the most important of the Major gentians. Of the numerous species, those of particular pharmacological and botanical interest belong to the Greater or Major gentians, including *G. lutea*, *G. purpurea*, and *G. pannonica*. The well-known species *G. acaulis*, with its brilliant blue flowers, is known by the Italian name gentianella. The beautiful yellow gentian grows in alpine meadows in chalky soil in central and southern Europe. The drug is obtained from the dried fermented rhizome and roots (*Gentianae radix*) of *G. lutea* which should be collected in the fall or spring. The preparation of gentian is a particularly effective tonic for digestive disorders and has been used for many centuries. It is widely employed in the manufacture of confectionery and liqueurs, especially *Gentiane*, a digestive liqueur made in Switzerland and parts of France. Those who wish to prepare gentian bitters domestically should not confuse it with the poisonous *Veratrum* or hellebore. Another less known but ancient use of gentian in folk medicine is as an antimalarial, because of its antifever properties. Small doses of gentian stimulate the central nervous system, but large doses are a depressant and can cause paralysis.

One of the easiest gentians to cultivate is the willow gentian (*G. asclepiadea*) which flowers in July and August. In the United States in midsummer, parts of the prairies are covered with a rose-colored gentian (*Sabbiata campestris*). The amarella gentian with little lavender flowers also grows well in America. The old country names for the gentian plants are baldmoney, butterwort, and fillwort.

A branch of willow gentian, the brilliant blue gentianella, and the root of yellow gentian. Gentian is widely used in liqueurs and in the manufacture of confectionery.

Valerian · Restharrow

Wild Valerian (*Valeriana officinalis*) has tremendous medicinal properties that earned it the name All-heal. It was also known as Drunken Sailor in certain ports where it was used as an aphrodisiac. Wild valerian is indigenous to Europe and Siberia. It was used by monks in their herbal remedies, hence the name *officinalis*. *Valeriana* comes from the Latin *valere*, "to be well." Its fame spread, particularly in the Middle Ages, and it was prescribed for a variety of illnesses from tuberculosis to gout and poisonous snake bites. At the end of the sixteenth century a Neapolitan claimed that it had cured his epilepsy. Other epileptics used this treatment, apparently with good results. Valerian acts as a sedative on the whole nervous system. It is a fast-acting drug which does not linger in the body. Red valerian (*Centranthus ruber*) has a similar sedative effect. This herbaceous perennial is native to Mediterranean regions but is also found in southern England. The drug is obtained from the red rhizome which resembles a large radish.

Restharrow (*Ononis arvenis*) and prickly restharrow (*O. spinosa*) are so called because their long tough roots frequently broke plough blades. They are leguminous plants. It is the prickly restharrow which is particularly valuable for its diuretic and emollient action. It is effective for urinary and renal disorders and dissolving kidney stones. Its reputation for curing kidney stones goes back to ancient Rome when it was mentioned by Pliny and Dioscorides. During the sixteenth century an eminent Italian physician used the bark of the root mixed with wine as a cure for renal disorders and as a tonic for the liver. The young shoots can be cooked as a vegetable.

Mallow · Hollyhock

The blue or common mallow (*Malva sylvestris*) is found throughout Europe and western Asia, Siberia, and North Africa. Its importance is more of historical than current interest as its pharmacological use is declining. The emollient properties of the leaves and flowers are useful in relieving inflammation of the digestive tract and urinary organs. Applied externally as a poultice, it reduces inflammation. The dwarf mallow (*M. rotundifolia*) has similar medicinal action, and its leaves may be eaten raw in salads, or cooked as spinach. Renaissance herbalists used marsh mallow to cure coughs, sore throats, stomach troubles, gonorrhea, and toothache. Today, although it is listed in all pharmacopoeias, it is rarely employed. However, in country districts where herbal lore persists, the roots are boiled with honey to make a soothing decoction that alleviates sore throats and bronchial complaints. The flowers are picked in summer and dried. The roots should be dug up in the fall, scraped free of their cork-like outer covering, and dried.

This tall and stately plant with its large, bright flowers caused Gerard to call it Outlandish Rose, or *Rosa ultramarine*. The hollyhock (*Althaea rosea*) is another member of the *Malvaceae*, believed by some authorities to have originated in such far-flung places as China and the Lebanon. Hollyhocks do not grow wild. The plant has similar properties to marsh mallow, and is believed to help relieve gastritis, enteritis, and cystitis. A purple dye is obtained from the flowers.

Left: hollyhock. Right: a tall branch of common mallow and two marsh mallow flowers.
Mallow leaves are effective as infusions and make good anti-inflammatory poultices. They are also delicious lightly boiled or raw in salads.

153

Flax · Lavender · Manna ash

Left: flax. Right: lavender. A few seeds of fresh lavender flowers can be sprinkled on to salads for an unusual and delicious flavor. The edible seeds of the flax plant can be added to soups, muesli, and cakes. They have a taste slightly similar to almonds.

SOUP WITH FLAX SEEDS

1 carrot; 2 potatoes; 1 leek; 1 lettuce; 1 cup/5 oz/150 g peas; 1 tbsp chopped parsley; 1 tbsp crushed flax seeds; 2 tbsp oat flakes; 3 pints/1½ liters stock; oil; salt and pepper.

Finely chop the carrot and leek. Put them into the heated stock together with the peas and whole peeled potatoes. Add the lettuce cut into fine strips and the flax seeds. Cook for 30 minutes, mash the potatoes, add the oat flakes and parsley. Cook for a further minute, season, and serve. A teaspoon of oil and some freshly ground pepper can be added to the individual servings.

Flax (*Linum usitatissimum*) originated in southern Europe and is now extensively cultivated for textile fiber (linen) and for the seeds which yield linseed oil. The shiny oval seeds are also used in pharmacy to alleviate constipation.

Lavender (*Lavandula vera*), more than any other herb, evokes summer days. Small bags of the dried flower have been traditionally kept in linen closets. The Romans scented their baths with it. Since ancient times it has been valued as a calming and digestive medicine. The fresh flowers yield an oil widely used in medicine and perfume.

English lavender is more esteemed than the continental species. Lavender has a sedative and antiseptic action and is useful for healing wounds, aiding the digestion, and relieving flatulence. Manna ash (*Franxinus ornus*) is commonly found in dry, sunny woods, on hillsides, and mountains. It is cultivated in southern Europe, particularly Sicily, for the sweetish juice called *manna* which has a gentle laxative action. In summer the bark of the tree is cut to allow the juice to drip out. The laxative obtained from *manna* can be safely given to children.

Manna ash keys. A sugary liquid is extracted from the bark of the manna ash.

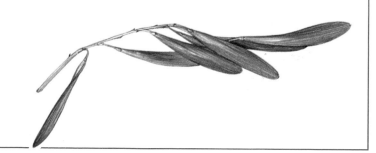

Periwinkle

"**F**resh pervenke rich of hue" was Chaucer's vivid description of the periwinkle (*Vinca major* or *V. minor*), whose brilliant little blue flowers may be seen blooming at any time of the year, no matter how cold the climate. This herb is thought to be an escape from the physick gardens of monasteries where it was grown for its astringent properties. The active principles are contained in the leaves, which are collected when fully grown and dried on wire trays in a warm place. The lesser periwinkle (*V. minor*) is favored by herbalists today as a tonic, and as a cure for intestinal complaints. Mixed with other herbs, it is a useful remedy for skin diseases, especially for the scalp. It is still employed by herbalists to treat uterine hemorrhage, and at one time was valued as a cure for diphtheria. It was believed that if a husband and wife ate the leaves together, it would bind them more closely to one another. This superstition may be connected with the plant's name, over which there is some controversy. "Periwinkle" comes either from the Latin *pervincire*, "to bind closely," or from *pervincere*, "to overcome." This could refer either to the practice of binding the legs with the trailing stems to relieve muscular cramp, or to the plant's astringent properties which helped to overcome internal bleeding.

Flowers and leaves of the periwinkle. The flowers can be crystallized like other edible flowers. Lightly brush the petals with egg white and dip the flowers into confectioners' sugar. Dry them in a cool oven and use them to decorate desserts.

Sweet fern · Elder

The sweet fern, also called wood licorice or common polypody (*Polypodium vulgare*), is commonly found in the temperate regions of Eurasia and Africa. The "sweet" part of the plant's name refers to the sweet taste of the rhizome which resembles licorice, and constitutes the pharmacologically active part of the *Polypodium*. It should be collected during the fall. By the time it has been well cleaned for commercial use, the flavor is considerably less sweet and tastes bitter if chewed. The active principles have a purgative and cholagogic action and can be administered to patients with jaundice or suffering from chronic constipation. Because the fern bore no flowers and the seeds were hidden on the back of the fronds, for many centuries people believed it had the power to make them invisible.

The elder (*Sambucus niger*) is probably the most necromantic tree in the world. Not only was it unthinkable for a witch of any standing not to have an elder in the garden; quite often they actually lived in it, and country folk rarely chopped down this tree for fear that the branches would drip blood, the witch having been hacked in error, with disastrous consequences for the woodsman. From this old belief stem others: that the elder should never be planted too near the house, nor used as firewood, nor to make a cradle. Every part of the elder is useful. The leaves are mixed with linseed oil to make an external emollient application called green oil of elder, and they are also used in insecticides; the distilled water of the flowers known as *Aqua sambuci* is an astringent used in eye and skin lotions; the flowers also go into drugs for bronchial troubles, influenza, and colds, and the berries, which are said to encourage longevity, have since ancient times been made into a "port" wine.

Another member of the *Caprifoliaceae* is the dwarf elder (*S. ebulus*) which rarely grows to more than 3 ft (1 m). One of its country names is ground elder. A decoction of the root produces urination, making it very helpful in the treatment of dropsy. The leaves used as poultices relieve inflammation. The dwarf elder is said to grow near or in battlefields and to spring up where blood has been shed.

Left: sweet fern. Below: red-berried elder. The sweet fern root has a flavor very similar to licorice: it is also known as wood licorice. Dry elder flowers are often used to flavor cookies and cakes.

Black mulberry

BLACK MULBERRY SYRUP

4½ lb/2 kg ripe black mulberries; sugar; juice of 2 lemons.

Wash the mulberries in cold water. Rinse well and dry on kitchen towels. Pass through a sieve using the base of a glass to push the berries through into a bowl.

Leave in the dark for 2 days allowing the sieved berries to ferment. Strain through a paper filter. Weigh the filtered berries and heat together with the same amount of sugar and the lemon juice. Boil gently for 5 minutes. Allow to cool and store the syrup in airtight bottles. It is delicious on ice cream and desserts or as a cool drink with soda and lemon.

The black mulberry (*Morus nigra*) originated either in the southern part of the Caucasus or in the mountains of Nepal. Today it is largely grown in Turkestan and Iraq where varieties with very large seedless fruits have been obtained. Like the white mulberry, *Morus nigra* was once widely cultivated to feed silkworms, and was certainly known to the ancient Greeks and Romans who prized it highly for its fruit. They are usually cooked rather than eaten raw. It has slightly laxative and expectorant properties, and can also be used in a soothing drink for feverish patients. The fruit is made into jams, jellies, and a slightly tart syrup.

Black mulberry. The berries are sweet and full of flavor. They can be used in the same way as other wood berries: to make jams, jellies, and syrups.

Nettle · White dead-nettle

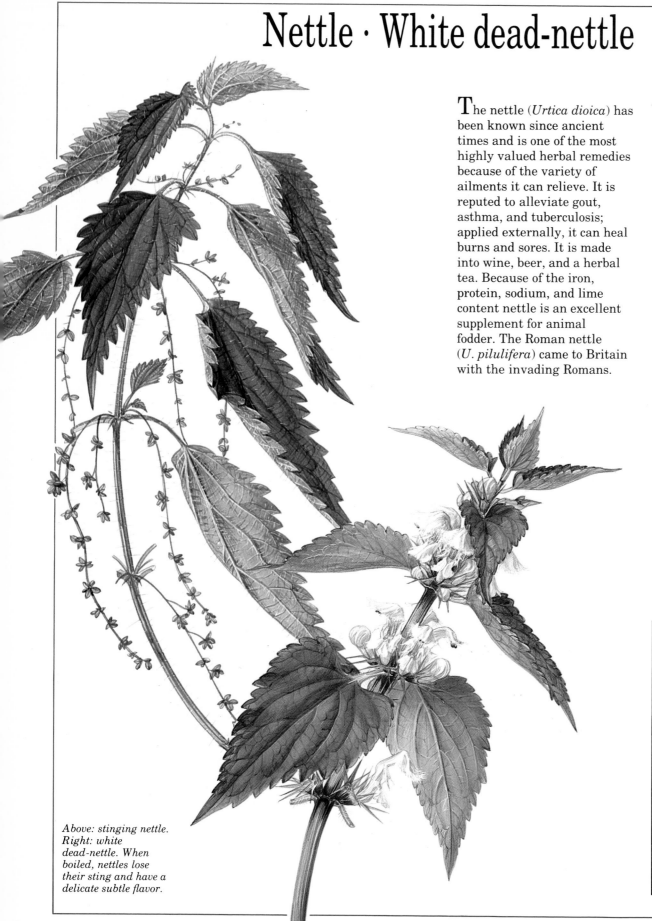

The nettle (*Urtica dioica*) has been known since ancient times and is one of the most highly valued herbal remedies because of the variety of ailments it can relieve. It is reputed to alleviate gout, asthma, and tuberculosis; applied externally, it can heal burns and sores. It is made into wine, beer, and a herbal tea. Because of the iron, protein, sodium, and lime content nettle is an excellent supplement for animal fodder. The Roman nettle (*U. pilulifera*) came to Britain with the invading Romans.

The soldiers planted seeds and used to keep warm by flogging their limbs with the nettles to stimulate the circulation. Before cotton was imported people spun flax from the fibers.

White dead-nettle (*Lamium album*), despite its common name, is not a member of the *Urticaceae*, but a labiate. In medieval times it was known as white archangel and its flowers were baked with sugar to make a pudding called sugar roset. White dead-nettle makes a good astringent and is effective in arresting hemorrhage. The fresh plant emits a foul smell which disappears on drying. According to Pliny it was this fearful scent which kept gardens free of snakes.

Above: stinging nettle. Right: white dead-nettle. When boiled, nettles lose their sting and have a delicate subtle flavor.

NETTLE SOUP

16 oz/450 g stinging nettles (only the tips and tender leaves should be picked); 1 onion, diced; 1 potato, diced; 3 pints/ 1½ liters chicken or vegetable broth; butter; nutmeg; 4 tbsp light cream.

Heat the butter and gently sauté the onion. Add the potato and shredded nettles. Mix well with the butter. Pour in the broth and cook for 30 minutes. Before serving add the cream and nutmeg. Serve with toasted wholemeal bread.

Wild orchid · Hart's tongue fern

Possibly only those who have visited the Near East, Greece or Russia will have heard of salep, and might even have tasted it, either in the form of a refreshing jelly or a spicy soup. This substance that provides the basis of these foods is also endowed with definite medicinal properties. Pharmaceutically salep is a food or drug made from the dried tubers of various species of wild orchid: the early purple orchid (*Orchis mascula*), and two other species, *O. latifolia* and *O. maculata*. They are collected when the plant is in flower, and the tubers are swollen with nutritious substances. They are then washed in boiling water to prevent germination, and dried, threaded together in small bunches until needed, when they are reduced to a powdery consistency.

It was popular with the Persians and the Turks, and has remained so to this day. Salep was unknown in Europe until around the fifteenth century. Its medicinal virtues soon began to be appreciated. It is an easily digested food for those suffering from gastric complaints. At one time salep was prescribed for serious cases of infantile diarrhea because of its supposed sedative and nutritive qualities.

Culpeper, who knew the wild orchid well, called it "one of the most valuable plants growing . . . the salep contains the greatest quantity of nourishment in the smallest bulk, and will support the system in privation and during famine."

"The distilled water is very good against the passions of the heart," wrote Culpeper of the Hart's tongue fern (*Scolopendrium vulgare* or *Asplenium scolopendrium*), and it also stopped hiccoughs. Hart's tongue fern grows in damp, shady locations, at the mouths of caves and wells, and in rock fissures, in most of the northern hemisphere. The large distinctive leaves contain tannins and mucilage which give them diuretic, expectorant, and astringent properties. An infusion of the fronds may be recommended for bronchial catarrh.

From left to right: hart's tongue fern and two species of wild orchid (lady orchid and green-winged orchid). The drug used pharmacologically is obtained from the dry tubers and also a flour, which has been used since ancient times.

Nasturtium · Pellitory of the wall

The buds and seeds of nasturtium or Indian cress (*Tropaeolum majus*) can be pickled and used as a substitute for capers. This plant is more frequently grown in gardens as a decorative plant than as a food. It was brought to Europe by the Jesuits who traveled across the world converting "heathens." It is sometimes called "Jesuits' cress" after them.

Both the brightly colored flowers and young tender leaves can be used in salads. The leaves have a bitter taste slightly similar to watercress. Nasturtium flowers will add a splash of color to summer salads. Nasturtium is rich in vitamin C and has antiseptic properties. The leaves can be dried and drunk as an infusion. The flowers can also be crystallized by lightly brushing the petals with egg white, dipping them in confectioners' sugar, and drying the flowers in a cool oven. They can be used to decorate desserts and ice cream.

Pellitory of the wall (*Parietaria officinalis*), as both its generic and botanical names imply, is found growing in the crevices of the old stone walls in most temperate zones of Europe and the British Isles. For many centuries it has been included in pharmacopoeias for its demulcent properties. It contains abundant potassium nitrate and is diuretic and reduces fever. It is good for diseases of the bladder and kidneys and for certain kinds of dropsy. Old books of husbandry also recommend it for getting rid of weevils if corn is placed with it. Early face-creams contained pellitory, and it was believed to "comfort the body." A very old remedy for this purpose entails sitting for two hours in three gallons of milk in which sprays of pellitory, rosemary, nettles, and violets have been immersed.

Nasturtium flower and bud. Nasturtium is used in soups because of its slightly peppery flavor. The flowers are delicious as well as being visually attractive in salads. The pickled buds and seeds can be used instead of capers.

POTATO AND NASTURTIUM SOUP

2 medium-sized potatoes; handful of nasturtium leaves; 1½ oz/30 g lean bacon; 4 oz/110 g small pasta shapes; 4 tbsp olive oil; 3 tbsp grated Parmesan cheese; salt.

Peel the potatoes and wash the nasturtium leaves. Dice the potatoes and bacon. Heat 2 tbsp oil in a saucepan and gently cook the potato and bacon for 15 minutes, adding a little boiling water from time to time. Pour in 2 pints/1 liter water, the nasturtium leaves, and salt. When it has reached boiling point add the pasta. When the soup is ready add the remaining oil and the Parmesan cheese.

Everlasting · Horsetail

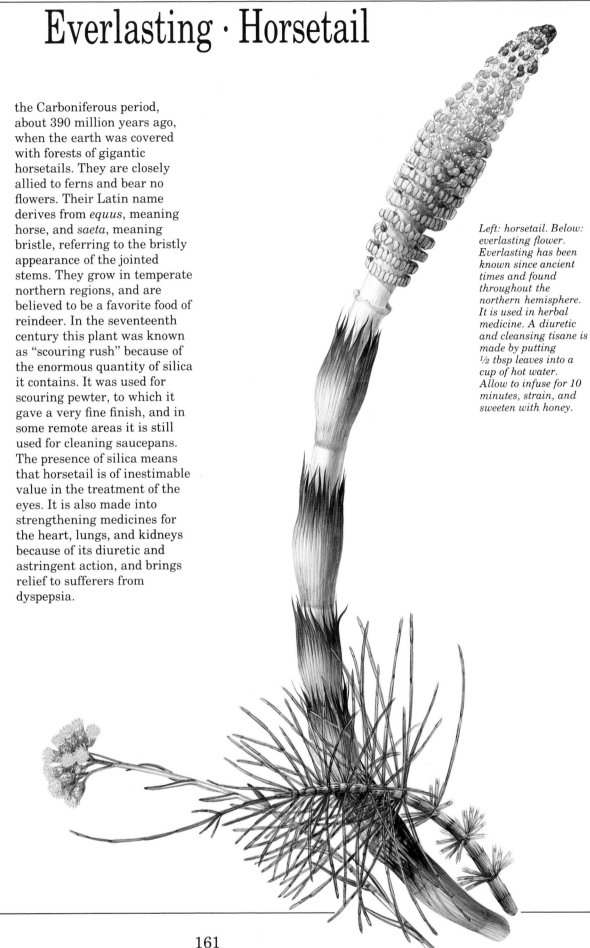

The genus *Helichrysum* is called everlasting because of the perpetual radiant yellow of some of its species, e.g. *H. italicum*; the name comes from the Greek *helios*, "sun," and *khrysos*, meaning "golden." Many other plants are also known as everlasting flowers, including cudweeds (*Gnaphalium*). The Romans put the downy leaves and stems into pillows and mattresses as a substitute for feathers, but the plants were also used medicinally in very early times. Pliny recommended the everlasting flower as a cure for quinsies and mumps with the certainty that there would never be a recurrence of either disease. The entire plant is used today for its astringent, pectoral, and discutient action. In homeopathy everlasting is recommended for some forms of sciatica, and is an excellent gargle. It is also useful for cramp in the feet and legs, and for stiffness of the joints in all parts of the body, either if the herb is rubbed on the affected parts, or if a decoction is drunk. Everlasting grows in most parts of Europe and America. Some of the cudweeds are to be found in Africa and the Levant. The plant, which symbolizes everlasting remembrance, is to be seen in large quantities in French cemeteries, where it is fittingly called *immortelle*. The horsetail (*Equisetum telmateia*), described by Culpeper as "but knotted rushes, some with leaves and others without," belongs to the sole surviving family and genus of an order of plants that can be traced back in fossils to

the Carboniferous period, about 390 million years ago, when the earth was covered with forests of gigantic horsetails. They are closely allied to ferns and bear no flowers. Their Latin name derives from *equus*, meaning horse, and *saeta*, meaning bristle, referring to the bristly appearance of the jointed stems. They grow in temperate northern regions, and are believed to be a favorite food of reindeer. In the seventeenth century this plant was known as "scouring rush" because of the enormous quantity of silica it contains. It was used for scouring pewter, to which it gave a very fine finish, and in some remote areas it is still used for cleaning saucepans. The presence of silica means that horsetail is of inestimable value in the treatment of the eyes. It is also made into strengthening medicines for the heart, lungs, and kidneys because of its diuretic and astringent action, and brings relief to sufferers from dyspepsia.

Left: horsetail. Below: everlasting flower. Everlasting has been known since ancient times and found throughout the northern hemisphere. It is used in herbal medicine. A diuretic and cleansing tisane is made by putting ½ tbsp leaves into a cup of hot water. Allow to infuse for 10 minutes, strain, and sweeten with honey.

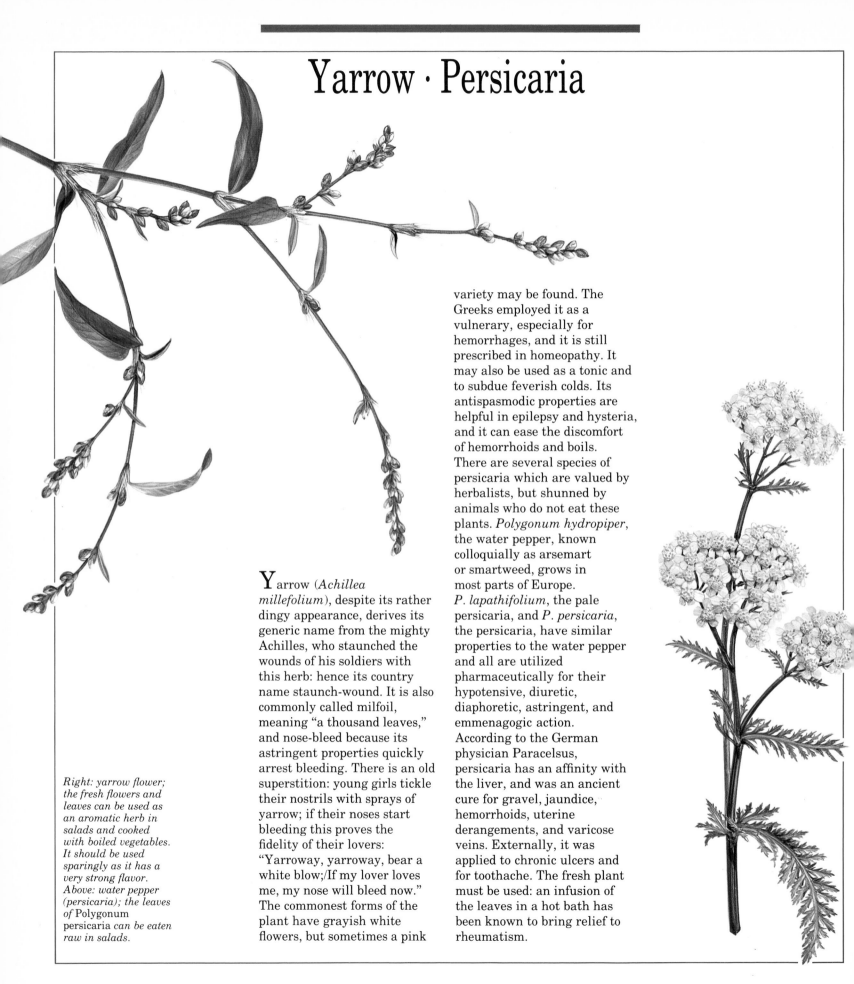

Yarrow · Persicaria

Yarrow (*Achillea millefolium*), despite its rather dingy appearance, derives its generic name from the mighty Achilles, who staunched the wounds of his soldiers with this herb: hence its country name staunch-wound. It is also commonly called milfoil, meaning "a thousand leaves," and nose-bleed because its astringent properties quickly arrest bleeding. There is an old superstition: young girls tickle their nostrils with sprays of yarrow; if their noses start bleeding this proves the fidelity of their lovers: "Yarroway, yarroway, bear a white blow;/If my lover loves me, my nose will bleed now." The commonest forms of the plant have grayish white flowers, but sometimes a pink variety may be found. The Greeks employed it as a vulnerary, especially for hemorrhages, and it is still prescribed in homeopathy. It may also be used as a tonic and to subdue feverish colds. Its antispasmodic properties are helpful in epilepsy and hysteria, and it can ease the discomfort of hemorrhoids and boils. There are several species of persicaria which are valued by herbalists, but shunned by animals who do not eat these plants. *Polygonum hydropiper*, the water pepper, known colloquially as arsemart or smartweed, grows in most parts of Europe. *P. lapathifolium*, the pale persicaria, and *P. persicaria*, the persicaria, have similar properties to the water pepper and all are utilized pharmaceutically for their hypotensive, diuretic, diaphoretic, astringent, and emmenagogic action. According to the German physician Paracelsus, persicaria has an affinity with the liver, and was an ancient cure for gravel, jaundice, hemorrhoids, uterine derangements, and varicose veins. Externally, it was applied to chronic ulcers and for toothache. The fresh plant must be used: an infusion of the leaves in a hot bath has been known to bring relief to rheumatism.

Right: yarrow flower; the fresh flowers and leaves can be used as an aromatic herb in salads and cooked with boiled vegetables. It should be used sparingly as it has a very strong flavor. Above: water pepper (persicaria); the leaves of Polygonum persicaria *can be eaten raw in salads.*

Convolvulus · Comfrey

The root and green part of the larger bindweed or convolvulus (*Convolvulus sepium*) have a purgative and cholagogic action. The basic active principle is derived from a gum resin similar to that of *C. scammonia*, which is also used in pharmacy. It has a gentle purgative effect and the powder mixed with honey is readily taken by children. Its other names are morning glory and bindweed. *C. sepium* is native to Europe and the United States, and is one of the most common weeds. Pliny in his *Historia Naturalis* likened the convolvulus to the lily: "for whiteness they resemble one another very much, as if Nature in making this flower were a learning and trying her skill how to frame the Lilly indeed" (Bk xxi, ch. 10). Comfrey (*Symphytum officinale*) is another ancient healing herb known to the Greeks and Romans. Its old name was knitbone, the leaves, made into poultices for sprains, swellings, and bruises. The term *officinale* denotes that this plant was cultivated in monastery gardens in the days when monks were the only physicians the common people had recourse to. Comfrey was reputed to suppress bleeding, and was used for bronchial and other inflammatory complaints. Old herbalists made an infusion to relieve colds and bronchitis.

Left: convolvulus; common throughout the United States and Europe on open waste ground, its root contains a purgative drug. Right: comfrey, an effective remedy for sprains and bruises.

Iris · Wall germander

The beautiful iris, despite its botanical name, *Iris florentina*, is actually derived from *I. pallida*. It is a perennial cultivated for commercial and decorative purposes. It grows well in gardens and flourishes in the wild in arid rocky places in continental Europe, around the Mediterranean, and in Mexico, from where it was originally imported. The dried root provides Orris powder which is used in cosmetics. It has a fragrance similar to that of violets.

Another variety, *I. germanica*, has darker colored flowers and is used in medicine. It is employed as a diuretic and expectorant, and in the liqueur industry.

The iris is Gerard's Floure de-luce, which "in two daies at the most take away the blacknesse or blewnesse of any bruise."

The wall germander (*Teucrium chamaedrys*) of the *Labiatae* or mint family owes its specific name, the ancient Greek word for "ground oak," to the resemblance of its leaves to those of the oak tree. It is found growing on walls and ruins in southern Europe, western Asia, and North Africa. In ancient times it was known chiefly as a vulnerary, and is still prescribed today for healing sores and ulcers. In medieval times it was also known as a cure for dropsy, jaundice, and gout. It is now used as a remedy for digestive and liver troubles, anemia, and bronchitis, because of its astringent, stimulant, diuretic, and antiseptic qualities. Taken as a tisane this herb reduces inflammation anywhere in the body.

Iris flower and rhizome. The dried root has a similar fragrance to violets. Orris powder is obtained from the iris root and used in toothpastes and cosmetics.

Wall germander (above) is used in a diuretic and digestive infusion. 1 tbsp of the leaves and flowers to two pints (1 liter) water. Sweeten with clear honey.

Hemp agrimony · Violet

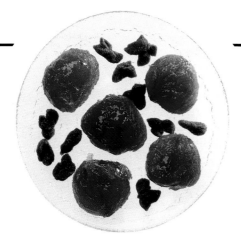

CANDIED VIOLETS

Prepare a sugar syrup by boiling 3 cups sugar and 1½ cups water for 5 minutes. Immerse the violet flowers and boil for a further minute. Remove the violets with a slotted spoon and leave to dry on waxed paper. Leave in a warm dry place for 48 hours until they are dried. They should be stored in glass jars. Candied violets are a classic accompaniment to *marrons glacés.*

Hemp agrimony (*Eupatorium cannabinum*) is widespread throughout the Old World and Australia. In the past it was used by Greeks and Romans and during medieval times to help digestion and relieve constipation, as well as remove stray earwigs from ears. The roots possess cholalogic and laxative properties. The leaves have a diuretic effect. The leaves and flowers should be used shortly after picking or the effects will be much reduced.

One of the best-loved flowers of all is the violet (*Violeta odorata*) with its haunting fragrance. Some old pharmacopoeias list species for their fragrance and beauty, neglecting their therapeutic value. The Greek physician Galen prized it for its emollient and expectorant properties. Commercially, violet petals are candied for confectionery.

The little wild pansy (*Viola tricolor*) owes its scientific name to the mixed colors of its corolla. The name pansy is derived from the French word for thought, *pensée.* The drug extracted from the flowers is made into cough extracts and syrups. A preparation can be made from the entire plant for treating acne and milk scab in small babies.

Above: hemp agrimony. Left: violet. Violet petals (or any other fragrant flower such as rose, nasturtium, and lavender) can be steeped in olive oil or vinegar for at least 10 days. Use the aromatic violet-scented oil and vinegar to dress salads.

165

Balm · Common centaury · Hawthorn

Hawthorn is an ancient plant. In prehistoric times the ripe berries were eaten. The young tender leaves have a slightly nutty taste.

From left: balm and common centaury. Balm contains essential oils and other principles, and is believed to have an antispasmodic, sedative and digestive action.

Balm or lemon balm (*Melissa officinalis*) has been popular with herbalists from time immemorial. It was also used in medieval times by the monks who manufactured aromatic liqueurs. The drug is prepared from the flowers or young leaves. As an infusion it is an effective remedy for nervous stomach cramps, vomiting, and insomnia. Culpeper recommended a syrup of balm and sugar to "be kept in every gentlewoman's house to relieve the weak stomachs and sick bodies of their poor and sickly neighbors."

The generic name of common centaury (*Centaurium erythraea*) derives from the legend that the centaur Cheiron had a foot wound healed by the application of the leaves and flowers of this plant. Applied externally to sores, ulcers, and eczema it is found to have valuable healing properties. It is often prescribed internally for digestive disorders. Its bitter quality makes it a popular ingredient of alcoholic drinks.

Hawthorn (*Cratageus oxyacantha*) is native to Europe, western Asia, Siberia, and North Africa. It is often found in hedgerows. The drug is obtained chiefly from the flowers, which are gathered just as they begin to open. It has antispasmodic and sedative properties and does not linger in the body. The berries are sometimes used to make a cardiac tonic. Hawthorn is also delicious in soups; the slightly nutty flavor of the young leaves can be combined with cucumber and cream.

Cowslip · Wall mustard

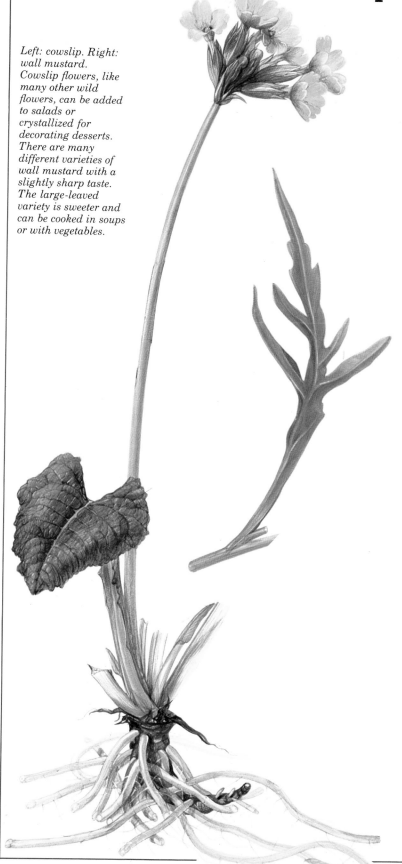

Left: cowslip. Right: wall mustard. Cowslip flowers, like many other wild flowers, can be added to salads or crystallized for decorating desserts. There are many different varieties of wall mustard with a slightly sharp taste. The large-leaved variety is sweeter and can be cooked in soups or with vegetables.

PASTA AND WALL MUSTARD SALAD

10 oz/300 g pasta shapes (e.g. macaroni); 5 fresh, ripe tomatoes; 1 scallion; 1½ oz/50 g wall mustard; olive oil; salt and pepper.

Place the tomatoes in boiling water for 2 minutes and remove the skin, seeds, and liquid; cut into strips. Place the tomato in a bowl adding the finely chopped scallion, salt, and 5 tbsp oil. Cook the pasta, drain, and leave to cool. Mix the pasta with the tomato sauce adding the wall mustard and freshly ground black pepper.

According to Gerard the cowslip is known botanically as *Primula veris* "because they are among those plants that doe floure in the spring, or because they floure with the first." This elegant little flower has many country names, the most common being paigles, which is believed to come from the Anglo-Saxon for keys, the pendant flowers symbolizing St Peter's bunch of keys. Two other names for cowslip are the Keys of Heaven and Our Lady's Keys.

Early herbalists claimed that users of this plant would become beautiful. It was believed to remove wrinkles and freckles, and, used with linseed oil, would heal burns. From very ancient times it was used for its soothing effect against fits and convulsions, and today is still employed in pharmacy as an antispasmodic and sedative. The active ingredients are contained in the flowers, which are gathered during May and June when in full bloom. Cowslip wine is still a popular home-made drink in the country, although its original use was as a cure for insomnia. The cowslip is no longer easy to find in the countryside and is one of the many victims of urbanization.

Wall mustard (*Brassica tenuifolia*) has similar expectorant properties to coltsfoot. Like coltsfoot it abounds on wasteland, ruins, and walls. It is also known familiarly as rocket but must not be confused with garden rocket (*Eruca sativa*) which it resembles. Wall mustard may be used in spring salads to give a slightly aromatic flavor, or the leaves can be cooked in the same way as spinach. Like other members of the *Cruciferae* this rocket contains sulfurated glucosides, and the juice of the fresh plant may be drunk as an expectorant to aid catarrh. The leaves have stimulant, diuretic, antiscorbutic, and revulsant properties.

Succory · Dandelion

Succory (*Cichorium intybus*), one of the *Compositae* of Eurasia and North Africa but naturalized all over western Europe, was already known at the time of Pliny, who recognized its value as a food plant and also its blood-purifying properties. The medicinal content comes from the leaves, which should be picked at the start of flowering, and the root harvested in the late fall. The leaves are used where there is a lack of gastric tone, bile deficiency, and chronic skin trouble. The leaves applied externally are thought to be good for boils and abscesses. Commercially, the dried root is used as a coffee substitute but has a very bitter taste.

The dandelion (*Taraxacum officinale*) has many therapeutic virtues as well as being an edible plant eaten raw in salads or cooked like spinach. In France the root is used in soups. Its distribution was originally confined to Europe, north and central Asia, North Africa, and North America. It is now naturalized in all the cool and temperate zones of the world. Medicinally the dandelion has a tonic, diuretic, and purgative action and is recommended for its beneficial effect on the liver. It is often prescribed for gastritis, kidney disease, inflammation of the gall bladder, and dyspepsia. It is also used as an astringent. Externally it has been used to treat eczema and ulcers. A form of coffee is made from the root which is good for those with digestive problems.

Succory. Right: a young dandelion; only small tender leaves should be used for salads.

DANDELION AND SMOKED SALMON SALAD

Young tender dandelion leaves; 1½ oz/50 g chopped smoked salmon; 4 tbsp light cream; 4 tbsp olive oil; juice of ½ lemon; ½ tsp mustard; salt.

Place the washed and drained dandelion leaves into individual dishes. Sprinkle the salmon over each portion. Beat together the oil, lemon, cream, mustard, and salt; pour over each plate. Mix well and accompany with brown bread and butter.

Burdock · Birch · Toad-flax

Burdock (*Arctium lappa*) is common on waste ground, in ditches, and on roadsides, growing in most parts of Europe and northern Asia. Every part of the plant is useful in pharmacy: seeds, flowers, leaves, and root. The herb influences the sebaceous and sweat glands, and is valuable in uterine displacements and for purifying the blood; it clears up eczema, acne, boils, and dandruff. If the stalks are picked before flowering they can be stripped of their rind and boiled like asparagus. They should be eaten with a little butter.

The birch (*Betula alba*) symbolizes good fortune and kindness. To the herbalist it is a purifier of the blood, a tonic and stimulant, and a pain-killer. It is found in North America, Russia, Scandinavia, parts of Germany, and in places where the climate is rather cool. The drug is derived from the bark and the leaves. Birch oil, obtained from the bark, is good for the skin. In Sweden poultices of the leaves are applied to ease rheumatic pains, and the Chinese use a decoction of the bark for jaundice and bilious fevers, and as a tonic for the middle-aged and elderly. Birch twigs are used to beat the limbs after sauna baths. Practically all parts of the toad-flax (*Linaria vulgaris*) contain active principles. One of the plant's old names was urinals, because of its powerful diuretic effect. In the form of an ointment it can cure boils, hemorrhoids, and fistulae; as an infusion it has been recommended for problems affecting the urinary tract, jaundice, and dropsy. The ivy-leaved toad-flax (*L. cymbalaria*) has similar properties, and adds a pungent cress-like flavor to salads.

Left: burdock. Below: birch. Right: toad-flax. Lightly steamed burdock leaves taste similar to beet.

Hellebore · Bearberry

Below: bearberry; a small dark green shrub with red berries. Left: black and green hellebore; only used for medicinal purposes.

Black hellebore or Christmas rose (*Helleborus niger*) is a herbaceous perennial with a creeping rhizome and sparse shiny leaves. It blooms between December and February, with the flowers being most profuse at Christmas, and in medieval times it was called Christ's herb because of the time of its flowering. Black hellebore grows in mountainous woods in central–southern Europe. The drug is obtained from the rhizome. This plant is toxic and should be used very carefully. It possesses various properties: the powdered rhizome has a sternutatory activity; helleborein is a cardiotonic; helleborin has a strong narcotic action.

In the sixteenth century Gerard prescribed "purgations of Hellebor . . . for mad and furious men" and for those that were "molested with melancholy." Green hellebore (*H. viridis*) is another herbaceous perennial growing in woods and thickets in western and central Europe. It produces abundant greenish flowers and flowering lasts from December to April. Green hellebore has similar properties to black hellebore. Today, because of its toxicity, it is no longer in much demand.

Bearberry or beargrape (*Arctostaphylos uva-ursi*) yields a drug from its leaves called arbutin, which is valuable for kidney diseases and digestive troubles. The leaves are gathered in early autumn and dried quickly so that they do not lose their dark green color. Bearberry is found mostly in Scotland and the north of England growing on high ground.

Black bryony · Asarabacca

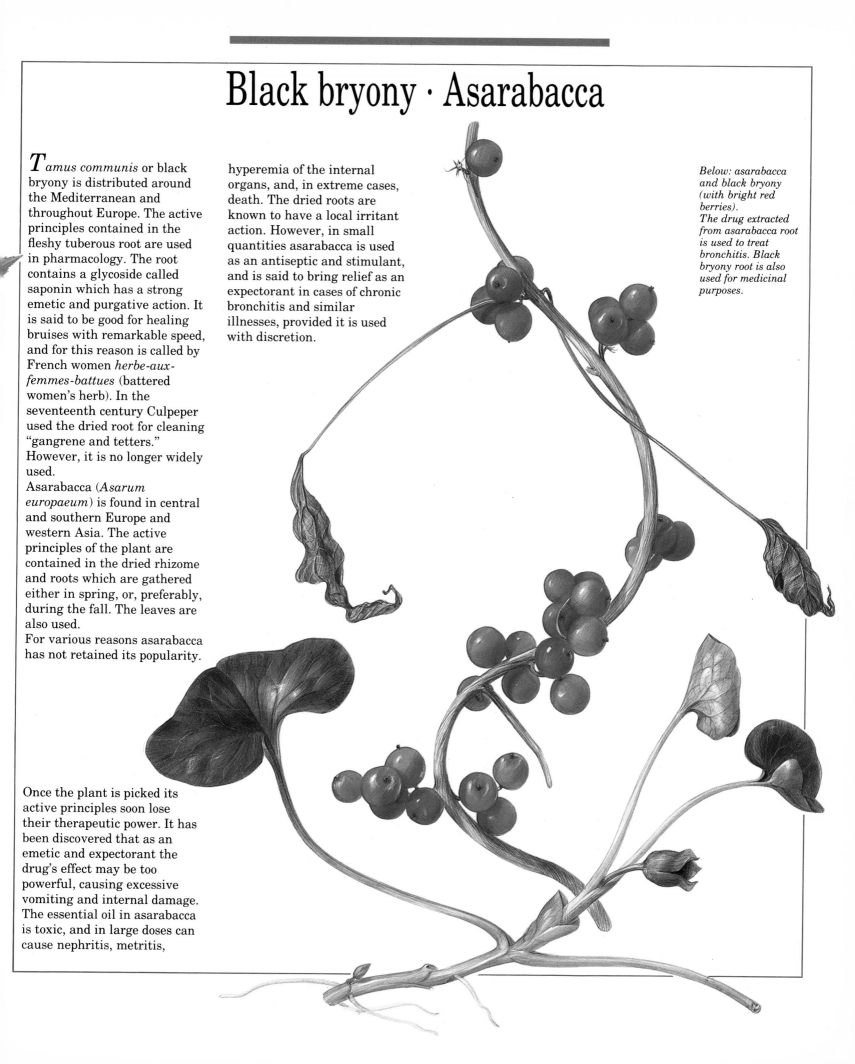

*T*amus communis or black bryony is distributed around the Mediterranean and throughout Europe. The active principles contained in the fleshy tuberous root are used in pharmacology. The root contains a glycoside called saponin which has a strong emetic and purgative action. It is said to be good for healing bruises with remarkable speed, and for this reason is called by French women *herbe-aux-femmes-battues* (battered women's herb). In the seventeenth century Culpeper used the dried root for cleaning "gangrene and tetters." However, it is no longer widely used.

Asarabacca (*Asarum europaeum*) is found in central and southern Europe and western Asia. The active principles of the plant are contained in the dried rhizome and roots which are gathered either in spring, or, preferably, during the fall. The leaves are also used.

For various reasons asarabacca has not retained its popularity.

Once the plant is picked its active principles soon lose their therapeutic power. It has been discovered that as an emetic and expectorant the drug's effect may be too powerful, causing excessive vomiting and internal damage. The essential oil in asarabacca is toxic, and in large doses can cause nephritis, metritis,

hyperemia of the internal organs, and, in extreme cases, death. The dried roots are known to have a local irritant action. However, in small quantities asarabacca is used as an antiseptic and stimulant, and is said to bring relief as an expectorant in cases of chronic bronchitis and similar illnesses, provided it is used with discretion.

Below: asarabacca and black bryony (with bright red berries).
The drug extracted from asarabacca root is used to treat bronchitis. Black bryony root is also used for medicinal purposes.

Ivy · Ground ivy

Below: ground ivy; it is rich in vitamin C and has diuretic and sedative properties. An infusion is made from one teaspoon of dried leaves and flowers for every 2 pints (1 liter) of water. Applied to the skin it relieves inflammation.
Right: ivy; a poultice of hedera helix *stimulates circulation.*

In the Middle Ages ivy (*Hedera helix*) formed part of the "soporific sponge," a foul mixture of hemlock, mandrake, poppy, lettuce, and other herbs, poured onto a sponge and held under the patient's nose as an anesthetic. The victim could not have failed to pass out after sniffing such a combination of evil smells. Ivy is a liana and is credited with strong antiseptic properties. It was used to ward off the plague. It is also thought to have some influence on the brain, and is used in homeopathic medicine against depression caused by intercranial pressure. In medieval England liquid was left to steep in cups made of ivy wood and then drunk to benefit the spleen. The leaves contain saponins, rutin, and a balsamic resin. They are manufactured into an ointment which is believed to bring relief to swollen feet and to cure corns. The berries are eaten by birds but poisonous to man. However, they can be made into an infusion to help rheumatic sufferers.

Ground ivy (*Nepeta hederacea*) is a pretty plant with mauvish blue flowers. Despite its name it is not related to ivy. Its country names, Gill-go-over-the-ground, Robin-run-in-the-hedge, and cat's-foot, describe this little herb which sprawls profusely over hedges and fields. For hundreds of years ground ivy has been esteemed as a cure for catarrh and colds, and was made into a herb tea mixed with honey or sugar to disguise its dreadfully bitter taste. Gerard mixed it with other herbs and used it as an eye lotion equally efficacious for humans and cattle. He praised the plant highly, claiming that it removed "any griefe whatsoever in the eies, yea although the sight were nigh hand gone: it is proved to be the best medicine in the world." It was widely believed that the constant use of ground ivy would eventually cure hardness of hearing. If sniffed up the nose the juice or powder could relieve catarrhal headaches, and although it is no longer official in the *British Pharmacopoeia* it is thought to relieve indigestion. The leaves provide the drug and are gathered in spring and summer.

Eucalyptus · St John's wort

One of the most enormous trees in the world is the eucalyptus, which is indigenous to Australia and Tasmania. It can reach a height of 250 ft, and has pinkish white flowers which grow either singly or in clusters. The leaves contain oil glands and have an antiseptic smell with germ-killing properties. The best-known species is the fast-growing blue gum tree (*E. globulus*). It provides the oil used in pharmacy for the treatment of malaria and typhoid, and harmful germs in general. Eucalyptus oil tastes of camphor and has a high cineol content. The fresh leaves are more efficacious than the dried. They are collected in summer. Because of the presence of tannin eucalyptus has a tonic and astringent action. A tincture of the leaves is used to treat asthma and chronic bronchitis, and as an antiseptic in respiratory, urogenital, and intestinal infections. *E. citriodora* provides the lemon-scented oil used in the perfume industry. St John's wort (*Hypericum perforatum*) was universally

known. In England it cured mania; in Russia it gave protection against hydrophobia; and the Brazilians knew it as an antidote to snake bite. It was the herb always called upon to cure madness, especially if the patient was thought to be possessed by a devil, and was collected on St John's Eve (23 June) to be hung in the house to ward off evil spirits. Hypericon oil, made from the flowers and leaves, is good for cuts. Dioscorides made great use of this herb when he was physician to the Roman army because of its pain-killing properties. It is particularly effective after operations; for the after-effects of shock; and for spinal injuries. It helps brain-fag, neurasthenia, and melancholia. The flowers are put into gargles and infusions for chest complaints; at one time the aromatic, resinous fragrance and bitter taste of these flowers made them popular in the liqueur industry. The herb's action is aromatic, astringent, nervine, and expectorant.

Eucalyptus (below) was introduced into Europe in 1870 to clear malaria-infested land. The oil extracted from the leaves is widely used in pharmacy. Eucalyptus is also used to flavor pastilles.
Below, left: St John's wort, popularly believed to ward off evil spirits.

173

Lungwort · Hyssop

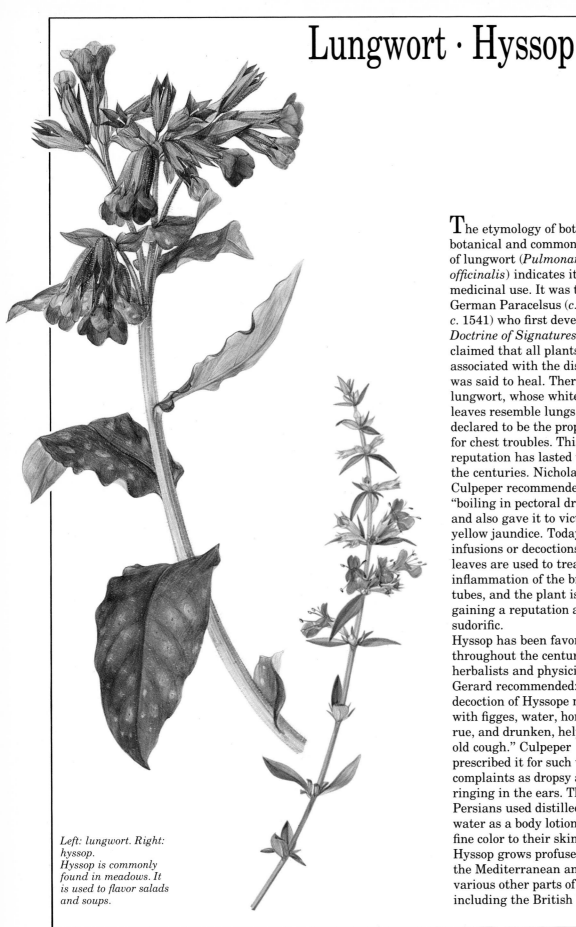

Left: lungwort. Right: hyssop.
Hyssop is commonly found in meadows. It is used to flavor salads and soups.

The etymology of both the botanical and common names of lungwort (*Pulmonaria officinalis*) indicates its medicinal use. It was the German Paracelsus (*c.* 1490–*c.* 1541) who first developed the *Doctrine of Signatures* which claimed that all plants must be associated with the disease it was said to heal. Therefore lungwort, whose white-spotted leaves resemble lungs, was declared to be the proper cure for chest troubles. This reputation has lasted through the centuries. Nicholas Culpeper recommended it for "boiling in pectoral drinks" and also gave it to victims of yellow jaundice. Today infusions or decoctions of the leaves are used to treat inflammation of the bronchial tubes, and the plant is also gaining a reputation as a sudorific.

Hyssop has been favored throughout the centuries by all herbalists and physicians. Gerard recommended: "A decoction of Hyssope made with figges, water, honey, and rue, and drunken, helpeth the old cough." Culpeper prescribed it for such varied complaints as dropsy and ringing in the ears. The Persians used distilled hyssop water as a body lotion to give a fine color to their skin.
Hyssop grows profusely around the Mediterranean and in various other parts of Europe including the British Isles, where it was probably introduced by the Romans. It is found as far afield as Siberia and the Himalayas. Today this little plant with its aromatic smell is used as a carminative and to treat coughs.
It is also used in the distilling industry to flavor many liqueurs.
Hyssopus officinalis was called "a holy herb" in ancient times and is mentioned in the Psalms (51: 7): "Purge me with hyssop, and I shall be clean."

HYSSOP SALAD

1 small cauliflower; 1 carrot; 1 green apple; 1 scallion; 1 tbsp finely chopped hyssop; natural yoghurt; 4 tbsp olive oil; salt and pepper.

Divide the cauliflower into florets. Mix together with the roughly chopped carrot and scallion, diced apple, and hyssop. Make a dressing with the yoghurt, oil, salt, and pepper. Pour over the salad and toss.

Foxglove

The foxglove (*Digitalis purpurea*) is a beautiful wayside plant found throughout central Europe. Today it is renowned as the source of the drug digitalin which is used in heart medicine. Both the purple and the yellow foxglove have been used for many hundreds of years for their cleansing effects. Culpeper claimed that foxglove could remove obstructions from the liver and spleen, cure falling sickness and King's evil (tuberculosis of the skin), and heal "a scabby head." But it was only in the seventeenth century that its cardiotonic action was discovered.

The leaves for the manufacture of the drug are picked at the beginning of the second growing year. Digitalin's beneficial action on the heart includes a toning effect and a slowing of the pulse; it regulates the working of the cardiac muscle while relieving disorders caused by obstructed circulation, such as congestion and edema. Near toxic doses are needed however, and sometimes cause gastric side-effects. It is important that the drug be used only under medical supervision. In addition to *D. purpurea* there is a small group of related species commonly called yellow foxglove (*D. ambigua*, *D. lutea*, *D. ferruginea*, and *D. micrantha*) with similar properties.

It was only recently discovered that foxgloves contain an important drug for heart problems. The beautiful flowers are also used in flower arrangements.

Boldo · Cornel · Castor-oil plant

Pharmacological studies of boldo (*Peumus boldus*) only began in the nineteenth century. The dried leaves of the plant are used as a diuretic and stimulant of the liver, bladder, and urethra, and for hepatic illnesses, and kidney stones. The fruit is edible. The plant is indigenous to South America, especially Chile and Peru. From these countries it was introduced into Europe and has now become acclimatized to the dry zones of the Mediterranean. Among the many species belonging to the genus *Cornus*, the cornel or cornelian cherry (*Cornus mas*) produces the best fruits. It is native to south-central Europe and western Asia, and has been known for many centuries. Today it is not widely cultivated. Its fruits have an acid taste and are pickled or made into a pleasant-tasting preserve with a bland astringent action because of their tannic and gallic acid content.

Seeds of the castor-oil plant have been found in ancient Egyptian tombs. It is thought that its usage dates back even further, perhaps as oil for lamps. Today castor oil is known as a purgative, but this medicinal role is fairly recent in Europe, dating only to the eighteenth century. The plant's scientific name comes from the Latin word for tick, a parasite the castor seed is supposed to resemble. *Ricinus communis* belongs to the *Euphorbiaceae* and is a half-hardy shrubby herb which flowers in July. It originated in tropical Asia, possibly India, but is now cultivated all over the world, and in some places has run wild. The drug comes from the seed which contains a high percentage of a fatty oil that gives it its purgative action. Castor oil has a gentle action especially beneficial in cases of constipation due to inflammation of the abdominal organs. The seeds are extremely toxic. If eaten they cause a burning sensation in the mouth, and two or more will cause gastroenteritis with congestion of the liver, and jaundice, speedily followed by death.

Above: cornel fruit; often made into a tart jelly.
Below: a castor-oil fruit and seed.
Right: boldo, used to flavor drinks.

Horse chestnut · Aloe

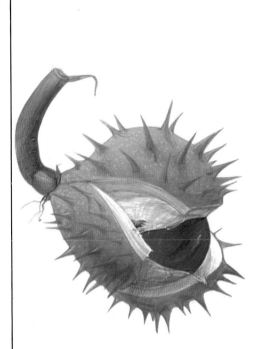

The fruit of the horse chestnut is similar to the edible chestnut but the two should never be confused. The horse chestnut is poisonous and is only used for medicinal purposes.

No one seems to know for certain why the horse chestnut (*Aesculus hippocastanum*) is so called. Today decoctions of the bark are used to treat hemorrhoids and varicose veins, and homeopaths employ it for sensitive nasal passages, coated tongues, and pharyngitis. It is a useful medicine for a distended abdomen, having a specific action on the capillary circulation of the lower bowel. France and Britain welcomed the horse chestnut with the greatest enthusiasm, and it was widely planted in both countries as an ornamental tree, for its immense size and the beauty of the flowering "candles." It will grow in almost any kind of soil and adapts easily to varying climatic conditions. Pharmacologically the term aloe covers a variety of products obtained from the fleshy leaves of the plant; a xerophyte of the *Liliaceae*. The most interesting species commercially are the *Aloe vera* which, with *A. chinensis*, a West Indian species, provides Barbados aloes. *A. ferox* from South Africa yields Cape aloes; *A. perryi*, a species from the island of Socotra, is the source of one of the oldest medicines, Socotrine aloes. *A. vera* or *A. vulgaris* is indigenous to Africa but is cultivated widely in the West Indies and on the northern shores of the Mediterranean.

An aloe flower. The juice extracted from the leaves is used in the food and pharmaceutical industries. Incorrect use can produce serious side-effects so best not to use it at home.

Alder buckthorn · Medlar · Angelica

The sweet-smelling angelica flowers (above) yield an essence which has a wide range of uses in the production of perfumes and liquors. The stems are used for flavoring in cookery. Below: a medlar fruit. Right: alder blackthorn leaves and berries.

Alder buckthorn (*R. frangula*) belongs to the *Rhamnaceae*, and is a deciduous shrub or small tree growing to 18 ft. in height, found in Europe, North Africa, Asia Minor, and the Caucasus and Siberia. The drug is derived from the bark of the tree and is collected in the spring. Although milder than either the aloe or rhubarb, it is considered to be an excellent purgative with a prolonged effect which makes it useful in the treatment of chronic constipation. It is usually taken in the form of a liquid extract. The bark is known medicinally as frangula bark. At one time its charcoal was in great demand for gunpowder-making.

The medlar (*Mespilus germanica*) is never planted in orchards, but only singly, usually as an ornamental plant, near country houses or in parks. Several varieties are cultivated in Britain. Immediately after picking, the fruits have a pinkish white pulp: hard, sour, strongly astringent, and therefore inedible. To become edible they must be spread for some time over straw where they undergo the beginning of a decomposition process that will make the pulp soft, changing its color from green to brownish, while the tannic compounds are transformed into sweet, tasty substances. The medlar has always enjoyed a certain reputation because of its diuretic and astringent properties. It is used in jams and jellies, and sometimes as a table fruit.

Angelica, called more poetically angelic herb, after its botanical name *Angelica archangelica*, is a large biennial herb of the *Umbelliferae*. It is indigenous to northern Russia, Lithuania, Bohemia, and Germany, but will thrive in gardens everywhere.

Medicinally angelica has always been recognized for its carminative, stomachic, sudorific, stimulant, and antispasmodic properties. It is mainly cultivated for the roots and stalks and is chiefly used in bronchial ailments, coughs, colds, and digestive troubles. Angelica is highly prized in the liqueur industry where it is used in chartreuse, strega, vespetro, English bitters, gin, and melissa cordial.

Wild rose · Azarole

The fruits of wild rose (rose hips) are rich in vitamin C. The dried fruit can be made into a refreshing tea which may be drunk hot or cold with a little honey and lemon.
Azarole fruits (below) are used in preserves.

Wild roses (*Rosa selvatica*) include numerous species such as climbing rose, meadow rose, dog rose, and sweet briar. They bear fruits or hips of little use which are used almost exclusively to make preserves and syrups which have a gentle laxative effect and are thought to be good for children. The Azarole (*Crataegus azarolus* of the *Rosaceae*) is a close relative of the hawthorn. It grows in scattered locations in southern Europe where the fruit can fully mature thanks to the favorable climate. The plant produces fruits which resemble a small fleshy apple either red or yellowish. The fragrant sugary pulp has a slightly acid flavor so the fruit can only be eaten raw if fully ripe. It is used to make preserves and jellies. The azarole flowers in May and the fruits are ripe in the early fall.

ROSE HIP SYRUP

15 oz/450 g washed and crushed rose hips; 7 oz/200 g sugar; 1 tbsp clear honey.

Bring 5 cups/ 2 pints/1 liter water to a boil. Add the crushed rose hips; remove from the heat and leave for 20 minutes. Strain, reserving the liquid. Place the rose hip pulp in 2¼ cups/ 1 pint/½ liter of water and bring to a boil. Remove from the heat and leave for 10 minutes. Strain and reserve the liquid. Boil all the reserved liquid until it has reduced to half. Add the sugar and boil for a further 5 minutes. Remove from the heat and add the honey. Store the syrup in glass bottles.

Agrimony · Henbane

Agrimony (*Agrimonia eupatoria*) is one of the herbs named botanically after King Mithridates Eupator, a great herb-collector, especially of poisonous species, which he took in small prophylactic doses to such good effect that he was eventually unable to end his life by poison. The plant's generic name is Greek and may refer to its supposed power of removing cataracts. It has been known to remove certain films from the eyes, and is employed in homeopathy and herbal medicine in various eye treatments. Agrimony, or church steeples as it is also called, has vulnerary, febrifuge, and astringent action, and at one time was included in the London *Materia Medica* as a certain cure for ague. Long before that, it appeared in Anglo-Saxon herbals under the name *garclive* as a remedy for wounds, warts, and snake bites. Today it is still popular with herbalists as a blood-purifier and liver tonic, a freshener of the breath, a soporific, and for the eyes. In the sixteenth century Gerard made a decoction of the leaves "for them that have naughty livers." Henbane (*Hyoscyamus niger*) has earned its common name from the lethal effect it has on poultry. It was widely used as a sedative by the ancient Egyptians, Babylonians, Greeks, and Romans, and in the Middle Ages was one of the ingredients of the dreaded "soporific sponge." In the twentieth century a drug containing hyoscine known as "Twilight sleep" was administered to women in labour and those suffering from nervous breakdowns. In ancient times the plant was used "against the phrenzy of madness," especially when the patient was believed to be possessed by a demon. All parts of the plant are poisonous and toxic doses will produce aggression, suspicion, and other manic symptoms. Prescribed under medical supervision it is helpful in overcoming shocks to the nervous system. It has antispasmodic, anodyne, and hypnotic action. Pilgrims, before starting on their journeys, put leaves of henbane in their shoes to alleviate weariness, and a decoction of the leaves in a footbath relieves aching feet. Henbane's deadliness is vividly described by the ghost of Hamlet's father: ". . . thy uncle stole,/With juice of cursed hebenon in a vial/And in the pouches of mine ear did pour/The leperous distilment; whose effect/Holds such an enmity with blood of man. . . ."

Holly · Butcher's broom

Holly (*Ilex aquifolium*) is widespread in Europe, western Asia, and North Africa. The pharmacological action derives from the leaves which are bitter-tonic, febrifuge, and sedative. According to some authorities they may be collected throughout the year; other herbalists believe that the best time is just before flowering. Before the advent of patent medicines holly was made into infusions or decoctions for colic, digestive difficulties, and malarial fevers, and for a long time was one of the chief remedies for smallpox. Extracts of the berries have a purgative and emetic activity, and have occasionally caused cases of serious poisoning in children, characterized by vomiting, diarrhea, and eventual collapse.

Culpeper, the seventeenth-century English herbalist, recommended the bark or leaves "used in fomentations, for broken bones and such members as are out of joint." Butcher's broom (*Ruscus aculeatus*) earned its generic name from the practice long ago of scrubbing butchers' chopping blocks with bunches of the twigs tied together. It is a curious plant with tiny scale-like leaves. What, at first, seem to be the leaves are actually flattened branches. The large scarlet berries are responsible for its other local names of knee holly and box holly. The young shoots may be cooked and eaten in the same way as asparagus. The roots possess diuretic properties and are manufactured into drugs for kidney and liver complaints.

At one time the plant had many uses in folk medicine; it was thought to be helpful for jaundice, headaches, menstrual pains, and chest ailments. Culpeper also advised: "The decoction of the roots drank, and a poultice made of the berries and leaves being applied are effectual in knitting and consolidating broken bones or parts out of joint."

The roots of butcher's broom are used in herbal remedies. Combined with other roots, they can be used to make an excellent aperitive decoction.

The holly's medicinal properties are to be found in the leaves. A tisane made from the leaves has a bitter taste and is an effective diuretic.

Mistletoe

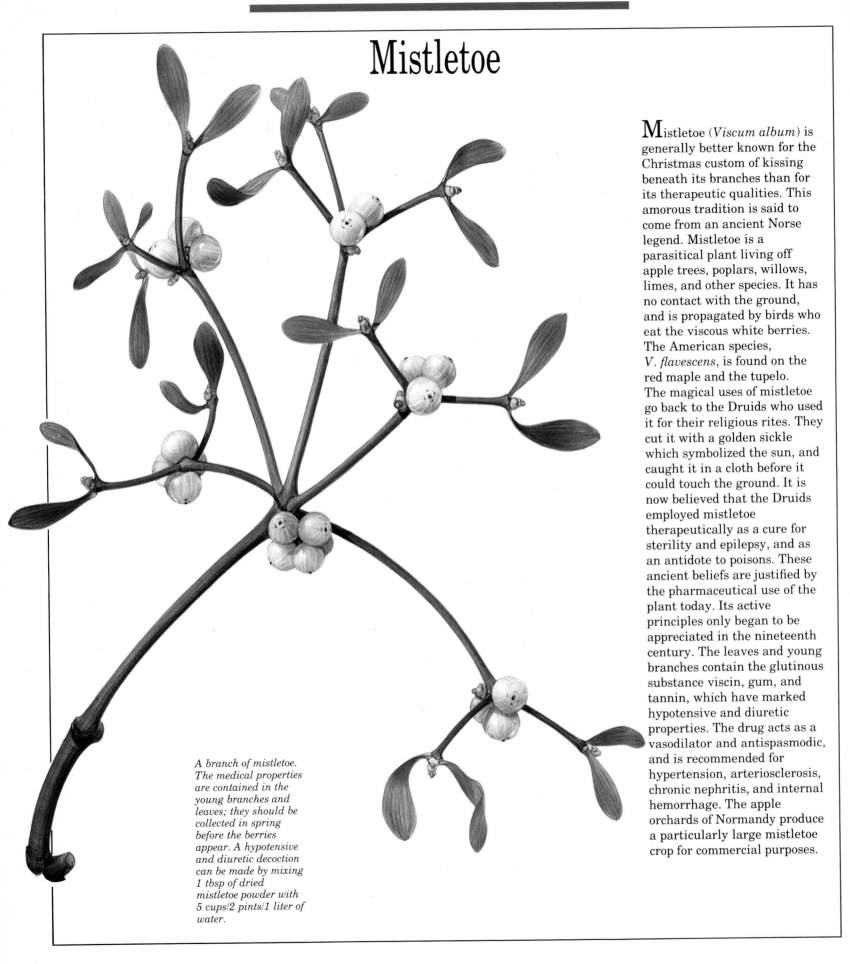

A branch of mistletoe. The medical properties are contained in the young branches and leaves; they should be collected in spring before the berries appear. A hypotensive and diuretic decoction can be made by mixing 1 tbsp of dried mistletoe powder with 5 cups/2 pints/1 liter of water.

Mistletoe (*Viscum album*) is generally better known for the Christmas custom of kissing beneath its branches than for its therapeutic qualities. This amorous tradition is said to come from an ancient Norse legend. Mistletoe is a parasitical plant living off apple trees, poplars, willows, limes, and other species. It has no contact with the ground, and is propagated by birds who eat the viscous white berries. The American species, *V. flavescens*, is found on the red maple and the tupelo. The magical uses of mistletoe go back to the Druids who used it for their religious rites. They cut it with a golden sickle which symbolized the sun, and caught it in a cloth before it could touch the ground. It is now believed that the Druids employed mistletoe therapeutically as a cure for sterility and epilepsy, and as an antidote to poisons. These ancient beliefs are justified by the pharmaceutical use of the plant today. Its active principles only began to be appreciated in the nineteenth century. The leaves and young branches contain the glutinous substance viscin, gum, and tannin, which have marked hypotensive and diuretic properties. The drug acts as a vasodilator and antispasmodic, and is recommended for hypertension, arteriosclerosis, chronic nephritis, and internal hemorrhage. The apple orchards of Normandy produce a particularly large mistletoe crop for commercial purposes.

Botanical glossary

Pharmacological glossary

Index of plants

Index of recipes

Botanical glossary

Achene A dry, one-seeded fruit that does not open when mature.

Acuminate Tapering to a slender point.

Acute Pointed, but not tapering.

Adventitious Growing from some part of a plant other than the main root.

Aerial Above ground level.

Alternate Arranged not opposite each other on the central stem, but singly at regular intervals at different levels.

Ament (also **amentum**) A dry scaly spike of small, closely clustered flowers, usually unisexual, such as the inflorescences of willows, birches, poplars. Commonly known as a catkin.

Amplexicaul With a base clasping the stem.

Annual Completing its life cycle in the course of a year.

Anther Pollen-bearing tip of a stamen.

Apex Tip of a stem or other organ.

Apothecium Spore-holding body of certain fungi and lichens.

Appressed Lying flat against the surface.

Aril Fleshy formation enclosing the seed of some gymnosperms.

Auricle Small appendage at the base of a leaf.

Awn Bristle-shaped appendage (*v.* **arista**), e.g., seen on the glumes of many grasses.

Axil The angle formed between two organs, e.g., between a branch or leaf and the axis from which it arises.

Berry Indehiscent fruit, usually with the seed or seeds surrounded by a fleshy or pulpy pericarp.

Bicarpellate Formed from two carpels.

Biennial Completing its life cycle in the course of two years.

Bifid Cleft into two, no deeper than halfway.

Bilobate Two-lobed.

Bipinnate Pinnately divided, with the leaflets themselves also pinnate.

Blade (also **lamina**) The expanded green portion of a leaf.

Bract Modified leaf growing just below the calyx.

Bulb Modified subterranean bud with fleshy leaf-bases, acting as an organ of storage and vegetative reproduction.

Bullate Blistered or puckered, usually applied to foliage.

Calcareous Growing on limy soil.

Calyx The outer covering of a flower, its separate leaves called sepals.

Campanulate Bell-shaped.

Capsule A dry fruit that opens to release seeds when mature.

Carpel A simple pistil, or a division of a pistil, regarded as a modified leaf, forming and bearing ovules.

Caryopsis A grain, the typical seedlike fruit of all grasses, including cereals, with pericarp and seed coat firmly united.

Catkin Dry, scaly spike of small, clustered flowers, usually unisexual. Also known as an ament or amentum.

Cladophyll A leaflike branch.

Composite Made up of numerous florets.

Compound Divided into separate leaflets, or formed of several ripened ovaries, e.g. blackberries.

Cone Pollen- or seed-bearing organ of most gymnosperms, usually composed of woody scales.

Cordate Heart-shaped.

Coriaceous Having a leathery texture.

Corm Short, fleshy, bulb-like subterranean stem.

Corolla Inner ring of a flower, composed of petals.

Corymb Flat- or round-topped inflorescence of flowers on stalks of different lengths.

Cotyledon Embryonic leaf present in the seed. Monocotyledonous plants have one, dicotyledonous plants two, gymnosperms several.

Cremocarp Bicarpellate fruit splitting when ripe into two mericarps which remain hanging from the plant.

Crenate With rounded teeth on the margin.

Cryptogamous Flowerless.

Cultivar A variety obtained through cultivation; a horticultural selection.

Cuneate Wedge-shaped.

Cyme Inflorescence in which the stem terminates in a flower, the other flowers being at the end of lateral branches.

Deciduous Falling off; shedding its leaves in autumn.

Decurrent Extending downward from the point of insertion.

Decussate Arranged in pairs at right angles to each other.

Dehiscent Opening or splitting at maturity to discharge seeds (used of a seed pod), or opening to discharge pollen (used of an anther).

Dentate Toothed. A doubly dentate leaf has marginal teeth that are themselves dentate.

Diclinous Unisexual, of flowers having stamens in one flower and pistils in another.

Dioecious Having male flowers on one plant, female on another.

Drupe Fruit with a hard kernel or stone and a fleshy pericarp.

Elliptical Oval, acute at the ends.

Emarginate With the margin slightly notched at the apex.

Endocarp (also **apicarp**) The inner layer of the pericarp, i.e., fruit wall, often different in texture.

Epicarp (or **exocarp**) The outer layer of the pericarp, often different in texture from the rest e.g., marrow.

Epigynous Having sepals, petals, and stamens growing above the ovary (used of a flower). In this flower the ovary is called inferior.

Epiphyte A plant that grows upon another without deriving any nourishment from it, e.g., ferns, mosses, and some orchids.

Evanescent Soon withering.

Exfoliating Peeling off in thin layers, as the bark of a birch or plane tree.

Exocarp see **epicarp.**

Filament Stalk of a stamen; microscopic thread forming vegetative part of a fungus.

Filiform Thread-like.

Floret Small flower, usually a component of a composite flowerhead.

Flowerhead Dense group of flowers; composite inflorescence in which the tubular disk florets surrounded by the ligulate ray florets give the appearance of a single flower.

Follicle Dry, monocarpellate many-seeded fruit, opening along one side when ripe.

Frond Leaf-like part of a fern.

Fruit Seed-bearing product of a plant. True fruits are produced by the transformation of the ovary; when any other part, e.g. receptacle, sepals, petals, bracts, is involved, the result is known botanically as a false fruit or pseudocarp.

Fruit body Spore-producing part e.g. of fungi.

Glabrous Smooth, especially not hairy or pubescent.

Glucoside A glycoside that yields glucose on hydrolysis.

Glumes Chafflike bracts; specifically one of a pair of dry bracts enclosing the flowers of grasses and sedges.

Gymnosperm Plant, e.g. coniferous tree, of the class Gymnospermae, with ovules and seeds not enclosed in an ovary.

Gynoecium The carpels taken collectively; the female organs.

Habitat The kind of locality in which a plant grows; its native country.

Head A group of flowers placed closely together; a dense cluster of sessile or nearly sessile flowers on a short receptacle, e.g., sunflower.

Herb A plant of which the stem dies to the ground at the end of the season. Also a plant used in cooking for its savory or aromatic qualities, or in medicine.

Hesperidium A fruit structured like an orange, pulpy within and with a leathery, separable rind.

Hip False fruit of a rose, formed from the receptacle.

Hirsute Hairy.

Hispid Bristly; with bristles.

Hymenium The fertile, spore-producing structure of certain fungi.

Hypocotyl The part of the axis of a plant embryo or seedling below the cotyledon (first leaves).

Hypogenous Growing upon the underside of anything; developing underground.

Imparipinnate Pinnately divided, with a single terminal leaflet.

Incised Cut sharply or irregularly more or less deeply.

Indehiscent Not opening in a definite manner when ripe to release seeds.

Indusium Membrane covering the sori in some ferns.

Inflorescence A cluster of flowers borne on one stalk.

Infructescence The fruiting stage of an inflorescence.

Integument Covering, usually of ovule or seed.

Involucre Ring of bracts surrounding an inflorescence.

Labiate Having petals fused to form a tube with two lips

Laciniate Irregularly divided into long, narrow segments.

Lamina Blade or expanded green portion of a leaf.

Lanceolate Lancehead-shaped; narrow, tapering at the apex, more rounded at the base.

Lateral At the side.

Leaflet Division of a compound leaf.

Legume Dry, monocarpellate.

Lenticel A pore on the young bark of the stem to allow air to reach the underlying tissue, especially during the winter. Often the color contrasts with the bark.

Lichen Compound plant arising from the mutually beneficial association (symbiosis) of an alga and a fungus.

Lignified Woody.

Ligulate Strap-shaped; having the petals fused into a single petal-like corolla or ligule

Linear Narrow and pointed.

Lipid Any of a group of substances soluble in a fat solvent, but only sparingly soluble in water, that with proteins and carbohydrates constitute the principle structural components of living cells. Fats are lipids.

Lobed Cleft, but not divided into leaflets.

Marbled Having irregular streaks of color.

Margin Edge of the lamina of a leaf.

Mericarp Half of a cremocarp, containing one seed.

Mesocarp The middle layer of the fruit wall (*see* **endocarp**).

Monoecious Having both male and female flowers on the same plant.

Must The juice of grapes or other fruit before and during fermentation.

Mycelium The thallus or vegetative part of a fungus, made of threadlike filaments called hyphae.

Nectary The part or organ of a flower where nectar is secreted.

Node Joint. The part of a branch or stem from which a leaf arises. Roots form more readily at a node when taking cuttings.

Nodules Small, hard lumps or swellings.

Nut Hard, indehiscent fruit, usually single-seeded.

Obovate Egg-shaped, with the narrow end at the base.

Obtuse Blunt-ended.

Opposite Arranged in pairs, one each side of the stem.

Orbicular Nearly circular.

Ovary The part of the pistil enclosing the ovules.

Ovate Flat and egg-shaped.

Ovoid Solid and egg-shaped.

Ovule Outgrowth of the ovary, developing after fertilization into the seed.

Palmate Radiating from a central point, e.g. veins from the base of a leaf; with lobes or leaflets so arranged. A palmately lobed leaf may be palmatifid, cleft to about halfway in from the margin; palmatipartite, more deeply cleft; or palmatisect, cleft almost to the midrib.

Panicle Loose, pyramidal inflorescence, usually a compound raceme, i.e. one with branching pedicels.

Papilionaceous With one erect petal, two side petals, and two petals below fused to form a keel.

Paripinnate Pinnately divided, with an even number of leaflets.

Pedicel Stalk of a single flower, especially in a branched inflorescence.

Peduncle Stalk of an inflorescence or a solitary flower.

Pentamerous Having five of each of its parts (sepals, petals, stamens, carpels).

Perennial Living for more than two years.

Perianth The envelope of a flower, consisting of calyx and corolla.

Pericarp Part of a fruit surrounding the seed, derived from the wall of the matured ovary. The outer layer is called the epicarp, the middle one the mesocarp and the inner one the endocarp.

Persistent Withering, but staying on the plant through the winter.

Petal Flower leaf, often colorful, forming part of the corolla.

Petiole Stalk of a leaf.

Pinnate Arranged on either side of a central vein or stalk; divided into leaflets so arranged. A pinnately lobed leaf may be pinnatifid, pinnatipartite or pinnatisect,

according to the depth of incision (*see* **palmate**).

Pistil Female organ of a flower, made up of one or more carpels and consisting of the ovary, style and stigma.

Pollen The fine, yellowish powder formed within the anthers in flowering plants; the male fecundating elements in seed plants.

Pubescent Covered with downy hairs.

Raceme An inflorescence in which the flowers are arranged on short stalks (*see* **pedicel**) at equal intervals along an elongated stem.

Rachis The axis or main stem of an inflorescence or of a compound leaf.

Receptacle The enlarged upper part of a stalk bearing a flower or an inflorescence.

Reticulated Having a network of veins.

Rhizome Root-like creeping subterranean stem, usually elongated horizontally. Also called a rootstock.

Rosette A cluster of leaves or other organs on an axis with very short internodes.

Runcinate Sharply incised or saw-toothed leaves with the segments directed backward (*see* **dentate**).

Scale Modified leaf or leaf-base.

Scape Leafless, flower-bearing stalk arising from the base of a plant.

Sclerotium Compact mass of hardened filaments forming the resting stage of certain fungi.

Scorpioid Curled up when immature, unrolling to bear flowers on one side only.

Sepal Modified leaf forming part of the calyx.

Septum Wall of tissue dividing an ovary, fruit etc. into cells.

Serrate Sharply toothed.

Sessile Without a stalk.

Shrub Low, woody plant.

Simple Not compound; unbranched.

Sinuate Deeply wavy.

Spathe Bract sheathing an inflorescence.

Spadix An inflorescence with a thick, fleshy spike thickly set with flowers embedded in pits.

Spike Raceme of sessile flowers.

Sporangium Spore case.

Spore Single-celled, asexual reproductive body of, e.g. fungi, ferns.

Sporophyll Leaf or frond bearing spore cases.

Stamen Male (pollen-bearing) part of a flower, consisting of the anther and filament.

Stigma Upper, pollen-receiving part of the pistil.

Striated Having narrow streaks or grooves.

Style Part of the pistil joining the ovary to the stigma.

Suture Line of junction between two parts; line along which a dehiscent fruit splits open.

Symbiosis A close association between two organisms, usually with benefit to both.

Taproot A long, usually central root directed vertically downward, bearing smaller lateral roots.

Tendril Coiling, stem-like climbing organ.

Terminal At the end.

Trifoliate With three leaves or leaflets.

Trilobate Three-lobed.

Tuber Thickened part of a subterranean stem or root.

Tubercle Small round swelling.

Umbel Flat-topped inflorescence with stalks arising from one point.

Undulate Wavy.

Unilateral Bearing flowers etc. on one side only.

Whorl Ring of leaves or flowers around a stem at one level.

Xerophyte Plant adapted to a limited water supply.

Zygomorphic Symmetrical on either side of a single plane.

Pharmacological glossary

Abortifacient Inducing abortion.

Active principle Constituent having a medicinal action.

Alkaloid Basic, bitter-tasting organic compound containing nitrogen and forming water-soluble salts with acids.

Anaesthetic Eliminating or reducing consciousness.

Analeptic Restorative or fortifying.

Analgesic Eliminating or reducing pain.

Anodyne Soothing or allaying pain.

Antibilious Effective against biliousness.

Antihemorrhagic Arresting or reducing bleeding.

Antiperspirant Reducing excessive sweating.

Antiscorbutic Preventing scurvy.

Antiseptic Preventing infection; killing germs.

Antispasmodic Calming nervous and muscular spasms.

Aperient Mildly purgative.

Aperitive Stimulating the appetite.

Aphrodisiac Increasing sexual stimulation and excitement.

Astringent Diminishing secretion; contracting the tissues.

Bacteriostatic Inhibiting the growth of bacteria.

Balsamic Soothing mucous inflammation, especially of the respiratory and urinary tracts.

Carminative Expelling gas from the stomach and intestines.

Cathartic Purgative.

Cicatrizing Encouraging the growth of new tissue over a wound.

Cordial A stimulant.

Corrective Additive, usually to improve the smell or flavor.

Decoction Liquid prepared by boiling the drug up with water and straining the cooled solution.

Depurative Expelling impurities by way of perspiration and urine.

Detergent Cleansing.

Digestive Aiding digestion.

Diuretic Increasing the flow of urine.

Draught Dose to be drunk.

Drug Part or parts of a plant in which the active principles are present.

Elixir Alcoholic tincture with sugar.

Essential oil Plant oil, usually scented, evaporating at a low temperature. Also known as volatile oil or ethereal oil.

Expectorant Helping to expel phlegm.

Extract Dry, soft or liquid preparation of a drug. A fluid extract may be prepared with alcohol, distilled water (aqueous extract), alcohol and water (hydralcoholic) or ether (ethereal).

Hemagogic Promoting the flow of blood; emmenagogic.

Hemostatic Arresting bleeding.

Hepatic Beneficial to the liver.

Hypnotic Inducing sleep.

Infusion Liquid prepared by pouring boiling water onto the drug and later straining the cooled solution.

Irritant Excessively stimulating; causing inflammation.

Laxative Mildly purgative.

Macerated Soaked in liquid to soften and dissolve.

Mucilage Gelatinous substance, swelling but not dissolving in water.

Narcotic Inducing sleep or drowsiness.

Oleo-resin Mixture of essential oil and resin.

Pectoral Relieving coughing and promoting expectoration.

Poultice Soft paste, hot or cold, wrapped in cloth and applied externally.

Sedative Having a calming and soothing effect.

Soporific Causing deep sleep.

Stimulant Exciting the functions of various organs.

Stomachic Beneficial to the stomach; promoting digestion.

Syrup Liquid containing a drug mixed in a strong sugar solution.

Tincture Extract of drug, usually dissolved in alcohol.

Tisane Dilute plant infusion or tea.

Tonic Stimulating the activity of an organ.

Vulnerary Curing wounds and sores.

Index of plants

Index of recipes